FEMINIST POLITICS AND HUMAN NATURE

FEMINIST POLITICS AND HUMAN NATURE

A K Singh

MD PUBLICATIONS PVT LTD
NEW DELHI
www.mdppl.com

Published by :

MD Publications Pvt Ltd
"MD House", 11, Darya Ganj,
New Delhi - 110 002
Phone : +91-11- 45355555
E-mail : contact@mdppl.com
Website: www.mdppl.com

ISBN : 978-81-7533-329-1

Published and Printed by Mr. Pranav Gupta on behalf of **MD Publications Pvt Ltd** at Repro India Limited.

PREFACE

Feminist theory is the extension of feminism into theoretical, or philosophical discourse, it aims to understand the nature of gender inequality. It examines women's social roles and lived experience, and feminist politics in a variety of fields, such as anthropology and sociology, psychoanalysis, economics, literary criticism, and philosophy. While generally providing a critique of social relations, much of feminist theory also focuses on analyzing gender inequality and the promotion of women's rights, interests, and issues. Themes explored in feminism include art history and contemporary art, aesthetics, discrimination, stereotyping, objectification, oppression, and patriarchy.

Modern feminism is illogical because it is based on the vanilla assumption that, but for lifelong gender socialisation and pernicious patriarchy, men and women are on the whole identical. An insurmountable body of evidence by now conclusively demonstrates that the vanilla assumption is false; men and women are inherently, fundamentally, and irreconcilably different. Any political movement based on such a spectacularly incorrect assumption about human nature that men and women are and should be identical is doomed to failure.

Feminism involves "the ideology of a female nature or female essence reappropriated by feminists themselves in an effort to revalidate undervalued female attributes". However, for the postmodern feminist the problem with the modernist feminist response is that it misses the way oppression works discursively - it does not criticize the fundamental mechanism of oppressive power used to perpetuate sexism and in fact reinvokes that mechanism in its supposed solution. The mechanism of power referred to here is the construction of the subject by a discourse that weaves knowledge and power into a coercive structure. By seeking to mobilize around some essential feminine identity, the modernist feminist is in danger of missing out on the Foucauldian sense in which identity can be constructed through a profound, discursively organised subjection. We therefore need to take a deconstructive line - to try to understand the use to which the discursive notion of an 'essential female identity' is being put, rather than simply accept it as given. It is this structure of signification that is the focus for deconstructing potentially oppressive frameworks.

In response to this criticism, modernist feminists point to the fact that for centuries women have been denied the position of subject, and have been defined as lacking, as other. They suggest that in order to gain strong political voice feminists need to steer clear of the postmodern trap which would deny us our own language and experiences. Instead the post-modern feminist would seek to replace unitary ideas about identity with the more fluid post-modern variety - "with plural and complexly constructed conceptions of social identity, treating gender as one relevant strand among others, attending also to class, race, ethnicity, age, and sexual orientation".

I am very grateful to Mr. Pranav Gupta, Director of MD Publications Pvt Ltd, New Delhi, for his kind cooperation and support for this book.

A K Singh

Contents

1

Feminist Politics and Human Nature

An Introduction

The 1960s and 1970s saw the resurgence of feminism as a social movement in virtually every Western nation. In each, the movement adapted to the history, culture, and politics of the society.This book focuses on how cultural traits and political institutions have shaped feminist movements in Britain, the United States, and Sweden. As Helga Hernes has pointed out, women in the state occupy similar roles regardless of national boundaries: they are citizens, consumers, clients, and employees. But they are also claimants in the arena of public policy, seeking to gain economic and political rewards and contesting for power and access. This study examines the mechanisms and impact of their role as political claimants helping to identify and influence policies that affect their lives as women.

The purpose of this inquiry is to demonstrate how differences in British, American, and Swedish feminism relate to systemic and cultural differences. A major hypothesis of this analysis is that such differences, in the respective "political opportunity structures", have patterned the development, goals, and values of feminist activists in each nation. In turn, it will be argued, movement structure and systemic differences have affected and constrained opportunities for movement impact within each nation. While the feminist activists in the United States, the United Kingdom, and Sweden share many objectives, they differ significantly in their style of political activism, leadership orientation, and organizational values. These differences interact with contrasting political opportunities to shape the success of feminist claims. The analysis defines alternate meanings for the concept of movement success. How the role of women activists themselves shapes political alternatives is a central question of this study.

Other political scientists have questioned the view that autonomous women's groups organized to fight for political power and policy gains are more likely to succeed than groups integrated into prevailing institutions. This study will argue, based on the British and American experience and with a briefer look at Sweden that gender-based women's groups that are separate from institutionalized interests such as parties and unions are more likely to develop independent strategies and political agendas of their own choosing, thus permitting greater political impact. This analysis seeks to demonstrate that autonomous feminist movements play a major role in the achievement of significant social change. Otherwise, women are acted upon as objects of social policy but are not participants in their own destinies.

The three countries studied here were selected because they are all postindustrial Western democracies, with policies that are superficially similar regarding women's rights. Each has legislation on abortion rights and labor force equality, and each has set up an administrative commission on equal opportunities to monitor sex discrimination laws, albeit with very different powers. Although all three societies have experienced similar trends, their significance for feminist politics differs. For example, while in all three nations women have simultaneously been mobilized and incorporated as new participants into the political process and into the expanding tasks of the modern state, particularly as these relate to women, these developments have proceeded in different ways and with different impacts in each nation.

The participation of women in the labor force has increased dramatically in each society, as have family "pathologies," such as divorce and female-headed families. Paradoxically, Sweden, which is noted world-wide for the equality in its progressive social policies, has the highest level of sex segregation in the labor force as well as the highest percentage of part-time workers who are women. In all three societies women and men are concentrated in specific occupations. Women are further segregated into a far smaller number of occupations than are men. These occupations are lower-paying; many are in the public sector service area. In one study an index of sex-based dissimilarity in employment reveals 70.7 for Sweden, 66.1 for Britain, and 65.1 for the United States. Another study has found Sweden to have a score of 60 per cent, the United States 46.8 per cent, and Britain 31.1 per cent.

This study will focus on 1) the sociopolitical context in which each movement operates,2) the organization and strategies utilized by each movement, and 3) the impact of each movement on the political process, public attitudes, and public policy. Within the context suggested, the study examines three Western countries that provide three different political models and therefore three different approaches to feminist politics.

To analyze the impact of women's movements on the political process and in helping to structure policy alternatives and outcomes, we will contrast three different models of women's participation and activism: 1) interest group feminism in the United States; 2) left-wing/ ideological feminism in the United Kingdom; and 3) state equality in Sweden.

Interest group feminism is characterized by a relatively open political system, a focus on equal rights and legal equality, and the creation of lobbying groups that may have a mass membership or be staff dominated. Networking and inclusiveness typify the approach to different political orientations within the women's movement.

Ideological, or left-wing, feminism is characterized by insistence on ideological purity and a reluctance to work with groups espousing different viewpoints. This type of feminist politics is decentralized and locally based, largely lacking a national political presence and impact. Fragmentation as well as enthusiastic commitments to sectarian views typifies this model. State equality is characterized by the absence of a visible and influential feminist movement. Instead, women are active via political parties and, to a lesser degree, trade unions. The state has tended to anticipate or co-opt women's concerns into public policy, even without significant pressure from women's groups. Policies related to women are generally discussed within the framework of "equality" or "family" policy.

In this analysis, movement development, effectiveness, and impact are seen as largely dependent on external factors such as political environment and available resources. Among the environmental variables that appear to be particularly significant are the current political complexions of government, the structure of the central administrative process, and the state of the economy. Examination of the structure of British politics, economics, and social life suggests a society highly traditional in its structure and values, a stagnant economy, and a centralized, secretive, and bureaucratically dominated system. These factors contribute to a political setting in which feminists tend to be isolated from the formal political system, from feminists with different perspectives and women in general, and from potential allies. Ideological divisions, rooted in class and other conflicts, inhibit the formation of coalitions dedicated to resolving women's political and economic needs.

We focus on the role and structure of feminism in the nations studied by examining two wings of feminism. The first is the women's liberation movement, often characterized as the more radical, or "younger," branch of the movement. Such groups in both the United States and Britain are distinguished by their emphasis on lifestyle change, provision of alternative services, and decentralization and anti-elitist values. The second wing of feminism is that segment of the movement operating within the traditional policymaking structure. In the case of Britain, this segment participates in parties and unions that play a dominant role in the political system. In the United States, women tend to be effective primarily as interest group activists, given the primacy of pressure groups in the American political arena. These two sets of feminist activists are roughly analogous to "militant" and "reformist" branches of contemporary feminism, although many British feminists would decline the honor of inclusion in the reformist camp. In Sweden, there is only one manifest face of feminism: that represented by women in parties and unions; the minute feminist movement is almost subterranean in character and visibility.

Among this study's major assumptions regarding the distinctions between the American, British, and Swedish systems are the importance in the United Kingdom and Sweden of centralized government and Parliament and the primacy of the administrative process.

Crucial variables affecting movement emergence and activism are the degree of corporatism/political centralization and pluralism. Schmitter's well-known definition characterizes corporatism as interest representation in which constituent units are organized into a limited number of singular, noncompetitive, hierarchically ordered and functionally differentiated categories, recognized or licensed by the state and granted a deliberate representational monopoly within their respective categories. Pluralism, in contrast, characterizes a society in which multiple, voluntary, competitive self-determined groups have access to state power. Table 1.1 makes the distinctions between the two approaches clearer. The United States, where strong or strongly structured pluralism prevails, is found on the pluralist/dispersed side of the continuum, while Britain and Sweden are placed close to the corporatist/centralist side.

Table: 1.1

Distinctions Between Pluralism and Corporatism		
Characteristic	Pluralism	Corporatism
Group unity/discipline	Low	High
Independence	High	Low
Character of state access	Open	Closed
Exclusivity of group participation	Unlimited	Limited
Character of state authority	Dispersed	Concentrated/ centralized
Consistency of issue resolution	Inconsistent	Consistent

In Table 1.2 we show how this structure may be supplemented to account for the organizational role of women's groups in the three nations studied.

The administrative process in the United Kingdom emphasizes ministerial responsibility and neutrality and operates behind closed doors, whereas in the United States there is far greater possibility for public scrutiny and intervention. British courts play a much more restricted role than their American counterparts. The American party system is looser and less dominant in the political system; and because power is fragmented both both in executive/legislative relations and in the federal structureit is more accessible to interest groups of all types. Swedish politics is usually characterized as a "consensual democracy" in which conflict and confrontation are customarily assiduously avoided. It resembles the British model of executive dominance and corporatism, although the political process incorporates a greater variety of groups.

Table: 1.2

Structure and Potential Role of Women's Groups			
Structure	Sweden	U.K.	U.S.
Strong labor unions	++	+	-
Strong political parties	++	+	-
Strong promotional interest groups	-	-	++
Women's section in parties/unions	++	+	-
Independent women's liberation group	-	++	+
Pluralist system	-	-	++
Politicized bureaucracy	+	-	++
Note :- −Limited; + = important; ++ = very important			

The scope of government differs as well. In the United Kingdom the role of national government intervention in family and welfare policies has been more firmly institutionalized, providing some support for British women in areas their American counterpart's lack. Examples are child benefits, maternity grants, and maternity allowances.

Welfare state benefits for women and children are greater in the United Kingdom than in the United States, including the non-means-tested child benefit of £5.25 per week, supplementary benefits, family income supplements, and rent rebates, although they are still far lower than those provided in most of the rest of industrialized Europe. After 1983, owing to a directive from the European Economic Community (EEC), married women on unemployment and sickness benefit could claim extra allowances for their children, although the new rights to Family Income Supplement and other benefits were significantly qualified by stringent requirements.

The United Kingdom has lower pay benefits for maternity and stricter eligibility conditions than any other European country. In comparison with the United States, Britain has legislated more extensive maternity benefits, but many women do not meet the benefit conditions. In the United States nearly half of women employees are provided with paid or unpaid maternity leavelarge corporations are most likely to provide such benefits. Thus, despite the existence of statutory maternity benefits in Britain, more American women appear to get such support because there are fewer restrictions in the United States.

The British have the least day-care space available for children of working mothers. American women are more likely to depend on paid and out-of-home child care than are their British sisters. British families tend to rely on family-based child care provided by husbands and grandmothers; few utilize institutional or nonfamily care.

In the United States, antipathy to centralized state power and reluctance to intervene in the family have resulted in a system of categorical grants; policies are fragmented and lack coordination, providing meanstested support only for poor women who are single parents. The United States is alone among these three nations in having no national insurance system for childbirth medical expenses, no children's allowances, and no statutory care benefits to cover pregnancy and childbirth. Civil/welfare rights activities in the 1960s did, however, expand the public sector's support of the poor.

In Sweden, a generous policy of support is available to parents for child care, housing, and other benefits to ease the burdens for working family members. In 1971, child allowances were $212 in Sweden, $62 in the United Kingdom, and $0 in the United States; the ratio has not changed much since then. The Swedes have sought to develop social programs with a view to labor force and market control; the British have tried to universalize social benefits but at a low level; the Americans have kept state intervention to a minimum. While the Swedish welfare state has sought to develop a minimum level of well-being for each citizen, the United States, via the "residual welfare" model, prefers reliance on the private market and family to meet individual needs.

In the United States, universal social welfare is not seen as a desirable social good; instead, the society provides remedial solutions to politically identified social problems.The concern of American policy is for the family as an institution but not for the individual member of the family. Family policy often tends to be dealt with at the state, rather than the federal, level; resistance to federal public spending in recent years has reinforced this trend.

The institutionalization of the welfare state in Britain has to some degree altered the nature of the debate about such feminist issues as abortion, because of the presence of the National Health Service (NHS). Nonetheless, less than 50 per cent of abortions are in fact performed by the NHS, a number that may be limited even further by cuts in the NHS under the Thatcher government. And there is a great variation in the availability and cost of abortions throughout Britain. As in the United States, politics in recent years has been dominated by conservative interests who have sought to slash budgets and "reprivatize" numerous public sector functions, including those specifically related to women dependent on the state. Even in Sweden, concern over financing the extensive welfare state in an era of a shrinking economy has emerged as a significant political issue.

The emphasis to be placed here on externally caused distinctions among the feminist movements in the three nations should not obscure the many similarities, particularly in comparing the movements in the United States and Britain. Among these have been virtually simultaneous historical developments, including the advent of the suffrage movement, the birth control movement, in which each country had a comparable leading figureStopes in the United Kingdom and Sanger in the United States and the "renaissance" of feminism in the 1960s. In addition, the Seven Demands of the women's liberation movement in the United Kingdom are markedly similar to those advocated by the National Organization for Women (NOW) in the United States:

1. Equal pay.
2. Equal education and job opportunities.
3. Free contraception and abortion on demand.
4. Free 24-hour nurseries, under community control.
5. Legal and financial independence.
6. An end to discrimination against lesbians.
7. Freedom from intervention by the threat of violence or sexual coercion, regardless of marital status. An end to the laws, assumptions, and institutions that perpetuate male dominance and men's oppression of women.

It is significant that in Sweden a major statement, "Toward Equality," was adopted in 1969 by the dominant Social Democratic Party. Among its major and primarily economically oriented goals are societies in which rights, obligations, and work are no longer allocated according to sex." This manifesto calls for equality in working life: eradication of sex discrimination in recruitment, promotion, and wages; economic independence for married partners, with the two-wage-earner family as a model; uniform taxes for all; and parental leave.

Analysis of public policy reveals similar trends. In the area of equal rights, the United Kingdom passed an Equal Pay Act, the latter establishing an Equal Opportunities Commission (EOC) to enforce the new laws. The Employment Protection Act of 1975 gave women a statutory right to paid maternity leave, protection from unfair dismissal during pregnancy, and a guaranteed maternity leave of 29 weeks. (However, these policies have been made more restrictive by the Thatcher administration institutionalized stringent requirements concerning prior work for would-be recipients). With regard to violence and victimization of women and the right to self-determination, the Domestic Violence and Matrimonial Proceedings Act (1976) strengthened procedures by which women could obtain injunctions to restrain violent husbands, while the Sexual Offenses Act of 1976 provided better safeguards for a rape victim's privacy during trial.The 1967 Abortion Act authorized abortion up to 28 weeks of pregnancy in cases where two doctors agreed either that the life of the mother or other children would be at risk or that the baby was likely to be handicapped.

In the United States, Title VII of the Civil Rights Act of 1964 and the establishment of the Equal Employment Opportunity Commission (EEOC) provided equal employment protection for women. The 1978 Pregnancy Discrimination Act gave pregnant women equal access to insured maternity benefits.

Abortion rights in the United States were established largely via Supreme Court decisions and have been the subject of congressional action. Domestic-violence legislation was enacted in 1984 at the federal level, and additional funding for victims and shelter expansion, as well as improved police and judicial intervention, has been the subject of considerable legislative activity at the state level.

In Sweden, legislation permitting women to choose abortion freely up to the eighteenth week of pregnancy was passed in 1975. After 1982, wife beating became open to public prosecution and, in March 1985, government grants were made available to aid some shelter activities. Equal opportunities legislation that prohibits sex-based discrimination in employment and requires employers to take steps to promote work equality was enacted into law in 1979. Despite the apparently similar nature of public policy related to women in the three nations, however, we will contend that the impact of such policy has depended in large measure on systemic factors and the strength of the organized feminist movement.

Social movements may be described as movements seeking to achieve social change through collective action. Directed groups have formal leadership, definitive ideology, stated objectives, and specific programs. Nondirected movements stress a reshaping of perspectives and values through personal interaction.

To a large extent, the most visible portion of the American feminist movement belongs to the "directed" category, at least in its formal leadership structure and definite programs of action. To a greater degree, British feminism is of a more "nondirected" nature, with greater emphasis on personal interaction, expression and articulation of feminist values, and the importance of internal democracy.

In addition, coalitional activities across issue and ideological lines are less well developed in the United Kingdom than in the United States. Hence, pressure group politics has not been the primary avenue for feminist involvement in Britain. However, the absence of formal, structured coalitional groups comparable to those in the United States should not obscure the existence of alternative groups actively involved in other aspects of political life.

As we have noted, in Sweden, feminist movement activity per se has been limited and women's organizations have tended to gravitate toward political parties. Some efforts to create all-party, gender-based groups have been made in recent years, and ad hoc activity has occurred around some women's issues.

The Political Opportunity Structure

This analysis rests on the premise that political structures provide the context for the development of social movement politics. Analysis of political structures includes the assessment of the significance of parties, pressure groups, the bureaucracy, the nature of state power, and the role of the judiciary. In addition, processes of socioeconomic change, including values and issue approaches, must be considered. External factors help structure the type of group mobilization that occurs as well as the character and success of a movement. Because British politics operate within a neocorporatist framework, large, economically labor-related pressure groups are primary actors in politics, although they are less well integrated into regimes dominated by the Conservative Party. There appears to be little support for Samuel Beer's view that British pressure groups are strong when promotional groups are considered. Most students of British politics agree that the nonorganized and lesser-organized are rarely consulted by policymakers. Gender, rather than economic sources of influence, is inevitably rendered less important in such a system.

Richardson and Jordan have characterized the British political system in terms of strategies for group influence; in their view, Whitehall is the primary target for influence; the legislative process comes second, and the public third. To a remarkable degree, the policy-making process is organized in an exclusive fashion. In fact, it may be suggested that the British political system tends to limit access for non-established, "promotional" groups, which seek social change. While producersor key economic groupsmay enjoy continued access to policy-making, based on sectional and economic roles and well-established relationships, the same is not true for groups, consumers, or others who may oppose them. A consequence of centralization and secrecy is to limit the role of "promotional" or attitude groups seeking changethey tend to be poor in size, finances, and the ability to obtain benefits.

Economic and technical problems are most often dealt with by a system that increasingly emphasizes executive dominance. The role of Parliament is diminishing in comparison to the administrative sector. Whereas in the United States political power is diffused, in Britain it is highly centralizedin both the horizontal and the vertical structures of policy-making. The administrative sector is characterized by limited public visibility and the absence of public scrutiny of decision-making. The core of "politically neutral" permanent civil servants and the relatively small size and narrow social backgrounds of the political elite often present significant barriers to change-oriented policies. Cabinet meetings are secret, and closed doors are the rule in most administrative proceedings.

The system of "tripartism," which includes the government, the Confederation of British Industries (CBI), and unions, limits possibilities for other groups to influence politics. Pressure groups may present views but may have little impact on the legislative process or the cabinet. Unlike the United States, where appointments to government, including administrative bodies, are often the product of "clientelism," or pressure group influence, in the United Kingdom such appointments are limited to "old boy" lists of the "Great and the Good." Confidentiality prevails, and there is virtually no opportunity for group activists to influence such processes. Traditional pressure group tactics are most successful for groups with high-level political or civil service contacts.. The absence of alternative methods of access to the political process virtually forces promotional groups out of the system. The secret process of nomination and appointment is made by the civil service in consultation with the prime minister and "leading mandarins". Little is publicly known about patronage politics. Policies are established behind theührenknowledge is hidden from Parliament and the people. The highly stratified administrative system means that many crucial steps in the policy-making process are unknown to ministers, the public, and groups interested in specific policies.Ashford has argued that because, traditionally, civil servants and politicians have not engaged in conflict, the political system has never confronted and subordinated the bureaucracy. The feedback and friction generated by implementation politics in the United States are almost entirely absent in Britain, owing to the primacy of appointed, not elected, officials.

Although parties are, by general consensus, declining in importance, they are major agents for the resolution of key political issues. Because of the significance of strong parties within Parliament, legislation of a controversial nature must enjoy government (party) support or at least sufficient neutrality to ensure that a private member's bill is given the time to introduce and nurture legislation. The final stages of the legislative process are less important than the negotiations that precede them.

British parties, more than those in the United States, tend to be parties of social integration rather than individual representation. Party policy does not seem to reflect group influence to the extent common in the United States, with the possible exception of the relationship between trade unions and the Labour Party. In the Conservative Party, the parliamentary structure plays a key role, and the organization is less federal than in the Labour Party. In Britain, where about 50 percent of workers are unionized, trade unions play a dominant political role, particularly in the Labour Party. Ninety percent of total Labour Party membership and 85 percent of the funds are derived from unions. The tradition of class-based ideology, socialism, and a strong organized left involves many British feminists in Labour Party and trade movement politics.

The passage of legislation is determined by the parliamentary timetable, individual M.P.'s, and the ruling party. Pressure groups may create a climate in which reform is possible but cannot make progress against a hostile government; they cannot dictate a bill's content or guarantee its passage, although they may generate a climate for reform and raise public consciousness about a special issue. The individual M.P. has little say in drafting or amending bills in parliamentary politics, so lobbying must have different goals than in the United States. The House of Commons creates or prevents a climate of opinion favorable to legislation proposed by the government. In the legislature, because of the absence of permanent standing committees, interest group relationships with specialized legislators are less common than in the United States, although contacts with M.P.'s are more frequent than with civil servants. The absence of regularly scheduled elections serves as an additional brake on opportunities for political pressure.

In Britain the courts define themselves as defenders more of the state and the general interest than of individual rights. The absence of distinct constitutional concepts and rules has limited the ability of courts to interpret law. Judicial review in the American sense does not exist in the British system. Class action suitssuch as those used to aid large groups in the United Statesare limited or nonexistent. The system of administrative justice is a tangled web of appeals tribunals and administrative agencies with indirect and ambiguous relationships to the courts. Judicial recourse is limited by the role of industrial tribunals which hear most discrimination-related cases. There is no general right of appeal from industrial tribunals.

New centers of powerincluding "quangos" such as the EOC,which are largely oriented toward achieving social goalsare autonomous organizations, with advisory, executive, and policy-making functions not unlike those of American regulatory agencies. Because they are not subject to parliamentary control, they have created new loci of power, reducing the role of elected politicians even further. Quangos were initially viewed as mechanisms for inadequately represented interests to gain a voice in government in the postwar period, but because of the systemic constraints outlined, they have in fact been hard pressed to play such a role. Appointments to quangos are, as already noted, at the discretion of the ministers and civil service.

In Britain, local government may sometimes provide greater opportunities for political participation than the national arena as there has been an increase in civic pressure-group activity concerned with the quality of life and services.

As noted earlier, the American party system is looser and less dominant in the political system, and the fragmented nature of power makes the system accessible to a wider variety of pressure groups. Politics is less "corporatist"; unions are less socialistic and less politically significant. Although in the United States there is no analogy to the strong labor union role linked to left and Labour Party politics in Britain, the Democratic Party most resembles the Labour Party in its organization as a party of groups rather than of individuals. The past decade has seen the further decline of political parties and the rise of single-issue pressure politics. The American political culture stresses incremental, nonradical change as well as compromise. With the step-up of federal policy on social and economic concerns in the 1960s, the number of interest groups involved in lobbying at the national level increased greatly. Citizen groups, in particular, expanded their activities, prompted in part by the social unrest of the time, which provided a powerful impetus for change. New regulatory legislation provided a route into the political process for hitherto excluded and unorganized groups. Jack Walker (1983) has shown that citizen groups, including women's groups, were able to gain patrons in the form of members, foundations, other groups, and/or government, which enabled them to organize and then maintain themselves as political activists.

The American process of interest group activity was given additional momentum with the passage of legislation on campaign finance reform, which helped to further institutionalize group formation in the electoral process in the 1970s and thereafter. In the United States, in contrast to Britain, decision-making is subject to considerable public scrutiny, in both legislative and bureaucratic politics, partly owing to the dispersed process of decision-making not only at the federal level but also at other levels of politics. Students of American public policy have pointed to policy networks, or "subgovernments", that permit specialists in Congress, in the relevant administrative sector, and in pressure group organizations to play a dominant role in policy-making. While policy networks in many areas have given way to broader and more open and penetrable "issue networks" in the 1980s, this development only accentuates the significance of interest group actors in U.S. policy-making. Interplay between several sets of political actors, both governmental and nongovernmental, is without parallel in the United Kingdom, and at least as far as noneconomic groups are concerned.

To sum up, American politics is responsive to interest group demands if they are seen as legitimate, whereas the

British government pays less heed to noneconomic-oriented group demands. (The Swedish government, to be discussed later, promotesand to a degree controlsinterest groups sympathetic to policies that are primarily economically based.)

A further aspect of movement politics in the constitutional/cultural setting is the role of third-party, or support, groups that may facilitate political access and provide needed assistance. Relationships with other reform/change-oriented groups may foster political consciousness and alliances that provide resources, access, and legitimacy for new movements. In the United Kingdom, movements such as the Campaign for Nuclear Disarmament (CND) helped set the stage for change-oriented politics in the 1950s and 1960s. The CND was probably the first major group to aim its strategies at the publicinstead of only at decisionmakersand in this way was a model for feminists who followed. However, the CND lacked a formal bureaucratic structure and formal membership, and although it was a major political presence and leading force in the mobilization of political consciousness for women, it was unable to provide a continuing institutional base on which emerging feminists could rely. In the 1960s numerous other social reform and environmental groups including those successful in promoting pro-abortion policy and legalization of homosexuality, and opposing capital punishmentemerged politically, as did groups of university students.

Like their American counterparts, traditional women's groups in the United Kingdom survived the doldrums of the '40s and '50s and continue to have a mass membership base, although it is declining. While they do not identify with women's liberation, they do support some feminist demands and efforts to achieve them. But such British women's organizations as the Women's Institutes and National Council of Women (NCW) by and large eschew relations with socialist and radical feminists. They have felt little in common with a women's liberation movement perceived by the media and general public as antimale. Hence, the links to civil rights and other movements that provided resources and access for feminists in the United States are weak in the United Kingdom, although there are important ties to such groups as the National Council for Civil Liberties, as well as a historic relationship to the socialist left, as we shall see.

In the United States, feminists were able to learn from the example of black civil rights groups and to rely on support from traditional women's groups. More recently, feminists have developed relations with a variety of political allies who have broadened their resource base and opportunities for access to the political system.

A final basis for contrast is the area of funding. Economic resources for promotional groups are scarce in the United Kingdom. In contrast, political scientists such as Jack Walker (1983) have stressed the crucial role played by patrons in the United States who contribute monetarily to both the formation and the maintenance of citizen-based promotional pressure groups, among them feminist groups.

In the United Kingdom, in contrast to the United States, there is relatively little money available for charitable gifts and little incentive for individual donors, who derive no direct financial benefit from contributions. Persons who wish to make annual payments to charities must sign a "covenant" for more than three years that obliges them to an annual payment (the charity receives the tax on earned income in lieu of the government; only individuals in the highest tax brackets are able to escape taxation up to £3,000). Apparently only a relatively few wealthy individuals are motivated to contribute in this manner. As in the United States, charitable status is not given to groups of a "primarily political" nature, although some campaigning is usually considered permissible by the Charities Commission. The limited nature of charitable income available in the United Kingdom is evident from a study revealing that 81 percent of charities have annual incomes of less than £500. Of the small number of charitable trusts, few contribute to feminist groups. In the main, only government agencies such as the EOC and the Manpower Services Commission (MSC) have provided any funds for feminist-related activity. Although American feminists are among the poorest of recipient groups, the infrastructure of contributors in the United States from both private and public sources supplies far more resources to emergent groups and movements than is the case in the United Kingdom.

American feminists have been able to rely on continuing, and in some periods even expanding, contributions from members, wealthy individuals, and foundations. For example, contributions increased in the post-1980 Reagan election period after the Equal Rights Amendment (ERA) failed to be ratified. Contributions have enabled groups to survive, and in some instances even expand, despite a very real decline in federal government support in the 1980s, although the fortunes of membership groups depend in part on issue visibility and changing political orientations. At the same time, lacking formal membership and funding, British feminist groups have tended to remain small and less bureaucratic, and thus further isolated from the centers of decision-making power.

The Economic and Cultural Setting

In this analysis, economic and social factors, including values, attitudes toward change, and receptivity to new movements, are viewed as variables that influence the emergence and impact of new political claimants. Thus, they help provide the context in which movements such as feminism may emerge and flourish or, instead, fail to gain political strength and importance. Cultural differences, then, interact with political institutions and ideology to produce a climate in which opportunities for change are structured. In turn, the type of movement that develops and what we have called the "political opportunity structure" create systemic possibilities and/ or constraints that either promote or retard positive policy outcomes and political impact. The concept of political economy suggests the relationship between the state and the ways in which citizens pursue their private ends and satisfy their wants. In Robert Keohane's terms, if the rules of the game in a particular society allow or require actors in the economy to exert power over one another then, the "economy is political".

As noted earlier, British society is distinguished by its traditional structure and values. The British social structure, with its low educational attainment for women, norms of "good" motherhood and marriage, low wages, and a stratified labor market and class system, has greatly narrowed opportunities for political involvements. The traditional family remains entrenched, to a degree unusual in Western society, with marriage rates high and divorce rates relatively low. The rates for divorce continue to be lower in Britain than in the United States, although they have risen dramatically in recent years, as have the rates of out-of-wedlock births. The divorce rate is roughly half that in the United States. By 1987, 21 percent of live births were out-of-wedlock in the United Kingdom, in contrast with 20 percent in the United States and 45 percent in Sweden. The link between female-headed families and poverty is blatantly apparent from an analysis of the data. In the United States, 17 percent of white families and over 50 percent of black families were headed by women in 1984, an increase from 8 percent and 33 percent, respectively, in 1970. Black and Hispanic female-headed families were especially likely to live in poverty. Nonetheless, while there are fewer single-parent families headed by women in the United Kingdom, their numbers doubled between 1961 and 1981, and over 60 percent of Supplementary Benefit recipients are women. Single parents received an extra £4.70 a week in Supplementary Benefits in 1987.

Participation in the labor force by women, including married women with small children, has increased dramatically in Britain, the United States, and Sweden, as it has in virtually all Western countries. About 59 per cent of British women are in the labor force, over 61 per cent in the United States, and almost 80 per cent in Sweden. Nonetheless, while in all three nations women are concentrated in lower-paying, lower-status jobs, the situation in Britain appears to be worse than that in the United States and Sweden, at least partly because of Britain's serious economic recession, which has resulted in an even greater increase in unemployment for women than for men.

In the United States, about 23 percent of women work part-time, limiting access to maternity leave, pensions, and job-training programs. In addition, part-time workers are usually first to be fired in cases of cutbacks and layoffs. In Britain the part-time component of the labor force is especially large compared with that of other European nations and the United States.The most accurate assessment places the number of female part-time workers at about 42 per cent in the United Kingdom, and rising steadily (the number is 46.2 per cent in Sweden.Women often experience downward mobility when returning to work and are more likely to work at semiskilled or manual jobs. In 1982, 14.9 percent of British women were unemployed, although the unemployment figures for all countries appeared to be lower by the mid-1980s.

In the United Kingdom, several studies suggest that female unemployment is less than that of men because men have been disproportionately affected by the decline in manufacturing opportunities. There was a perceptible narrowing of wage differentials between men and women during the 1970s when, perhaps in response to the passage of the Equal Pay Act, women's gross hourly earnings increased from 63 to 74 per cent of men's from 1970 to 1977.Nonetheless, even these figures reflect hourly wage rates for full-time employees over the age of 21, so they considerably exaggerate the scope of the gains made.More recent evidence suggests a falling back to widened wage gaps based on gender.

The backwardness of the economy has further constrained opportunities and value change for women in the class-ridden, elitist British society, reinforcing the concept of the "family wage," which entrenches the leading economic role of male breadwinners and limits opportunities for women in the labor force.At present the contracting nature of public-sector employment and concomitant reduction in education and social welfare subsidies have reinforced these tendencies.

Norms of political efficacy are unusually low in the United Kingdom, no doubt owing to difficulties of access in a centralized bureaucratic state, suggesting that political participation in general is likely to be limited.Participation and efficacy are related to high income and educational attainment, both of which are especially lacking for most British women.

Although the women in all three societies analyzed here are more likely to be clients of the state and workers for it than power wielders within it, this chapter has sought to suggest that opportunities for the British feminist movement are constrained by the values inherent in a traditional society, a declining economy, and a highly centralized, closed political system. The next three chapters will explore the two wings of feminism by examining the structure of women's liberation and mainstream feminist activities in both Britain and the United States in order to develop a sense of how the "political opportunity structure" has affected movement strategy, style, and impact. We will then consider a different model that posed by Sweden's "state equality," in which movement activism has tended to be absorbed by or incorporated in partisan and other institutions.

2

Early Feminist Thought

For most of recorded history, a key aspect of women's subordination has been their exclusion from public debate and the means of written expression. This means that we have little direct access to what they may have thought. Nevertheless, it seems likely that wherever women have been subordinated some have resisted, and it is possible to trace elements of feminist consciousness back to the first written expressions of women's thought in seventh century Europe. As Gerda Lerner has argued, any woman who wrote in this early period, or who claimed the ability to benefit from education or to contribute to theological, philosophical and political debate, was already challenging her society's teaching about women's God-given intellectual inferiority and their propensity for sin. It is therefore unsurprising that an identifiable theme in early writing by women is the attempt to re-interpret the scriptures to challenge such beliefs.

By the beginning of the fifteenth century, there was a European-wide public debate, which came to be known as the Querrelle des femmes, over the nature of women and their portrayal in literature. Of the pro-women writers, the best known is the Frenchwoman Christine de Pizan, who appealed to the authority of women's own experiences and to the record of 'great women' in history to assert her sex's innate intellectual equality with men and to defend women against the misogyny of contemporary literature and religious authority. Although the work of Pizan and her contemporaries did not produce any kind of political programme or analysis of power, they show that debates over women's role in society that include a recognisably feminist perspective go back much further than has until recently been assumed. While it is important not to impose current preoccupations on earlier periods, it is also possible to identify an early version of the difference/equality debate which recurs throughout this book, as some writers asserted their equal worth with men and others demanded respect for women's alleged sex-specific virtues, such as piety.

Seventeenth-century Feminism in Continental Europe and Britain

The Querelles had been primarily concerned with education, morality and manners, and participants frequently based their arguments on interpretations of the bible. Feminist theological arguments were further elaborated in the seventeenth century: for example, some writers used the creation story to argue that Eve was superior to Adam because she was created last, or because she was created out of Adam's rib rather than out of mud and slime.However, some writers also engaged directly with the increasingly secular arguments of mainstream philosophical and political debate, appealing to reason rather than existing authorities when making their claims, and employing concepts and terminology that are still with us today.

The inspiration for these new ways of thinking was the revolution in western philosophy which had been started in the first half of the seventeenth century by Descartes. According to Cartesian philosophy, all people possess reason, and true knowledge, which is based on experience and selfdiscovery rather than study of the classics or sacred texts, is in principle available to all. This means that traditional authority is rejected in favour of rational analysis and independent thought, and that customs and institutions which are not in accordance with reason should be rejected.

Although, as we shall see, the focus on reason has been criticised by some recent feminists, at the time it provided inspiration for many feminist writers, for it implied that women's exclusion from classical education need not also exclude them from philosophy, for what is important is good ideas, and not 'what fanciful people have said about them'.

It also meant that the questioning of authority could be extended to that of men over women, and that 'unreasonable institutions' might include those, such as seventeenth century marriage laws, that perpetuated women's subordination. Akkerman and Stuurman have described the seventeenth century as the age of 'rationalist feminism' in Europe, as writers such as the Frenchwoman Marie de Gourney and the Dutchwoman Anna Maria von Schurman used Cartesian principles to make increasingly egalitarian claims.

Such continental feminism was probably given its most systematic and radical philosophical exposition at this period by the Frenchman François Poulain de la Barre in his three famous treatises on sexual equality, first published in the 1670s. In these, de la Barre not only claimed that, since 'the mind has no sex', women are as capable of reason as men, he also argued that women are as capable as men of gaining the skills and knowledge that would enable them to participate equally in virtually all economic and social activities, including government and military command. Perhaps even more importantly, he suggested that because belief in male superiority was the most basic, widespread and deeply entrenched form of prejudice, a challenge to this could make other forms of prejudice questionable too.

The impact of continental debates extended to Britain where, by the second half of the seventeenth century, they had combined with more local influences to produce 'the first sizeable wave of British secular feminist protest', with significant numbers of women challenging received ideas about their sex in pamphlets and in books. Any attempt to 'read off' feminist theory from the social situation of women should be approached with extreme caution. However, it does seem that the increased scale and intensity of the debate in Britain stemmed at least in part from changes in gender roles that occurred in its early years of capitalist development, as well as from the political upheavals of this 'century of revolution'.

Changes in agriculture were creating a new and growing class of wage labourers and, as the division of labour became more complex and units of production larger, the old system of family-based domestic industry gradually declined, creating for the first time a distinction between the public world of employment and the private world of home and family. Meanwhile, working women were progressively excluded from trades and professions in which they had previously been active, such as brewing, printing and medicine, and aristocratic women, who had formerly played an important role in running their husbands' estates, were increasingly restricted to the domestic sphere. As it became increasingly difficult for women to earn their own living, marriage became an economic necessity and wives became increasingly dependent on their husbands for financial support.

Demographic factors were, however, increasing the numbers of 'surplus women' unable to find a husband, while the sixteenth century English reformation meant that the option of entering a convent was no longer available. In this context it is not surprising that the role of women should have been debated. Moreover, it was only now that the public and the private could be clearly distinguished that it made sense to ask about the appropriate sphere of women's activity; this distinction was alien to medieval society, but remains central to many discussions of feminism today.

Politically, the seventeenth century was one of the most turbulent periods of British history, as for a time the country was engulfed by civil war, and all political and religious authority was thrown into question It was almost inevitable that many women as well as men would become politicised and, in addition to the traditional 'behind the scenes' involvement, there is evidence of women demonstrating, rioting and petitioning parliament; these activities included a demonstration by 'Shoals of Peace Women' wearing white ribbons, who mobbed Westminster demanding an end to the civil war.Even more subversively, a number of the radical religious sects that sprang up challenged received notions as to appropriate sexual roles and behaviour: for example, the Ranters preached extreme sexual permissiveness, while the Quakers argued that men and women were not only equal in God's eyes, but were equally eligible for the ministry.

Questions of authority in state and family were, moreover, intimately linked in the political theory of the time. Conservative defenders of absolute monarchical power argued that the authority of the king over his people was sanctioned by God and nature in exactly the same way as that of a father over his family; this meant that 'patriarchy' in the home was used as justification for a parallel power in the state. Opponents of such state power, who argued that authority was not divinely ordained but must rest on reason and consent, were therefore forced to re-examine arbitrary power within the family as well; logically, it seemed, patriarchy in state and home must stand or fall together.

Perhaps unsurprisingly, this logic was not pushed to its conclusion by male writers. Although Hobbes and Locke, the foremost political theorists of the century, did examine relationships within the family at some length, they fell back on arguments of social convenience and men's superior strength to justify the continued subordination of women. This meant that, while they saw men as independent and rational individuals capable of perceiving and pursuing their own self-interest, they saw women as wives and mothers, weak creatures unable to escape the curse of Eve, whose interests were bound up with those of their family, and who therefore had no need for independent political rights.

This at first sight appears to be the kind of inconsistency that a more rigorous application of the underlying principles could rectify; some recent theorists have however suggested that, despite their universalistic pretensions, the basic premises of early liberal writers were inherently biased against women. Here it is argued that they were based on an essentially male view of human nature that ignored human interdependence and attributes such as nurturing that have traditionally been associated with women.It is further claimed that the whole approach was predicated upon a distinction between the public and private which involved the exclusion of women from the former and a devaluation of the latter,and that it perpetuated a view of rationality that excluded women, because it defined reason in terms of overcoming femininity (identified with nature, particularity, biology, passion and emotion; see Coole, 1993; Lloyd, 1984; Braidotti, 1986; Nye, 1990a; Jones, 1993; Frasier and Lacey, 1993).

Similar criticisms have been made of the more fundamental Cartesian revolution in philosophy despite Descartes' claim that 'even women' are capable of rational thought. Thus Susan Bordo has attacked his insistence that knowledge can only be achieved through disembodied reason, and describes his refusal to acknowledge the value of subjective, intuitive or 'sympathetic' knowledge as 'an aggressive intellectual flight from the female cosmos and "feminine" orientation towards the world' (Bordo, 1994:6; Lloyd, 1984; Ferguson, 1985; Perry, 1986; Hill, 1986; Kinnard, 1983; Smith, 1982; Rogers, 1982.; Springborg, 1996; Waters, 2000).

These are complex and contested arguments which will recur throughout the book: at this stage it is important to note simply that the extension of traditional theory to include women may not be as unproblematical as it at first sight seems, and that the concepts and assumptions made by male theorists may not be entirely adequate when it comes to expressing female needs and experiences.

As in earlier periods, mainstream political and philosophical debates in the seventeenth century were conducted almost exclusively by men. There were, however, exceptions, of which the most important is probably Mary Astell. Although she has been written out of histories of political thought, in her lifetime Astell was widely seen as a serious contributor to mainstream political theory; she has also recently been described as 'The First English Feminist' and 'arguably the first systematic feminist theoretician in the west.'

In Astell's writings on women, we find the new approach to philosophy and knowledge being used to produce a classic early statement of the core liberal feminist belief that men and women are equally capable of reason, and that therefore they should be equally educated in its use: 'Since God has given to Women as well as Men intelligent Souls, why should they be forbidden to use them?'.Here Astell anticipated the arguments of Mary Wollstonecraft and other later writers, by arguing that although women in the society of her day appeared frivolous and incapable of reason, this was the product of faulty upbringing rather than any natural disability: as such it was evidence of the need for improved female education rather than its impossibility.

However, although Astell based her arguments on the liberal idea of rationality, she did not accept the liberal idea of political rights. Like most of the seventeenth-century feminists, she was a staunch Tory and defender of the monarchy; as such, she was more concerned to deny political rights to men than to attempt to extend them to women. Indeed, the logic of her conservatism led her to a seemingly very unfeminist conclusion: accepting the parallel between authority in the state and in the home, she argued that a wife must obey her husband as a subject must obey the king; when a women enters marriage, she argued, she has chosen a 'monarch for life', and must therefore submit to his authority. Astell's writings are at times heavily ironic, so that not everything she says should be taken at face value; nevertheless her conservatism does seem genuine enough.

It has, however, more radical implications than at first sight appear, and in many ways she is carried beyond liberal feminist demands to a broader analysis of the relations between men and women.

Firstly, she insisted that a woman's duty to obey her husband did not involve any recognition of his superiority; indeed there is throughout her writings a marked tone of barely disguised contempt for the male sex (for example, she said that men are not fit to educate children, for 'precepts contradicted by example seldom prove effective'. Secondly, she argued that submission to male authority could not extend to single women, whether 'poor fatherless maids' like herself or 'widows who have lost their masters'.This meant, thirdly, that an educated woman should choose to reject the domestic slavery involved in marriage, and she therefore advised women to avoid matrimony (while cheerfully admitting that if they all followed her advice, then 'there's an End to the Human Race'; quoted in Perry, 1986:9). From this it followed, fourthly, that women's activities need not be limited by the need to attract a husband, and they could therefore concentrate on improving their minds rather than their beauty: 'Were not a morning more profitably spent at a Book than at a Looking Glass?' Finally, as a practical means of freeing women from marriage and dependence on men, she advocated the establishment of female communities, rather like secular nunneries, where women could live and learn together without men, knowing themselves 'capable of More Things than the pitiful Conquest of some Wretched Heart'.This idea excited considerable interest; it failed to attract sufficient financial support, not so much because of its feminism, but because of its dangerous associations with Roman Catholicism.

This entire means that, despite her political conservatism, Astell's work contains in embryonic form some of the core ideas of recent radical feminism: the idea that man is the natural enemy of woman; the idea that women must be liberated from the need to please men; the belief that this liberation can be achieved only if women are enabled to live separately from men; the perception that men have controlled and defined knowledge; and the understanding that women's experiences can give them a valuable and distinctive perspective on the world.Underlying all this there is a clear rejection of the whole scale of values in which man is the unquestioned measure of human worth in favour of a celebration of women: it was not for nothing that Astell's major work on education was entitled A Serious Proposal to the Ladies...by a Lover of her Sex. While Mary Astell been the most radical and systematic feminist of her time she was, as has already been said, certainly not an isolated voice. This means that by the early eighteenth century we have a quite widely established perception of women as a group in society whose situation is in need of improvement, and it is this consciousness of women's group identity which Smith thinks distinguishes writers of this period from their predecessors.

What we do not yet find, however, is any direct challenge to women's social and economic positions or to the sexual division of labour, nor do we find any coherent political programme or demand that the rights of male citizens be extended to women. For the most part socially and politically conservative, these early feminists addressed themselves almost exclusively to women of the upper and middle classes and there were few attempts to link the situation of women to other disadvantaged groups in society. For these writers, it was through education and the exercise of reason that women could be made independent of men; it is not until the third quarter of the eighteenth century that feminism was to become associated with wider demands for change.

The Enlightenment and early liberal feminism in some ways, the middle years of the eighteenth century seem to represent a retreat from feminism, as arguments for women's rationality became less fashionable than belief in their innate weakness and dependence on men, the ideas of Astell and her contemporaries fell into disrepute, and the very names of these early feminists were forgotten. Nevertheless, although there was no systematic analysis of women's situation or organised women's movement, individual complaints about their lot continued, as did discussion of women's abilities and social roles, and Karen Offen has argued that 'there was clearly a full-blown feminist consciousness in existence among some privileged women and men [in Europe], in dialogue with a mounting backlash'.

In Britain, many women continued to write and publish throughout the period; most famously, the 'bluestocking' group of 'salon intellectuals' debated and wrote on a range of contemporary issues. The bluestockings, whose best known member was Hannah More, have usually been seen as anti-feminist: they stressed the importance of women's domestic role, particularly their responsibility for nurturing virtue within the family, and they argued that, to a greater extent than men, women were motivated by 'sensibility' rather than reason.

However, they also argued that if women were to become good wives and mothers they must be educated, while arguments about women's greater emotional sensibility were both positively appraised and used to justify women's involvement in movements for moral and social reform, such as temperance and anti-slavery campaigns. Moreover, the very existence of the bluestockings as a group of intellectual women, publicly discussing and publishing from the 1750s onwards, could be seen as a statement about women's ability and role in society: no longer a silenced majority, women could not be entirely excluded from public debate.It is in this context that the ideas of the late Eighteenth-century feminists must be understood; although there is no direct line between them and the writers of Mary Astell's day, their ideas did not explode upon an entirely unsuspecting world.

The second half of the eighteenth century was a period in which the stress on rationality and the questioning of traditional authority which we saw beginning in seventeenth-century philosophy reached its fullest expression. It was also a period dominated by the experiences of the American and French revolutions, and in which philosophical debates on the nature of freedom and human rationality were to take tangible form in the American Declaration of Independence.What united the philosophers of this so-called 'Age of Reason' or 'The Enlightenment' was their optimism and their belief in progress through the onward march of human reason and knowledge; reason replaced God or antiquity as the standard of right or wrong, and no institution or authority was to be exempt from its judgement.

Although many of the leading philosophers were in fact socially and politically conservative, the radical implications of these principles are obvious, and they provided the basis for the liberal belief that, as rational beings, individual men have rights that must not be violated by arbitrary power; that therefore any authority must rest upon the consent of the governed; and that individuals should be as far as possible self-determining and free from government control.

Although always expressed in terms of the rights of man, it might at first sight seem that this could be understood as a generic term that includes women; for the most part, however, the philosophers of the Enlightenment and the leaders of the revolutions did not simply fail to make this extension, but they denied that it could be made. There was indeed a strikingly widespread consensus amongst leading philosophers that the principles of rational individualism were not applicable to women, for it was held that by their very nature women were incapable of the full development of reason; thus we can find in the writings of Voltaire, Diderot, Montesquieu and above all Rousseau, the idea that women are essentially creatures of emotion and passion, who have an important role to play as wives and mothers, but who are biologically unsuited for the public sphere. This consensus did not, however, go unchallenged, and by the end of the century there were a number of attempts to show its inconsistency, and to demonstrate that the liberal ideas of the Enlightenment could be applied to women as well as men.

The best known of these is Mary Wollstonecraft's Vindication of the Rights of Women (1792), but the fame of this work should not be allowed to obscure the extent of other feminist writing at the time. For example, the French writer Condorcet insisted that women were capable of reason and should be educated accordingly, that they should therefore have the same political rights as men, and that to deny this was an unacceptable tyranny. In practice he did not anticipate the widespread involvement of women in politics, but this he said was no reason to deny them political rights in principle – indeed he argued that women could no more be logically excluded from politics on the grounds of menstruation or pregnancy than could a man because he was suffering from gout (On the Admission of Women to the Right of Citizenship,

1790, and Sketch for a Historical Future of the Progress of the Human Mind, 1793, in Baker. Here we have a direct attempt to confront the inconsistencies of other writers and to claim that liberal principles have a universal application that includes women, so that 'Feminism was an integral part of the complete pattern of liberalism that Condorcet so enthusiastically advocated'.The German writer von Hippel similarly rejected the idea that women's exclusion from civil and political rights could be justified in terms of a biologically given nature; it was men, he claimed, who had made women what they were, and he demanded that men and women be given equal rights and education for citizenship rather than for their traditional sex roles. He went further than other writers of the time in blaming men for women's situation, and in denying that the traditional division of labour between the sexes was sanctioned by reason or nature; it was however, he argued, enlightened men who had to act to liberate women, for they themselves had been rendered incapable of independent political action.

However, women at this time were themselves far from silent, and their voices were to be heard on both sides of the Atlantic demanding equal treatment with men. Thus in America Abigail Adams wrote in 1776 to her husband, employing the language that he had used against English rule to point out that her sex too needed protection from tyranny and 'will not hold ourselves bound by any laws in which we have no voice or representation'. John Adams' reply that 'As to your extraordinary code of laws, I cannot but laugh ...' can have done little to change her opinion that 'all men would be tyrants if they could'.Other correspondence of the period suggests that such ideas were commonly discussed by women of Adams's class, while a more systematic analysis was given by Judith Murray.

Meanwhile in England the historian Catherine Macaulay was arguing on similar lines. In her Letters on Education (1790) she insisted that the differences between the sexes were a product of education and environment and not of nature: she attacked the way in which women's minds and bodies had been distorted to please men, and she demanded that boys and girls be given the same education - and here she went beyond uncritical acceptance of male values to demand that the education of boys too be changed to provide them with traditional female skills. Macaulay's work has been overshadowed by that of her close contemporary Mary Wollstonecraft, but at one time her fame extended across two continents: she was in correspondence with George Washington, and Abigail Adams asked a correspondent to find out all he could about her for 'One of my own sexes so eminent...naturally raises my curiosity'. Whatever the reason for her rapid disappearance from public memory (an indigestible prose style, the offence caused to polite society by her marriage to a much younger man, and the inability of male historians to cope with the existence of more than one feminist writer at a time have all been suggested - see Spender, 1983a), it is certain that at the time her ideas were widely read and anticipated many of Wollstonecraft's, a fact which the latter readily acknowledged.

By the late eighteenth century, a key source of 'progressive' ideas in England was provided by the Unitarians. Although their relationship with feminism was not unambiguous, they drew many women as well as men into campaigns against slavery and for education, and they were an important part of the radical circles which Wollstonecraft was to join. It was, however, in France that women of this period were to play the most dramatic role: the women of Paris demanding bread, the tricoteuses knitting under the guillotine and Charlotte Corday's assassination of Marat have passed into legend, while a number of individual women such as the moderate republican Madame Roland were involved in the struggle for political power. Feminism as such was always marginal to the revolution; demands for improved female education were however included in the first petitions to the National Assembly, and wider issues of women's rights and representation were soon fiercely debated in pamphlets and the radical press, and in the women's political clubs that sprang up between 1789 and 1793. Like Condorcet, women were arguing that principles of the Enlightenment applied to them too, and that political rights belonged to them as much as to men: Olympe de Gouges' Declaration of the Rights of Women is the clearest example of this approach. Such demands can seem a straightforward and 'common sense' application of existing principles.

However, as Joan Scott has argued, they were deeply paradoxical, for the claim to equal rights simultaneously denied the relevance of sex difference and affirmed the existence of women as a sexually differentiated group with identifiable interests and needs: '... in order to protest women's exclusion, they had to act on behalf of women and so invoked the very difference they sought to deny'.As we shall see, this paradox recurs throughout the history of feminism. As the revolution developed, demands were silenced; in an anti-feminist reaction the women's clubs were closed and the most prominent writers and spokeswomen imprisoned or put to death; in the light of her own fate, de Gouges' claim that 'since a woman has the right to mount the Scaffold, she must also have the right to address the House' has a terrible irony.

Although the articulation of feminist demands in the French revolution was short-lived, it had an impact on the public imagination that was to affect popular reaction to feminism in other nations: 'The feeling was that the French were bad, revolution was bad, and the French revolution had led to feminism, therefore feminism must be bad'.It is therefore important to remember that liberal feminism could be seen as a revolutionary ideology in the most literal sense, if we are to understand the reception given to Mary Wollstonecraft's ideas in England; for despite her own revulsion from the extremism and violence of the revolution, 'Viewed through the smoke of the Bastille, Wollstonecraft loomed like a bloodstained Amazon, the high-priestess of loose-tongued liberty'.This meant that although her work was less original than both her admirers and detractors have claimed, its effect was maximised by its timing – she wrote it two years after the outbreak of revolution; and it was written with a force and passion which reflected the tumultuous times through which she was living.

Mary Wollstonecraft's *Vindication of the Rights of Woman* at one level, is simply a continuation of the old debate about women's nature and their capacity for reason. Here Wollstonecraft was particularly concerned to refute the ideas of the philosopher Rousseau who, in his work Emile, which described the ideal education of a young man, had included a chapter on the very different education of 'Sophy', Emile's future wife. For Rousseau, men's and women's natures and abilities were not the same, and these biologically given differences defined their whole role in society, with men becoming citizens and women wives and mothers.

This meant that the education of boys and girls must both recognise natural differences in ability and inclination, and encourage the virtues appropriate to adult life: this involved training in rational citizenship for boys and lessons in how to please a man and bring up his children for a girl. Rousseau's democratic radicalism had marked him out from the other philosophers of the Enlightenment, and it is partly because she shared his passion for liberty and justice in other spheres that Wollstonecraft was so enraged by his views on women: it is the radical nature of Rousseau's views on politics which give a revolutionary edge to her insistence that girls and boys should be educated alike.

Her quarrel with Rousseau was fourfold. First, like earlier feminists, she refused to accept that women were less capable of reason than men, or that vanity, weakness and frivolity were the natural attributes of her sex: in phrases often strikingly reminiscent of Astell. She roundly condemned the mindless vanity of upper-class women of her day, but like Astell saw this 'femininity' as a social construct that distorted rather then reflected women's true ability. Secondly, Wollstonecraft argued that if men and women are equally possessed of reason they must be equally educated in its use: woman is not 'specially made for man's delight', but an independent being who is both capable of and entitled to a rational education. This much had, as we have seen, already been asserted by earlier feminists, but Wollstonecraft extended the argument in her third main point of disagreement with Rousseau: as men's and women's common humanity is based on their shared and God-given possession of reason, then virtue must be the same for both sexes – that isit must be based on reason and it must be freely chosen. This meant that for Wollstonecraft the virtues of the good wife and mother could not be seen as 'natural', nor could they be based upon a male-imposed ignorance cunningly disguised as innocence and she argued forcefully that a woman taught only passive obedience to her husband could never be fit to bring up children.

Women must be given knowledge and education so that they can make rational choices, for it is only then that it makes sense to talk of their goodness. This claim that women's actions must be freely chosen adds a radical new dimension to the debate, for it challenges the whole idea of ascribed social roles and the rights and duties that accompany them. It is this fourth and final area that distinguishes Wollstonecraft and her contemporaries from the earlier feminists, for the idea of equal worth now leads irrevocably to that of equal rights. In Astell's time, belief in women's rationality had been combined with political conservatism, but now it was firmly linked to political liberalism, and the principles were established that were to lead to later campaigns for women's suffrage and legal rights and, eventually, to the demand for equal participation with men in the worlds of politics and paid employment.

The systematic articulation of these demands was, however, still very much in the future, and Wollstonecraft was much more concerned to establish the principle than to elaborate a detailed programme for change. She was writing at a time when, although industrialisation was opening up new employment, this was, particularly for women, at very low wages and in appalling conditions, while in the middle ranks of society women's economic dependence on men had grown with the increased separation of home and work. As in Astell's day, employment prospects for middle-class women were almost non-existent, and Wollstonecraft's own experiences showed her how degrading and unsatisfactory were the only available options of teacher, companion and governess. Increasingly, a man's wife was seen as the purely ornamental symbol of his success and not in any sense his partner; this dependency was formalised in Blackstone's famous decree that within marriage 'the very legal existence of the wife is suspended or at least is incorporated and consolidated into that of the husband'.It was in this context that

Wollstonecraft insisted that women had an independent right to education, employment, property and the protection of the civil law; this she argued was needed to ensure that women were not forced into marriage through economic necessity, and that wives were not entirely dependent on the goodwill of their husbands. Women therefore needed legal rights in order to make independent rational choices and achieve virtue; a woman who is forced to perform the traditional female roles will do so very badly but if men would...but snap our chains, and be content with rational fellowship instead of slavish obedience, they would find us more observant daughters, more affectionate sisters, more faithful wives, more reasonable mothers – in a word, better citizens.

As the above quotation suggests, Wollstonecraft did not expect that education and freedom of choice would lead most women to reject their traditional role, but argued that they would enable them to perform it better. She did not accept the public/private split that runs through liberal thought and which insists on the superiority of the former over the latter; rather she sought to 'envalue' women's domestic responsibilities, and to show that domestic duties, properly performed, were a form of rational citizenship: that is, they were to be seen as public responsibilities rather than a source of private satisfaction or tribulation. The problem with this, of course, is that in a world in which domestic duties are unpaid, the economic dependence of a woman upon her husband remains; Wollstonecraft had perceived the dangers of this, but does not follow its implications through. Similarly, her insistence that motherhood is a form of citizenship does not solve the problem of the male monopoly of formal political and legal power, which leaves women dependent on the goodwill of men to 'snap their chains'. Here she did briefly suggest that women should have representatives in government, but this was in no way central to her argument, and although she argued that women must be free to choose a career in business or public life, she never suggested that individual successful women might use their power to benefit their sex as a whole. Carol Pateman has argued that Wollstonecraft was caught in an underlying dilemma which still traps liberal feminists today: she sought to claim citizenship for women on gender-neutral grounds at the same time as recognising their specific qualities and roles, within a framework that allowed women to become full citizens only by being like men.

Some recent feminist critics of liberalism and the Enlightenment have argued that Wollstonecraft's arguments are further confused by her uncritical acceptance of an inherently male model of rationality which, as discussed above, is bound up with the need to subdue qualities traditionally associated with women, such as passion and emotion, and which sees calculating self-interest rather than sympathy, emotion or imagination as the only legitimate basis for human motivation and conduct. Even Rousseau, who stressed the importance of passion in human affairs, insisted that public life must be ruled solely by reason.

He therefore argued that women can have no place in politics; his recent feminist critics argue that this exclusion is not simply a regrettable product of Rousseau's personal prejudices, which could be ignored by later theorists, but is basic to a view of rational citizenship which presupposes not only the exclusion of passion from public life, but its containment and expression within the family. This means that, from a Rousseau-ite perspective, if women enter political life they not only disrupt it, they also destroy its domestic foundations.

Critics argue that such an approach cannot provide an

adequate basis for a woman-centred theory or feminist politics. The problem is only compounded if domesticity too is seen as a source of civic responsibility to which the same public standards of rationality apply. Some feminist critics of liberal rationality have therefore criticised Wollestonecraft's apparent denial of any legitimate place to more unruly emotions and desires, and they have attributed her unhappy private life to an unworkable belief that even in marriage passion and love must be subordinated to reason, so that 'In the choice of a husband women should not be led astray by the qualities of a lover'. As Virginia Sapiro has pointed out, a problem with this body of feminist criticism is that it is often based on a caricature of Enlightenment thinking.

It also misrepresents Wollstonecraft, who employed the contemporary notion of sensibility to argue for the legitimacy of both emotion and reason 'so long as emotion was trained by reason and reason tempered by emotion', and whose belief in women's need to control their sexual impulses was simply common sense in an age when lack of reliable contraception or safe childbirth meant that 'Sexuality was – materially and not just conceptually – a life-and-death matter for women'. It is also self-evident that unhappy relationships are not confined to liberal feminists, and many a contemporary feminist whose heart or sexual desire refuses to obey the dictates of logic and political correctness will empathise with Wollstonecraft's unhappy love affairs and sympathise with the conflict between love and reason articulated in her private correspondence; many may also envy her eventual marriage to the philosopher Godwin, which appears to have been based on a high degree of mutual respect and independence as well as love.Ironically, it was the publication of her correspondence by Godwin shortly after her death in childbirth that did most to discredit her ideas for the next generations of women: the association of feminism with 'immorality' effectively banished it from consideration in 'respectable' society.

A further criticism that has frequently been made of liberal feminists is that they fail to recognise any non-sexual forms of oppression or to relate the situation of women to conditions in society as a whole; in particular they are accused of being class-blind, and interested only in the plight of middle-class women. Thus it has been said of Wollstonecraft that 'her feminism was basically a demand for equality with bourgeois man', and certainly the Vindication does address itself to women of the middle class, and she consistently seems to assume that the existence of servants is necessary if domestic work is to be more than mindless drudgery.

However, the ideas discussed in the radical circles in which Wollstonecraft moved were certainly not confined to the demand for formal legal rights, but encompassed a whole range of social, economic and religious concerns, with a clear overlap between the ideas of early liberal and socialist writers.If we look beyond the pages of the *Vindication of the Rights of Woman* to Wollstonecraft's earlier Vindication of the Rights of Man (1790), we see her rejecting arguments for hierarchy and privilege, and attacking inheritance and property as causes of poverty and misery for working people; her last novel was concerned to explore the predicament not only of the middle-class heroine, but also of a servant girl drawn into prostitution.

To describe Wollstonecraft as a socialist would be an exaggeration, for her ideas on economics remain latent rather than systematically articulated, but there is in her writings a consistent insistence that a good social order is incompatible with a high degree of inequality: 'From the respect paid to property flow, as from a poisoned fountain, most of the evils and vices which render this world such a dreary place to the contemplative mind' and 'the more equality there is among men, the more virtue and happiness will reign in society'.Thus she went well beyond the defence of equal property rights normally associated with liberalism, and provides an interesting link with the ideas of the 'utopian socialists' to which we now turn – indeed one of the foremost of these, Robert Owen was to say that he 'had never met with a person who thought as exactly as he did'.

The Utopian Socialists and Feminism

The term 'utopian socialist' was used by Marx and Engels to refer to those who believed that competitive capitalist society should be replaced by a more equitably organised, co-operative and rational one, and that this could be achieved by demonstrating the reasonableness and desirability of reform: persuasion and example, not class conflict and revolution, were to be the agents of social change. The best known of these early socialists were the Frenchmen St Simon and Fourier, and the British Robert Owen.They do not form a unified groupand some of their ideas were eccentric in the extreme; they had, however, an important influence on later writers and, unlike most later socialists, they saw relationships between the sexes and within the family as central issues - changes here were not seen as simply the by-products of social change or class struggle, but were themselves a necessary precondition for the transformation of society.

These feminist aspects of their thought were developed by some of their followers and attracted widespread interest and excitement in both Europe and America.There was lively debate in the press and, while previous generations of feminists had broken ground by going into print, women such as Frances Wright, Anna Wheeler, Frances Morrison and Flora Tristan were now stating their case in public and drawing huge crowds to their lectures and meetings.In the numerous but short-lived socialist communities that the movement inspired, the role of women was a central concern, while William Thompson and Anna Wheeler's 1825 Appeal on Behalf of Women remains an outstanding contribution to feminist theory.

In this context the ideas of Wollstonecraft and other liberal feminists were but a starting-point and, although socialist feminism was never a coherent movement, a number of key themes emerge. In the first place, the goal was not equal rights within the existing system, but within a radically transformed one in which private property was to be abolished or severely modified, and in which women would have economic as well as legal independence. Secondly, the traditional division of labour between the sexes was widely attacked: not only were women to be given a full place in productive life, but some even suggested that men should share communal responsibility for domestic work. Thirdly, the family as an institution was widely condemned: it was seen as a source of male power, a bastion of selfish individualism incompatible with socialist co-operation, and as a coercive restraint on free choice. Following from this, some stressed, fourthly, the importance of the free expression of sexuality, and argued that 'free love' was the necessary basis of a free society. All this meant that the liberal claim for equal rights was now placed firmly within a social–economic context of which Wollstonecraft had shown only passing awareness and power relationships were identified within the family as well as in public life.

Recent writers have also seen in the new ideas on sexuality a symbolic challenge to the dualism of Western political thought, for reason and virtue no longer seemed to require the denial of passion, but rather its fullest possible expression. Attempts to put this analysis into practice, however, met with little success. With their faith in reason and human perfectibility the leaders were very much children of the Enlightenment; they therefore expected that education and example would prove the moral and practical superiorityof their system, and that capitalist funding would be found to further the cause of social transformation. Perhaps not surprisingly, such support was seldom forthcoming.

Thus, although Owen claimed to have shown that benevolence was not incompatible with capitalist self-interest in his famous model factory at New Lanark in Scotland, where improved conditions, health and housing had produced not only a healthy workforce but healthy profits too, other capitalists remained unconvinced that this represented a sound return on investment, and were frightened off the scheme by Owen's increasingly radical ideas on religion and the family. Owen himself came to see the establishment of socialist communities as a speedier means of regenerating society: as with those inspired by Fourier, the idea was not to 'drop out' of existing society, but to change it by force of example; in practice, however, the communities were to prove more of a warning than an inspiration. America in the nineteenth century had seemed to offer an ideal opportunity for such experiments, and Emerson wrote in 1840 that 'Not a reading man but has a draft of a new community in his waistcoat pocket'.Of the five hundred or so secular and religious communities that were established, about 50 were inspired by Fourier and 16 by Owen; there were also at least 7 Owenite communities in England between 1821 and 1845. However, none of these socialist communities lasted for more than a few years; this was partly because optimism and idealism could not compensate for lack of practical skills and financial resources, and partly because they tended to attract all kinds of opportunists and misfits and were torn by personality clashes and policy disputes; attitudes to women and to the family also seem to have played a crucial role.

For Owen, private property, religion and marriage formed a kind of unholy and inseparable trinity: each was evil in itself, each upheld the others, and none could therefore be eradicated in isolation. Thus, to stop the married woman being treated as the property of her husband, it was necessary to abolish not only marriage but also private property. To abolish private property, it was necessary to remove the major source of individualism and selfish gratification - the family. To do this, it was necessary to attack the cement that bound them together and upheld them both - religion. However, although the three institutions were logically entwined in theory, Owen found himself unable to abolish the family in practice: most of those entering the communities wished to live as couples, communal childrearing and the separation of children from their parents were far too unpopular to carry out, and fear of scandal led him to downplay his attack on marriage.

The need for such caution was shown by the extent of public hostility to the Owenite community that had been established at Nashoba in 1825 by Frances Wright with the rehabilitation of former slaves as a major aim. Wright's unorthodox views on marriage ('she put an affirmation of sexual experience that no one else in nineteenth-century

America would approach', Eckhardt, 1984:156) provoked widespread condemnation and effectively removed any chances of attracting 'respectable' financial support. Fourier's ideas on the liberating effects of sensuality were downplayed for similar reasons: he had advocated extreme sexual permissiveness both as a means of breaking down the ethics of individualism and possessiveness, and because he thought repression was harmful and incompatible with harmonious society; clearly his ideas could all too easily become an excuse for sexual exploitation, but in practice the Fourierite communities largely ignored this aspect of his thought and adopted a relatively conservative attitude to the family.

This means that although the failure of the communities is often cited as proof of the inadequacy of the utopian socialists' theories, their theories on the family were never in fact put to the test. As with the family and sexuality, so too with the division of labour, socialist theory was never matched by community practice. Here Fourier's views were again the most radical, for he demanded a total end to all specialization and the entire division of labour: he argued that work could be fulfilling and creative only if it were freely chosen, and that an ideal community must be organised to allow all individuals to move freely from one occupation to another. He did seem to think that some jobs will naturally be more attractive to women and implied that they should care for very small children, but he also insisted that in any occupation at least some of the workers should be of the sex that does not normally perform it.

This meant that no man or woman would be bound to one task for life and that domestic tasks like all other work would be the willingly performed expression of creativity rather than mindless drudgery. In practice, however, Fourier's elaborate ideas were never systematically applied, and, despite the claims of the men to the contrary, it seems that responsibility for domestic life remained firmly with the women in all the communities. In this context it is perhaps not surprising that they should consistently be less enthusiastic in their support than the men; this was often taken as a sign of women's political backwardness, but, as Barbara Taylor has argued, it had less to do with any innate partiality for individual wash-tubs than a fear, often justified, of becoming embroiled in a hard life over which they would have too little control, and in which they would bear the brunt of utopian impracticality.

However, as indicated at the beginning of this section, the impact of utopian socialism and its importance for feminist theory was not limited to the experience of the communities, but became linked in the 1830s and 1840s to a revival of interest in feminist issues which although shortlived was international in character. Thus, for example, Frances Wright had contacts in England, France and America, while there were many direct links between Owenites in England and French feminists inspired by the ideas of Fourier and St Simon.The ferment of ideas around the time of the evolutions which swept across much of the European continent in 1848 also had a clear impact on the American feminists.

The St Simoniennes are of particular historical significance, both because they involved unprecedented numbers of working-class women, and because of their affinity with some late twentieth-century feminist thought. As well as firmly identifying the link between sexual and class issues, they rejected liberal arguments based on equal rationality, making their claims for women on the basis of their essential difference from men, and they saw sexual repression as central to women's subordination. They also took the unprecedented step of holding women-only meetings and setting up their own newspaper, which only published articles by women. Claire Moses argues that they were, therefore, asserting women's cultural autonomy and establishing what 'was most likely the first consciously separatist women's liberation movement in history'.

Although she too drew on St Simonian ideas to argue that women were both different from and superior to men, Flora Tristan took a rather different line on political activity, arguing that working men must be persuaded both to rise up in protest at their current situation and to liberate working women. In the early 1840s, Tristan was to be disappointed by most French workers' apparent indifference to both socialism and feminism, whilst even socialists frequently expressed suspicion of feminist concerns. Such tension between socialism and feminism was also apparent in England, where Owenism had by the 1830s built up a considerable basis of workingclass support strongly linked to the cooperative and trade union movements. Owenism never became a mass movement on the scale of the Chartist campaign for the vote which reached its peak at about the same period, but its feminism posed problems for working-class supporters at a time when the idea of the male breadwinner and domestic wife was becoming increasingly popular amongst the working class. Women had been widely involved in political activity such as food riots and strikes earlier in the century, but with increased sexual competition for jobs they became excluded from trade union activity, and although they played an active role in both Chartist and Owenite organisations, particularly in the earlier years, this was often in support of male activity and did not necessarily involve any kind of feminist consciousness. By the 1850s political involvement by working-class women had sharply declined and active hostility to feminism had increased.

Nevertheless, for a brief period socialism and feminism had been united not only with each other but with the idea that it is only by transforming personal life that wider political and socio-economic changes can occur, and that such personal change itself can only succeed in the context of wider social transformation - so that the personal, the political and the socio-economic are inextricably linked and intertwined. Although latent in all utopian socialist theories, especially those of Owen and the St Simoniennes, these interconnections were given their most sustained analysis in the work of Anna Wheeler, a leading socialist feminist lecturer, and her friend William Thompson,a leading Owenite and economist, who gave feminism a centrality lacking in other male writers; their most direct analysis of women's situation is to be found in the splendidly titled, Wheeler and Thompson's Appeal on Behalf of Women.

The Appeal was formally a reply to James Mill's Article on Government in which Mill had claimed that, because women have no interests separate from those of their husband or father, they have no need for independent political representation. As such, it ridiculed Mill's logic and vigorously restated the liberal case for equal rights; here Wheeler and Thompson went well beyond Wollstonecraft's tentative ideas on representation to insist that women are entitled to full political rights including representation and participation in affairs of state. Women's intellectual capacity is, they argued, at least as great as men's, and biological differences can never be an argument against political rights.

At present 'the law has erected the physical organisation into a crime', but in fact, they asserted, the consequences of female biology are much less incapacitating than the diseases of excess to which male legislators are prone, while is it possible to conceive that legislative power lodged exclusively in the hands of women could have produced atrocities and wretchedness equal to those with which exclusive male legislation has desolated the globe?

However, Wheeler and Thompson were not simply liberal feminists, and although they claimed equal political and legal rights for womenthey argued that these could become meaningful only when common ownership and co-operation replaced private property and competition as the basis of social organisation. Until such time, they claimed, women would still be disadvantaged, for formal equality takes no account of actual difference of condition,so that men will in practice be more successful than women and 'superiority in the production or accumulation of individual wealth will ever be whispering into man's ear preposterous notions of his relative importance over woman'.Economic independence for Wheeler and Thompson therefore involved far more than Wollstonecraft's insistence that women have the right to follow a career, for it included the independence of a wife from her husband. This they argued, could only be achieved in a cooperative society in which the full worth of women's contribution would be appreciated, and in which there would be no motives for men to practice injustices or for women to submit to them – for only without the distorting influences of possession and property could men and women relate to each other as free and equal human beings.

However, although women's oppression was therefore seen as a product of capitalism reinforced by unequal laws, Wheeler and Thompson also saw it as based on men's selfishness: Whatever system of labour…whatever system of government…under every vicissitude of MAN's condition he has always retained woman his slave. This led them to an analysis of the ways in which men have kept women as their slaves which has clear affinities with the radical feminist analysis of patriarchy and oppression in personal relationships. Thus, they argued that a husband does not simply use legal or physical coercion to dominate his wife but insists on controlling her mind, demanding her love as well as her obedience and 'exacting from her trained obsequiousness the semblance of a voluntary obedience'. They saw the family too as a means of male domination, where women are 'isolated and stultified with their children, with their fire and food-processing processes' and reduced by their despotic husbands 'to a state of stupidity and apathy, rendering them incapable of a greater degree of happiness than that of the brutes'.

All this is strong stuff, and provides an analysis of power in personal and family relations which is far removed from Wollstonecraft's ideal of the 'domestic citizen'. However it did not lead Wheeler and Thompson to condemn the male sex in perpetuity or to advocate the kind of separatist men visaged by some late twentieth-century radical feminists.Rather, they believed that the true interests of the sexes could be reconciled, for if women were free then men would find the pleasures of equal companionship far outweighed those of despotism; on a larger scale, the ending of relations of dependency and possession in personal life would make possible a new and higher order of society and as women's bondage has chained down man to the ignorance and vices of despotism, so will their liberation reward him with knowledge, with freedom and with happiness.

This conclusion blends liberal, socialist and radical analysis as it shows the interconnections of political, economic and personal power, and as such it has much in common with recent socialist feminist analysis. It also frequently bears a startling resemblance to the ideas put forward by John Stuart Mill in his famous *On the Subjection of Women* some twenty-four years later; and it is based on a philosophy, utilitarianism, which is usually associated with liberal theory but which Wheeler and Thompson use throughout their analysis. Wheeler and Thompson's use of utilitarian theory suggests that liberal concepts may be more flexible than some feminists have claimed, and not necessarily incompatible with other approaches. Although the utopian socialists failed to achieve their aims, and they have generally been seen as merely an eccentric footnote to the history books, their ideas represent an important if brief alliance of liberal, socialist and feminist ideals which challenged the distinction between the private and the public and saw the interconnections between legal, political, economic and personal subordination. As we shall see in the next chapter, they also had a direct influence on some later mainstream writers. Nevertheless, for the next 150 years, liberal campaigns for political and legal rights were often separate from socialist reoccupations with the class struggle, while the idea of personal oppression frequently disappeared from the agenda; it was only towards the end of the twentieth century that these strands were to be drawn systematically together again.

3

Feminist Political Philosophy

Feminist political philosophy is an area of philosophy focused on understanding and critiquing the way political philosophy is usually construed, often without any attention to feminist concerns, and to articulating how political theory might be reconstructed in a way that advances feminist concerns. Feminist political philosophy is a branch of both feminist philosophy and political philosophy. As a branch of feminist philosophy, it serves as a form of critique or a hermeneutics of suspicion.That is, it serves as a way of opening up or looking at the political world as it is usually understood and uncovering ways in which women and their current and historical concerns are poorly depicted, represented, and addressed. As a branch of political philosophy, feminist political philosophy serves as a field for developing new ideals, practices, and justifications for how political institutions and practices should be organized and reconstructed.

While feminist philosophy has been instrumental in critiquing and reconstructing many branches of philosophy, from aesthetics to philosophy of science, feminist political philosophy may be the paradigmatic branch of feminist philosophy because it best exemplifies the point of feminist theory, which is, to borrow a phrase from Marx, not only to understand the world but to change it.And, though other fields have effects that may change the world, feminist political philosophy focuses most directly on understanding ways in which collective life can be improved. This project involves understanding the ways in which power emerges and is used or misused in public life.As with other kinds of feminist theory, common themes have emerged for discussion and critique, but there has been little in the way of consensus among feminist theorists on what is the best way to understand them. This introductory article lays out the various schools of thought and areas of concern that have occupied this vibrant field of philosophy for the past thirty years.

Historical Context

Current feminist political philosophy is indebted to the work of earlier generations of feminist scholarship and activism, including the first wave of feminism in the English-speaking world, which took place from the 1840s to the 1920s and focused on improving the political, educational, and economic system primarily for middle-class women. Its greatest achievements were to develop a language of equal rights for women and to garner women the right to vote. It is also indebted to the second wave of feminism, which, beginning in the 1960s, drew on the language of the civil rights movements and on a new feminist consciousness that emerged through women's solidarity movements and new forms of reflection that uncovered sexist attitudes and impediments throughout the whole of society. As the entry on approaches to feminism notes, by 1970 feminism had expanded from activism to scholarship with the publication of Shulamith Firestone's *The Dialectic of Sex*; Kate Millett's *Sexual Politics*; and Robin Morgan's *Sisterhood is Powerful*.

As a branch of political philosophy, feminist political philosophy has often mirrored the various divisions at work in political philosophy more broadly. Prior to the fall of the Berlin Wall and the end of the Cold War, political philosophy was usually divided into categories such as liberal, conservative, socialist, and Marxist. Except for conservatism, for each category there were often feminists working and critiquing alongside it. Hence, as Alison Jaggar's classic text, *Feminist Politics and Human Nature*, spelled out, each ideological approach drew feminist scholars who would both take their cue from and borrow the language of a particular ideology.Jaggar's text grouped feminist political philosophy into four camps: liberal feminism, socialist feminism, Marxist feminism, and radical feminism. The first three groups followed the lines of Cold War global political divisions: American liberalism, European socialism, and revolutionary communism.Radical feminism was the most indigenous of the feminist philosophies, developing its own political vocabulary with its roots in the deep criticisms of patriarchy that feminist consciousness had produced in its first and second waves. Otherwise, feminist political philosophy largely followed the lines of traditional political philosophy. But this has never been an uncritical following. As a field bent on changing the world, even liberal feminist theorists tended to criticize liberalism more than to embrace it, and to embrace socialism and other more radical points of view more than to reject them. Still, on the whole, these theorists generally operated within the language and framework of their chosen approach to political philosophy.

Political philosophy began to change enormously in the 1980s, just before the end of the Cold War, with a new invocation of an old Hegelian category: civil society, an arena of political life intermediate between the state and the household. This was the arena of associations, churches, labor unions, book clubs, choral societies and manifolds other nongovernmental yet still public organizations. In the 1980s political theorists began to turn their focus from the state to this intermediate realm, which suddenly took center stage in Eastern Europe in organizations that challenged the power of the state and ultimately led to the downfall of communist regimes.

After the end of the Cold War, political philosophy along with political life radically realigned. New attention focused on civil society and the public sphere, especially with the timely translation of Jürgen Habermas's early work, the *Structural Transformation of the Public Sphere.*Volumes soon appeared on civil society and the public sphere, focusing on the ways in which people organized themselves and developed public power rather than on the ways that the state garnered and exerted its power. In fact, there arose a sense that the public sphere ultimately might exert more power than the state, at least in the fundamental way in which public will is formed and serves to legitimate- or not- state power.

In the latter respect, John Rawls's work was influential by developing a theory of justice that tied the legitimacy of institutions to the normative judgments that a reflective and deliberative people might make. By the early 1990s, Marxists seemed to have disappeared or at least become very circumspect (though the downfall of communist regimes needn't have had any effect on Marxist analysis proper, which never subscribed to Leninist or Maoist thought). Socialists also retreated or transformed themselves into "radical democrats."

Now the old categories of liberal, socialist, and Marxist feminisms were much less relevant. Along with political philosophy more broadly, more feminist political philosophers began to turn to the meaning and interpretation of civil society, the public sphere, and democracy itself.

Contemporary Approaches and Debates

Of Jaggar's categories, liberal feminism and radical feminism remain strong currents in feminist political thought. Care ethics, which was originally developed as an alternative to mainstream ethical theory, has been harnessed to counter liberal political theory.More recently, two other approaches have emerged: radical democratic or "agonistic" feminism and deliberative or communicative democratic theory.An even newer approach that might be termed "performative" is also developing.This section gives a brief overview of these various approaches and attendant issues.

Liberal Feminism

The first of these, liberal feminism, can be traced back to feminist efforts and theorizing around political and economic equality for women. This approach got a boost with the publication of John Rawls's *A Theory of Justice* and subsequently his *Political Liberalism*.Susan Moller Okin and Eva Kittay have used Rawls's work productively to extend his theory to attend to women's concerns. From a more critical perspective, several feminist theorists have argued that some of the central categories of liberalism occlude women's lived concerns; for example, the central liberal private/public distinction sequesters the private sphere, and any harm that may occur there to women, away from political scrutiny.Perhaps more than any other approach, liberal feminist theory parallels developments in liberal feminist activism.

While feminist activists have waged legal and political battles to criminalize, as just one example, violence against women, feminist political philosophers who have engaged the liberal lexicon have shown how the distinction between private and public realms has served to uphold male domination of women by rendering power relations within the household as "natural" and immune from political regulation. Such political philosophy uncovers how seemingly innocuous and "commonsensical" categories have covert power agendas. For example, old conceptions of the sanctity of the private space of the household and the role of women primarily as child-bearers and caregivers served to protect male domination of women in the household from public scrutiny. Feminist critiques of the public/private split supported legal advances that finally led in the 1980s to the criminalization in the United States of spousal rape.

Radical Feminism

A second approach, radical feminism, remains committed to getting at the root of male domination by understanding the source of power differentials, which some radical feminists, including Catharine MacKinnon, trace back to male sexuality and the notion that heterosexual intercourse enacts male domination over women. "Women and men are divided by gender, made into the sexes as we know them, by the requirements of its dominant form, heterosexuality, which institutionalizes male sexual dominance and female sexual submission. If this is true, sexuality is the linchpin of gender inequality".Radical feminists tend to see power as running one-way, from those with power over those who are being oppressed. As Amy Allen puts it, "Unlike liberal feminists, who view power as a positive social resource that ought to be fairly distributed, and feminist phenomenologists, who understand domination in terms of a tension between transcendence and immanence, radical feminists tend to understand power in terms of dyadic relations of dominance/subordination, often understood on analogy with the relationship between master and slave." Unlike the more reformist politics of liberal feminism, radical feminists have largely sought to reject the prevailing order altogether, sometimes advocating separatism.

Maternal Feminism

A third important approach in feminist political philosophy draws on what is called care or maternal ethics. Drawing on feminist research in moral psychology, this field explores the ways in which the virtues that society and mothering cultivate in women can provide an alternative to the traditional emphases in moral and political philosophy on universality, reason, and justice. Some maternalists have sought to take the virtues that had long been relegated to the private realm, such as paying particular attention to those who are vulnerable or taking into consideration circumstances and not just abstract principles, and use them as well in the public realm. This approach has led to intense debates between liberals who advocated universal ideals of justice and maternalists who advocated attention to the particular, to relationships, to care. By the 1990s, though, many maternalists had revised their views. Rather than seeing care and justice as mutually exclusive alternatives, they began to recognize that attention to care should be accompanied by attention to fairness in order to attend to the plight of those with whom we have no immediate relation.

The maternalist approach raises the question of whether and, if so, how women have distinct virtues. Feminists as a whole have long distanced themselves from ideas that women have any particular essence, choosing instead to see femininity and its accompanying virtues as social constructs, dispositions that result from culture and conditioning, certainly not biological givens. So for maternalists to champion the virtues that have inculcated femininity seems also to champion a patriarchal system that relegates one gender to the role of caretaker. The maternalist tactic has largely been to flip the hierarchy, to claim that the work of the household is more meaningful and sustaining than the work of the polis. But critics, such as Drucilla Cornell, Mary Dietz, and Chantal Mouffe, argue that such a revaluation keeps intact the dichotomy between the private and the public and the old association of women's work with childcare.

Such concerns are part of a larger set of concerns and criticisms that have run through feminist theorizing since the 1970s, with non-white, non-middle-class, and non-American women starting to question the very category of "woman" and the notion that this title could be a boundary-spanning category that could unite women of various walks of life. Criticisms of a unitary identity of "woman" have been motivated by worries that much feminist theory has originated from the standpoint of a particular class of women who mistake their own particular standpoint for a universal one.

In her 1981 book, Ain't I a Woman?: Black Women and Feminism, bell hooks notes that the feminist movement pretends to speak for all women but was made up of primarily white, middle class women who, because of their narrow perspective, did not represent the needs of poor women and women of color and ended up reinforcing class stereotypes.What is so damning about this kind of critique is that it mirrors the one that feminists have leveled against mainstream political theorists who have taken the particular category of men to be a universal category of mankind, a schema that does not in fact include women under the category of mankind but marks them as other.

Hence, one of the most vexing issues facing feminist theory in general and feminist political philosophy in particular is the matter of identity.Identity politics in general is a controversial political practice of mobilizing for change on the basis of a political identity.The philosophical debate is whether such identities are based on some real difference or history of oppression, and also whether people should embrace identities that have historically been used to oppress them. Identity politics in feminist practice is fraught along at least two axes: whether there is any real essence or identity of woman in general and even if so whether the category of woman could be used to represent all women. Women at the intersection of various identities have raised questions about which identity is foremost or whether either identity is apt. Such questions play out with the question of political representation- what aspects of identity are politically salient and truly representative, whether race, class, or gender.The ontological question of women's identity gets played out on the political stage when it comes to matters of political representation, group rights, and affirmative action.

The 2008 U.S. Democratic Party primary battle between Senators Barack Obama and Hillary Clinton turned this philosophical question into a very real and heated one from black women throughout the United States. Was a black woman who supported Clinton a traitor to her race, or a black woman who supported Obama a traitor to her sex? Or did it make any sense to talk about identity in a way that would lead to charges of treason? Of the approaches discussed above, radical and maternal feminism seem particularly wedded to feminist identity politics.

Democratic Feminism

Fourth is feminist democratic theory, perhaps best known through the works of Seyla Benhabib, greatly inspired by the work of the German critical theorist, Jürgen Habermas. Like other feminist democratic theorists, Benhabib's work engages democratic theorists quite broadly, not just feminist theorists. This passage of hers helps to clarify what she takes to be the best aim of a political philosophy: a state of affairs to which all affected would assent. As she writes, Only those norms can be said to be valid,which would be agreed to by all those affected by their consequences, if such agreement were reached as a consequence of a process of deliberation that had the following features: 1) participation in such deliberation is governed by norms of equality and symmetry; all have the same chances to initiate speech acts, to question, to interrogate, and to open debate; 2) all have the right to question the assigned topics of conversation; and 3) all have the right to initiate reflexive arguments about the very rules of the discourse procedure and the way in which they are applied or carried out.

Democratic theorists such as Benhabib and Habermas contend that certain conditions need to be in place in order for members of a political community to arrive at democratic outcomes, namely the proceedings need to be deliberative. Some take deliberation to be a matter of reasoned argumentation; others see it as less about reason or argumentation but more about an open process of working through choices.

Deliberative theory is not the only prominent form of feminist democratic theory. Iris Young's pioneering book, *Justice and the Politics of Difference* and several of her subsequent works have been very influential and have led to a good deal of hesitance in feminist theoretical communities about the claims of deliberative theory where Benhabib is confident that conditions can be such that all who are affected can have a voice in deliberations, Young points out that those who have been historically silenced have a difficult time having their views heard or heeded. Young is skeptical of the claims of mainstream democratic theory that democratic deliberative processes could lead to outcomes that would be acceptable to all.

Young, along with Nancy Fraser and others, worried that in the process of trying to reach consensus, the untrained voices of women and others who have been marginalized would be left out of the final tally. Young's criticisms were very persuasive, leading a generation of feminist political philosophers to be wary of deliberative democratic theory. Instead of deliberative democracy, in the mid 1990s Young proposed a theory of communicative democracy, hoping to make way for a deliberative conception that was open to means of expression beyond the rational expression of mainstream deliberative democratic theory. Young worried that deliberation as defined by Habermas is too reason-based and leaves out forms of communication that women and people of color tend to use, such as greeting, rhetoric, and storytelling. Young argued that these alternative modes of communication, modes that women and people of color and other marginalized people tended to use, could provide the basis of a more democratic, communicative theory. In her last major book, *Inclusion and Democracy*, Young had clearly moved to embrace deliberative theory itself, seeing the ways in which it could be constructed to give voice to those who had been otherwise marginalized. More recent feminist democratic theory has engaged deliberative theory more positively.

Agonistic Feminism

A fifth approach is agonistic feminism, which draws from a certain reading of the work of Hannah Arendt and from Antonio Gramsci, among others. Leading theorists of this approach include Chantal Mouffe, Bonnie Honig, and Ewa Ziarek.Where liberal feminists inspired by John Rawls and democratic feminists inspired by Jürgen Habermas and/or John Dewey hold out the hope that democratic deliberations might lead to democratic agreements, agonistic feminists maintain that any kind of agreement is inherently undemocratic.

Agonistic feminist political philosophy comes out of poststructural continental feminist and philosophical traditions. It takes from Marxism, especially western Marxism, the hope for a more radically egalitarian society. It takes from contemporary continental philosophy notions of subjectivity and solidarity as malleable and constructed. Along with much of postmodern thought, it repudiates any notion of pre-existing moral or political truths or foundations. Its central claim is that feminist struggle, like other struggles for social justice, is engaged in politics as battle or war. Agonistic views see the nature of politics as inherently conflictual, with battles over power and hegemony being the central tasks of democratic struggle. Advocates of agonistic politics worry that the kind of consensus sought by democratic theorists will lead to some kind of oppression or injustice by silencing new struggles. As Chantal Mouffe puts it, "We have to accept that every consensus exists as a temporary result of a provisional hegemony, as a stabilization of power, and that it always entails some form of exclusion".

Performative Feminism

A sixth approach to feminist political philosophy is emerging, what could be called performative feminist political philosophy. Performative feminist politics doesn't worry about whether it is possible to come up with a single definition of "woman" or any other political identity; it sees identity as something that is performatively created. "How we assume these identitites," Drucilla Cornell writes, "is never something 'out there' that effectively determines who we can be as men and women- gay, lesbian, straight, queer, transsexual, transgender, or otherwise". It is something that is shaped as we live and externalize identities. From a performative feminist perspective, feminism is a project of anticipating and creating better political futures in the absence of foundations. As Linda Zerilli writes, "politics is about making claims and judgments- and having the courage to do so- in the absence of the objective criteria or rules that could provide certain knowledge and the guarantee that speaking in women's name will be accepted or taken up by others".Drawing on the works of Arendt, Butler, and Joan Copjec, Zerilli calls for a "freedom-centered feminism" that "would strive to bring about transformation in normative conceptions of gender without returning to the classical notion of freedom as sovereignty" that feminists have long criticized but found difficult to resist.

In its feminist incarnations, this view also takes its cue from Judith Butler's performative account of gender as well as Hannah Arendt's concern with the anticipatory nature of rights, as well as other thinkers' ideas, to describe an anticipatory ideal of politics. Linda Zerilli describes this kind of feminist politics as "the contingently based public practice of soliciting the agreement of others to what each of us claims to be universal".From a performatve perspective, normative political claims appeal to other people, not to supposed truths or foundations. This view recuperates many of the ideals of the Enlightenment- such as freedom, autonomy, and justice- but in a way that drops the Enlightenment's metaphysical assumptions about reason, progress, and human nature. Instead of seeing these ideals as grounded in some metaphysical facts, this new view sees them as ideals that people hold and try to instantiate through practice and imagination. Where many ancient and modern ideals of politics were based on suppositions about the nature of reality or of human beings, contemporary political philosophies generally operate without supposing that there are any universal or eternal truths. Some might see this situation as ripe for nihilism, arbitrariness, or the exercise of brute power. The performative alternative is to imagine and try to create a better world by anticipating, claiming, and appealing to others that it should be so. Even if there is no metaphysical truth that human beings have dignity and infinite worth, people can act as if it were true in order to create a world in which it is seen to be so.

What Zerilli does with the concept of freedom, Drucilla Cornell does with the idea of autonomy. Her work in ethics and political philosophy is also in this vein, arguing for seeing old Enlightenment notions such as autonomy, dignity, and personhood, in a new performative capacity, as ideals that people aspire to rather than as moral facts waiting to be discovered, applied, or realized. Peformative feminist political philosophy shares liberal feminism's appreciation for Enlightenment ideals but in a way that is skeptical about foundations, just as agonistic feminism repudiates foundations. It has less in common with radical and maternalist feminisms for these very reasons.

In sum, feminist political philosophy is a still evolving field of thought that has much to offer mainstream political philosophy. In the past two decades it has come to exert a stronger influence over mainstream political theorizing, raising objections that mainstream philosophers have had to address, though not always very convincingly. And in its newest developments it promises to go even further.

4

Identity Politics

The laden phrase "identity politics" has come to signify a wide range of political activity and theorizing founded in the shared experiences of injustice of members of certain social groups. Rather than organizing solely around belief systems, programmatic manifestoes, or party affiliation, identity political formations typically aim to secure the political freedom of a specific constituency marginalized within its larger context. Members of that constituency assert or reclaim ways of understanding their distinctiveness that challenge dominant oppressive characterizations, with the goal of greater self-determination.

History and Scope

The second half of the twentieth century saw the emergence of large-scale political movements - second wave feminism, Black Civil Rights in the U.S., gay and lesbian liberation, and the American Indian movements, for example - based in claims about the injustices done to particular social groups. These social movements are undergirded by and foster a philosophical body of literature that takes up questions about the nature, origin and futures of the identities being defended. Identity politics as a mode of organizing is intimately connected to the idea that some social groups are oppressed; that is, that one's identity as a woman or as a Native American, for example, makes one peculiarly vulnerable to cultural imperialism, violence, exploitation, marginalization, or powerlessness.Identity politics starts from analyses of oppression to recommend, variously, the reclaiming, redescription, or transformation of previously stigmatized accounts of group membership. Rather than accepting the negative scripts offered by a dominant culture about one's own inferiority, one transforms one's own sense of self and community, often through consciousness-raising. For example, in their germinal statement of Black feminist identity politics, the Combahee River Collective argued that "as children we realized that we were different from boys and that we were treated different - for example, when we were told in the same breath to be quiet both for the sake of being 'ladylike' and to make us less objectionable in the eyes of white people. In the process of consciousness-raising, actually life-sharing, we began to recognize the commonality of our experiences and, from the sharing and growing consciousness, to build a politics that will change our lives and inevitably end our oppression".

The scope of political movements that may be described as identity politics is broad: the examples used in the philosophical literature are predominantly of struggles within western capitalist democracies, but indigenous rights movements' worldwide, nationalist projects, or demands for regional self-determination use similar arguments. Predictably, there is no straightforward criterion that makes a political struggle into an example of "identity politics;" rather, the term signifies a loose collection of political projects, each undertaken by representatives of a collective with a distinctively different social location that has hitherto been neglected, erased, or suppressed. It is beyond the scope of this essay to offer historical or sociological surveys of the many different social movements that might be described as identity politics, although some references to this literature are provided in the bibliography; instead the focus here is to provide an overview of the philosophical issues in the expansive literature in political theory.

The phrase "identity politics" is also something of a philosophical punching-bag for a variety of critics. Often challenges fail to make sufficiently clear their object of critique, using "identity politics" as a blanket description that invokes a range of tacit political failings.From a contemporary perspective, some early identity claims by political activists certainly seem naive, totalizing, or unnuanced. However, the public rhetoric of identity politics served useful and empowering purposes for some, even while it sometimes belied the philosophical complexity of any claim to a shared experience or common group characteristics. Since the twentieth century heyday of the well known political movements that made identity politics so visible, a vast academic literature has sprung up; although "identity politics" can draw on intellectual precursors from Mary Wollstonecraft to Frantz Fanon, writing that actually uses this specific phrase, with all its contemporary baggage, is limited almost exclusively to the last twenty years.

Thus it was barely as intellectuals started to systematically outline and defend the philosophical underpinnings of identity politics that we simultaneously began to challenge them. At this historical juncture, then, asking whether one is for or against identity politics is to ask an impossible question. Wherever they line up in the debates, thinkers agree that the notion of *identity* has become indispensable to contemporary political discourse, at the same time as they concur that it has troubling implications for models of the self, political inclusiveness, and our possibilities for solidarity and resistance.

Philosophy and Identity

From this brief examination of how identity politics fits into the political landscape it is already clear that the use of the controversial term "identity" raises a host of philosophical questions. Logical uses aside, it is likely familiar to philosophers from the literature in metaphysics on personal identity - one's sense of self and its persistence. Indeed, underlying many of the more overtly pragmatic debates about the merits of identity politics are philosophical questions about the nature of subjectivity and the self.Charles Taylor argues that the modern identity is characterized by an emphasis on its inner voice and capacity for *authenticity* - that is, the ability to find a way of being that is somehow true to oneself.While doctrines of equality press the notion that each human being is capable of deploying his or her practical reason or moral sense to live an authentic live qua individual, the politics of difference has appropriated the language of authenticity to describe ways of living that are true to the identities of marginalized social groups. As Sonia Kruks puts it:

> What makes identity politics a significant departure from earlier, pre-identarian forms of the politics of recognition is its demand for recognition on the basis of the very grounds on which recognition has previously been denied: it is *qua* women, *qua* blacks, *qua* lesbians that groups demand recognition. The demand is not for inclusion within the fold of "universal humankind" on the basis of shared human attributes; nor is it for respect "in spite of" one's differences. Rather, what is demanded is respect for oneself *as* different?

For many proponents of identity politics this demand for authenticity includes appeals to a time before oppression, or a culture or way of life damaged by colonialism, imperialism, or even genocide. Thus for example Taiaiake Alfred, in his defense of a return to traditional indigenous values, argues that:

> Indigenous governance systems embody distinctive political values, radically different from those of the mainstream. Western notions of domination are noticeably absent; in their place we find harmony, autonomy, and respect. We have a responsibility to recover, understand, and preserve these values, not only because they represent a unique contribution to the history of ideas, but because renewal of respect for traditional values is the only lasting solution to the political, economic, and social problems that beset our people.

What is crucial about the "identity" of identity politics appears to be the experience of the subject, especially his or her experience of oppression and the possibility of a shared and more authentic or self-determined alternative. Thus identity politics rests on unifying claims about the meaning of politically laden experiences to diverse individuals. Sometimes the meaning attributed to a particular experience will diverge from that of its subject: thus, for example, the woman who struggles desperately to be attractive may think that she is simply trying to be a better person, rather than understanding her experience as part of the disciplining of female bodies in a patriarchal culture. Making sense of such disjunctions relies on notions such as false consciousness - the systematic mystification of the experience of the oppressed by the perspective of the dominant. Thus despite the disagreements of many defenders of identity political claims with Marxism and other radical political models, they share the view that individuals' perceptions of their own interests may be systematically distorted and must be somehow freed of their misperceptions by group-based transformation.

Concern about this aspect of identity politics has crystallized around the transparency of experience to the oppressed, and the univocality of its interpretation. Experience is never, critics argue, simply epistemically available prior to interpretation; rather it requires a theoretical framework - implicit or explicit - to give it meaning. Moreover, if experience is the origin of politics, then some critics worry that what Kruks (2001) calls "an epistemology of provenance" will become the norm: on this view, political perspectives gain legitimacy by virtue of their articulation by subjects of particular experiences. This, critics charge, closes off the possibility of critique of these perspectives by those who don't share the experience, which in turn inhibits political dialogue and coalition-building.

From these understandings of subjectivity, it is easy to see how critics of identity politics, and even some cautious supporters, have feared that it is prone to *essentialism*. This expression is another philosophical term of abuse, intended to capture a multitude of sins. In its original contexts in metaphysics, the term implies the belief that an object has a certain quality by virtue of which it is what it is; for Locke, famously, the essence of a triangle is that it is a three-sided shape. In the contemporary humanities the term is used more loosely to imply, most commonly, an illegitimate generalization about identity.In the case of identity politics, two claims stand out as plausibly "essentialist:" the first is the understanding of the subject that characterizes a single axis of identity as discrete and taking priority in representing the self- as if being Asian-American, for example, were entirely separable from being a woman. To the extent that identity politics urges mobilization around a single axis, it will put pressure on participants to identify that axis as their defining feature, when in fact they may well understand themselves as integrated selves who cannot be represented so selectively or even reductively.

The second form of essentialism is closely related to the first: generalizations made about particular social groups in the context of identity politics may come to have a disciplinary function within the group, not just describing but also dictating the self-understanding that its members should have. Thus, the supposedly liberatory new identity may inhibit autonomy, as Anthony Appiah puts it, replacing "one kind of tyranny with another".Just as dominant groups in the culture at large insist that the marginalized integrate by assimilating to dominant norms, so within some practices of identity politics dominant sub-groups may, in theory and practice, impose their vision of the group's identity onto all its members. For example, in his films *Black Is, Black Ain't* and *Tongues Untied* Marlon Riggs eloquently portrays the exclusion of Black women and gay Black men from heterosexist and masculinist understandings of African-American identity politics.

Or, theorizing the experience of hybridity for those whose identities are especially far from norms of univocality, Gloria Anzaldúa, for example, famously writes of her *mestiza* identity as a Chicana, American, raised poor, a lesbian and a feminist, living in the metaphoric and literal Borderlands of the American Southwest.Some suggest the deployment of "strategic essentialism:" we should act *as if*an identity were uniform only to achieve interim political goals, without implying any deeper authenticity.Others argue that a relational social ontology, which makes clear the fluidity and interdependence of social groups, should be developed as an alternative to the reification of other approaches to identity politics.These accounts of subjectivity, ontologies, and ways of understanding solidarity and relationships are at the forefront of contemporary philosophical scholarship in identity politics.

Liberalism and Identity Politics

A key condition of possibility for contemporary identity politics was institutionalized liberal democracy.The citizen mobilizations that made democracy real also shaped and unified groups previously marginal to the polity, while extensions of formal rights invited expectations of material and symbolic equality. The perceived paucity of rewards offered by liberal capitalism, however, spurred forms of radical critique that sought to explain the persistence of oppression. At the most basic philosophical level, critics of liberalism suggested that liberal social ontology - the model of the nature of and relationship between subjects and collectives - was misguided. The social ontology of most liberal political theories consists of citizens conceptualized as essentially similar individuals, as for example in John Rawls' famous thought experiment using the "original position," in which representatives of the citizenry are conceptually divested of all specific identities or affiliations in order to make rational decisions about the social contract.

To the extent that group interests are represented in liberal polities, they tend to be understood as associational, forms of interest group pluralism whereby those sharing particular interests voluntarily join together to create a political lobby. Citizens are free to register their individual preferences, or to aggregate themselves for the opportunity to lobby more systematically.These lobbies, however, are not defined by the identity of their members so much as by specific shared interests and goals, and when pressing their case the marginalized subjectivity of the group members is not itself called into question. Finally, political parties, the other primary organs of liberal democratic government, critics suggest, have few moments of inclusivity, being organized around party discipline, responsiveness to lobby groups, and broad-based electoral popularity. Ultimately conventional liberal democracy, diverse radical critics claim, cannot effectively address the ongoing structural marginalization that persists in late capitalist liberal states, and may even be complicit with it.

On a philosophical level, these understandings of the political subject and its relationship to collectivity came to seem inadequate to ensuring representation for women, gays and lesbians, or racial-ethnic groups.Critics charged that the neutral citizen of liberal theory was in fact the bearer of an identity coded white, male, bourgeois, able-bodied, and heterosexual.This implicit ontology in part explained the persistent historical failure of liberal democracies to achieve anything more than token inclusion in power structures for members of marginalized groups. A richer understanding of political subjects as constituted through and by their social location was required. In particular, the history and experience of oppression brought with it certain perspectives and needs that could not be assimilated through existing liberal structures. Individuals are oppressed by virtue of their membership in a particular *social group* - that is, a collective whose members have relatively little mobility into or out of the collective, who usually experience their membership as involuntary, who are generally identified as members by others, and whose opportunities are deeply shaped by the relation of their group to corollary groups through privilege and oppression.

Oppression, then, is the systematic limiting of opportunity or constraints on self-determination because of such membership: for example, Frantz Fanon eloquently describes the experience of being always constrained by the white gaze as a Black man: "I already knew that there were legends, stories, history, and above all *historicity*... I was responsible at the same time for my body, my race, for my ancestors".Conversely, members of dominant groups are *privileged* - systematically advantaged by the deprivations imposed on the oppressed. For example, in a widely cited article Peggy McIntosh identifies whiteness as a dominant identity, and lists 47 ways in which she is advantaged by being white compared with her colleagues of color. These range from being able to buy "flesh-colored" Band-Aids that will match her skin tone, to knowing that she can be rude without provoking negative judgments of her racial group, to being able to buy a house in a middle-class community without risking neighbors' disapproval.

Critics have also charged that *assimilation* is a guiding principle of liberalism. If the liberal subject is coded in the way Young suggests, then attempts to apply liberal norms of equality will risk demanding that the marginalized conform to the identities of their oppressors. For example, many gays and lesbians have objected to campaigns to institute "gay marriage" on the grounds that these legal developments assimilate same-sex relationships to a heterosexual model, rather than challenging its historical, material, and symbolic terms. If this is *equality*, they claim, and then it looks suspiciously like the erasure of socially subordinate identities rather than their genuine incorporation into the polity. This suspicion helps to explain the affiliation of identity politics with *separatism*. This latter is a set of positions that share the view that attempts at integration of dominant and marginalized groups so consistently compromise the identity or potential of the less powerful that a distinct social and political space is the only structure that will adequately protect them.

In Canada, for example, Québec separatists claim that the French language and francophone culture are persistently erased within an overwhelmingly dominant Anglo-American continent, despite the efforts of the Canadian state to maintain its official bilingualism and to integrate Québec into the nation. Given their long history of conflict and marginalization, a separate and sovereign Québec, they argue, is the only plausible solution.Analogous arguments have been made on behalf of Native American and other indigenous peoples and African Americans.Lesbian feminist separatists have claimed that the central mechanism for the oppression of women under patriarchy is heterosexuality. Understanding heterosexuality as a forced contract or compulsory institution, they argue that women's relationships with men are persistently characterized by domination and subordination. Only divorce and the creation of new geographic and political communities of woman-identified women will end patriarchal exploitation, and forge a liberatory female identity.

One of the central charges against identity politics by liberals, among others, has been its alleged reliance on notions of sameness to justify political mobilization. Looking for people who are *like* you rather than who share your political values as allies runs the risk of sidelining critical political analysis of complex social locations and ghettoizing members of social groups as the only persons capable of making or understanding claims to justice. After an initial wave of relatively uncompromising identity politics, proponents have taken these criticisms to heart and moved to more philosophically nuanced accounts that appeal to *coalitions* as better organizing structures. On this view, separatism around a single identity formation must be muted by recognition of the internally heterogeneous and overlapping nature of social group memberships. The idea of a dominant identity from which the oppressed may need to dissociate themselves remains, but the alternative becomes a more fluid and diverse grouping, less intent on guarantees of internal homogeneity and more concerned with identifying "family resemblances" than literal identity.

This trajectory - from formal inclusion in liberal polities, to assertions of difference and new demands under the rubric of identity politics, to internal and external critique of identity political movements - has taken different forms in relation to different identities. Increasingly it is difficult to see what divides contemporary positions, and some commentators have suggested possible *rapprochements* between liberalism and identity politics.A problem in sorting through such claims is the vagueness of philosophical discussions of identity politics, which are often content to list their rubric under the mantra of "gender, race, class, etc." although these three are not obviously analogous, nor is it clear which identities are gestured toward by the predictable "etc.".Class in particular has a distinctively different political history, and contemporary critics of identity politics, as I'll discuss below, often take themselves to be defending class analysis against identity politics' depoliticizing effects. Of those many forms of identity politics to which large academic literatures attach, however, I'll briefly highlight key issues concerning gender, sexuality, and a complex cluster of race, ethnicity and multiculturalism.

Gender and Feminism

Twentieth century feminism has consistently opposed biological determinism: the view that shared biological features among a certain group lead inevitably to certain social roles or functions. For example, one early opponent of women's suffrage suggested that women and men had different metabolic systems - katabolic in men, and anabolic in women - that precluded women's effective or informed participation in politics.Feminist identity politics, then, takes up the task of articulating women's understandings of themselves without reducing femininity to biology. Whatever experiences women share will be experiences of femininity not necessarily resulting from an immutable sexual difference but rather from social injustice.

Put less usefully, perhaps, although sex may be biological, gender is "socially constructed." Claims about the "social construction" of the identities of identity politics permeate the field as a logical extension of its mandate, although with tremendous philosophical vagueness attaching to the content of the phrase, which serves primarily to emphasize the contingency of any particular category or concept.The fear of biological determinism has led to tremendous caution in feminist theorizing: any invocation of features of female bodies as a basis for identity political claims risks being seen as complicit with sexist views. Furthermore, the very idea of reclaiming women's identities from patriarchy has been criticized as merely an affirmation of a slave morality - a Nietzschean term describing the attachments of the oppressed as they rationalize and valorize their condition. Attempts from various quarters to capture and revalue the distinctively feminine risk, critics claim endorsing existing power relations. Thus the heated debates surrounding the"ethic of care" in moral psychology, for example, line up around two constellations of positions: on the one hand, advocates of the ethic of care as a distinctively feminine contribution to moral reasoning point to its benefits for negotiating a human social world characterized by webs of relationship, and to the pathologies of the dissociation that is culturally linked to masculinities. Carol Gilligan is the best known proponent of this position. Her critics charge that she reifies femininity - were women not oppressed, they would not speak in the voice of care, thus casting doubt on the desirability of attempts to reclaim it as part of a liberatory framework. In other words, the current construction of femininity is so deeply imbricated with the oppression of women that such attempts will always end up reinforcing the very discourse they seek to undermine; this critique has strong affiliations with post-structuralism.

The narrative of feminist interpretation of gender relations most commonly offered points to universalizing claims made on behalf of women during the so-called "second wave" of the feminist movement in the late 1960's and 1970's in Western countries. The most often discussed second wave feminist icons- women such as Betty Friedan or Gloria Steinem - are white, middle-class, and heterosexual, although this historical picture too often neglects the contributions of lesbian feminists, feminists of color, and working-class feminists, which were less visible in popular culture, perhaps, but arguably equally influential in the lives of women. For some early radical feminists, women's oppression *as women* was the core of identity politics, and should not be diluted with other identity issues. For example, Shulamith Firestone, in her classic book *The Dialectic of Sex*, argued that "*racism is sexism extended*," and that the Black Power movement represented only sexist cooptation of Black women into a new kind of subservience to Black men. Thus for Black women to fight racism was to divide the feminist movement, which properly focused on challenging patriarchy, understood as struggle between men and women, the foundational dynamic of all oppressions.

Claims about the universality of gender made during the second wave have been extensively criticized in feminist theory for failing to recognize the specificity of their own constituencies. For example, Friedan's famous proposition that women needed to get out of the household and into the professional workplace was, bell hooks pointed out, predicated on the experience of a post-war generation of white, middle-class married women confined to housekeeping and child-rearing by their professional husbands.Many women of color and working-class women had worked outside their homes for decades; some lesbians had a history of working in traditionally male occupations or living alternative domestic lives without a man's "family wage." Similarly, some women from the less developed world have been critical of Northern feminist theory for globalizing its claims. Such moves construct "Third World" women, they argue, as less developed or enlightened versions of their "First World" counterparts, rather than understanding their distinctively different situation; or, they characterize liberation for Northern women in ways that exacerbate the exploitation of the global poor: by supporting economic conditions in which increasing numbers of western women can abuse immigrant domestic workers, for example.

Thus feminist claims made about the oppression of women founded in a notion of shared experience and identity is now invariably greeted with philosophical suspicion. Some critics have charged that this suspicion itself has become excessive, undercutting the very possibility of generalizations about women that gives feminist theory its force, or that it marks the distancing of feminist philosophy from its roots in political organizing. Others suggest alternative methods for feminist theory that will minimize the emphasis on shared criteria of membership in a social group and stress instead the possibilities for alliances founded on non-identical connections.It is commonplace to hear that "identity" is a term in serious crisis in feminist thought, and that feminist praxis must move beyond identity politics.Nonetheless, sex-gender as a set of analytical categories continues to guide feminist thought, albeit in troubled and troubling ways.

From Gay and Lesbian to Queer

Nowhere have conceptual struggles over identity been more pronounced than in the lesbian and gay liberation movement. The notion that sexual object choice can define who a person is has been profoundly challenged by the advent of queer politics. Visible early lesbian and gay activists emphasized the immutable and essential natures of their sexual identities. For some, they were a distinctively different natural kind of person, with the same rights as heterosexuals to find fulfillment in marriage, property ownership, and so on. This strand of gay organizing with its complex simultaneous appeals to difference and to sameness has a genealogy going back to pre-Stonewall homophilic activism.While early lesbian feminists had a very different politics, oriented around liberation from patriarchy and the creation of separate spaces for woman-identified women, many still appealed to a more authentic, distinctively feminist self. Heterosexual feminine identities were products of oppression, yet the literature imagines a utopian alternative where woman-identification will liberate the lesbian within every woman.

The paradigm shift that the term "queer" signals, then, is a shift to a model in which identities are more self-consciously historicized, seen as contingent products of particular genealogies rather than enduring or essential natural kinds.Michel Foucault's work, especially his *History of Sexuality*, is the most widely cited progenitor of this view: Foucault famously argues that "homosexuality appeared as one of the forms of sexuality when it was transposed from the practice of sodomy onto a kind of interior androgyny, a hermaphrodism of the soul. The sodomite had been a temporary aberration; the homosexual was now a species".Although Foucault is the most often cited as the originator of such genealogical arguments about homosexuality, other often neglected writers contributed to the emergence of this new paradigm.

In western popular culture such theories co-exist uneasily with biologically essentialist accounts of sexual identity, which look for a particular gene, brain structure, or other biological feature that is noninteractive with environment and that will explain same-sex sexual desire. At stake are not only epistemological and metaphysical questions about how we can know what kind of thing "sexual orientation" might be, but also a host of moral and political questions. If sexual identity is biologically caused, then it is as hard to hold an individual morally responsible for being homosexual as it is to blame someone for being Black. Some gay activists thus see biological explanations of sexuality as offering a defense against homophobic commentators who believe that gays can voluntarily change their "immoral" desires. Indeed, much of the intuitive hostility to genealogical or social constructionist accounts of sexuality within gay and lesbian communities seems to come from the dual sense of many individuals that they could not have been other than gay, and that anything less than a radically essentialist view of sexuality will open the door to further attempts to "cure" them of their homosexuality.

Whatever the truth of these fears, Eve Sedgwick is right, in my view, to say that no specific form of explanation for the origins of sexual preference will be proof against the infinitely varied strategies of homophobia.That sexual orientation takes on a metaphysical life of its own, for example, elides the fact that it is generally sexual behavior - not an abstract "identity" - that is the object of moral disapprobation. *Queer* politics, then, works to trouble the categories "gay" and "lesbian," as well as "heterosexual", and eschews a genetic quest for the origins of homosexuality. In addition to historicizing and contextualizing sexuality, including the very idea of sexual identity, the shift to queer is also characterized by deconstructive methods. Rather than understanding sexual identities as a set of discrete and independent social types, queer theorists adduce evidence and read to emphasize their mutual implication: for example, such thinkers love to point out that the word "homosexuality" first appears in English in 1897, but the term "heterosexuality" is back-formed, first used some years later.Heterosexuality comes into existence as a way of understanding the nature of individuals *after* the homosexual has been diagnosed; homosexuality *requires* heterosexuality as its opposite, despite its self-professed stand-alone essence. Queer theorists point out that the homo/hetero dichotomy, like many others in western intellectual history that it arguably draws on and reinforces, is not only mutually implicated, but also hierarchical and masquerades as natural or descriptive. The task of a more radical "identity politics," on this vision, is to constantly denaturalize and deconstruct the identities in question, with a political goal of their subversion rather than their accommodation.

An exemplary conflict within the identity politics of sexuality focuses on the expansion of gay and lesbian organizing to those with other queer affiliations, especially bisexual and transgendered activists. Skepticism about inclusion of these groups in organizational mandates, community centers, parades, and festivals has origins in more traditional understandings of identity politics that see reclaiming lesbian and/or gay identity from its corruption in a homophobic society as a task compromised by those whose identities are read as diluted, treacherous, ambiguous, or peripheral. Some lesbian feminist critiques of transgender, for example, see male-to-female transsexuals in particular as male infiltrators of women's space, individuals so intent on denying their male privilege that they will modify their bodies and attempt to pass as women to do it; bisexual women dabble in lesbian life, but flee to straight privilege when occasion demands.These arguments have been challenged in turn by writers who see them as attempts to justify purity of identity that merely replace the old exclusions with new dictatorships and inhibit coalitional organizing against conservative foes.

Race, Ethnicity, and Multiculturalism

Similar debates in philosophy of race highlight the contingent and historical nature of "race" as a category of identity. Despite a complex history of biological essentialism in the presentation of racial typologies, the notion of a genetic basis to racial difference has been largely discredited; the criteria different societies use to organize and hierarchize "racial formations" are political and contingent.While skin color, appearance of facial features, or hair type are in some trivial sense genetically determined, the grouping of different persons into *races* does not pick out any patterned biological difference (although see the debate "Is Race Real?" in the internet resources. What it does pick out is a set of social meanings with political ramifications.The most notorious example of an attempt to rationalize racial difference as biological is the) U.S. "one-drop rule," under which an individual was characterized as Black if they had "one drop" or more of "Black blood." Adrian Piper points out that not only does this belief persist into contemporary readings of racial identity, it also implies that given the prolonged history of racial mixing in the US - both coerced and voluntary - very significant numbers of nominally "white" people in the U.S. today should be re-classified as "Black".

In those countries that have had official racial classifications, individuals' struggles to be re-classified are often invoked to highlight the contingency of race, especially at the borders of its categories. And a number of histories of racial groups that have apparently changed their racial identification - Jews, Italians, or the Irish, for example - also illustrate social constructionist theses.The claim that race is "socially constructed," however, does not in itself mark out a specific identity politics. Indeed, the very contingency of race and its lack of correlation with categories that have more meaning in everyday life may circumscribe its political usefulness: just as feminists have found the limits of appeals to "women's identity," so Asian-Americans may find with ethnicities and cultures as diverse as Chinese, Indian, or Vietnamese that their racial designation itself provides little common ground. That a US citizen of both Norwegian and Ashkenazi Jewish heritage will check that they are "white" on a census form says relatively little about their experience of their identity, or indeed of their very different relationship to anti-Semitism. Tropes of separatism and the search for forms of authentic self-expression are related to race via ethnocultural understandings of identity: for example, the U.S. Afro-centric movement appeals to the cultural significance of African heritage for Black Americans.

Racial categories are perhaps most politically significant in their contested relation to racism. Racism attempts to reduce members of social groups to their racial features, drawing on a complex history of racial stereotypes to do so. Racism is arguably analogous to other forms of oppression in being both overt and institutionalized, manifested both as deliberate acts by individuals and as unplanned systemic outcomes. The specific direction of US discussion of the categories of race has been around color-blind versus color-conscious public policy.Color-blindness - that is, the view that race *should* be ignored in public policy and everyday exchange - has hegemony in popular discourse. Drawing attention to race - whether in a personal description or in university admissions procedures - is unfair and racist. Advocates of color-consciousness, on the other hand, argue that racism will not disappear without proactive efforts, which require the invocation of race. Thus affirmative action, for example, requires statistics about the numbers of members of oppressed racial groups employed in certain contexts, which in turn requires racial identification and categorization. Thus those working against racism face a paradox familiar in identity politics: the very identity they aim to dispel must be invoked to make their case.

The literature on multiculturalism takes up questions of race, ethnicity, and cultural diversity in relation to the liberal state. Some multicultural states - notably Canada - allegedly aim to permit the various cultural identities of their residents to be preserved rather than assimilated, despite the concern that the over-arching liberal aims of such states may be at odds with the values of those they claim to protect. For example, Susan Moller Okin argues that multiculturalism is sometimes bad for women, especially when it works to preserve patriarchal values in minority cultures. If multiculturalism implies a form of cultural relativism that prevents judgment of or interference with the "private" practices of minorities, female genital mutilation, forced marriage, compulsory veiling, or being deprived of education may be the consequence. Okin's critics counter that she falsely portrays culture as static, internally homogeneous, and defined by men's values, allowing liberalism to represent a culturally unmarked medium for the defense of individual rights.For many commentators on multiculturalism this is the nub of the issue: is there an inconsistency between defending the rights of minority cultures, while prohibiting those cultural practices that the state judges illiberal? Can liberalism sustain the cultural and value-neutrality that some commentators still ascribe to it, or to what extent should it embraces its own cultural specificity? Defenders of the right to cultural expression of minorities in multicultural states thus practice forms of identity politics that are both made possible by liberalism and sometimes in tension with it.

Other Challenges to Identity Politics

Since its 1970s vogue, identity politics as a mode of organizing and set of political philosophical positions has undergone numerous attacks by those motivated to point to its flaws, whether by its pragmatic exclusions or more programmatically as liberals, Marxists, or poststructuralists. For many leftist commentators, identity politics is something of a *bête noire*, representing the capitulation to cultural criticism in place of analysis of the material roots of oppression. Marxists, both orthodox and revisionist, and socialists - especially those who came of age during the rise of the New Left in western countries - have often interpreted the perceived ascendancy of identity politics as representing the end of radical materialist critique.Identity politics, for these critics, is both factionalizing and depoliticizing, drawing attention away from the ravages of late capitalism toward superstruc-tural cultural accommodations that leave economic structures unchanged.

For example, while allowing that both recognition and redistribution have a place in contemporary politics, Nancy Fraser laments the supremacy of perspectives that take injustice to inhere in "cultural" constructions of identity that the people to whom they are attributed want to reject. Such recognition models, she argues, require remedies that "valorize the group's 'groupness' by recognizing its specificity," thus reifying identities that themselves are products of oppressive structures. By contrast, injustices of distribution require redistributive remedies that aim "to put the group out of business as a group".

The reasons given for this alleged turn away from economic oppression to themes of culture, language, and identity in contemporary politics differ. First, the institutionalization of North American radicalism in the middle-class bastion of academia creates incentives for intellectuals to minimize the political importance of their own class privilege, and focus instead on other identities.Second, Wendy Brown suggests that capitalist suffering has been displaced onto other identities, interpreted through the lens of class aspiration.Third, the turn away from economic analysis may be less dramatic than some critics believe: recent activism against global capitalism indicates a resurgence in economic critique that is now arguably more fully imbricated with identity politics.Finally, the rise of diverse "postmodern" paradigms offers sophisticated theoretical alternatives to Marxism for those on the left.

Of these, poststructuralist challenges to identity politics are perhaps the most philosophically developed and profound. Poststructuralists charge that identity politics rests on a mistaken view of the subject that assumes a *metaphysics of substance* - that is, that a cohesive, self-identical subject is ontologically prior to any form of social injustice.This subject has certain core essential attributes that define her or his identity, over which are imposed forms of socialization that cause her or him to internalize other nonessential attributes. This position, they suggest, misrepresents both the ontology of identity and its political significance. The alternative view offered by poststructuralists is that the subject is itself always already a product of discourse, which represents both the condition of possibility for a certain subject-position and a constraint on what forms of self-making individuals, may engage. There is no real identity- individual or group-based- that is separable from its conditions of possibility, and any political appeal to identity formations must engage with the paradox of acting from the very subject-positions it must also oppose. Central to this position is the observation that any claim to identity must organize itself around a constitutive exclusion:

> An identity is established in relation to a series of differences that have become socially recognized. These differences are essential to its being. If they did not coexist as differences, it would not exist in its distinctness and solidity. Entrenched in this indispensable relation is a second set of tendencies, themselves in need of exploration, to conceal established identities into fixed forms, thought and lived as if their structure expressed the true order of things. When these pressures prevail, the maintenance of one identity involves the conversion of some differences into otherness, into evil, or one of its numerous surrogates. Identity requires differences in order to be, and it converts difference into otherness in order to secure its own self-certainty.

The dangers of identity politics, then, are that it casts as authentic to the self or group an identity that in fact is defined by its opposition to other. Reclaiming such an identity as one's own merely reinforces its dependence on this dominant other, and further internalizes and reinforces an oppressive hierarchy. While the charge that identity politics promotes a victim mentality is often a facile pot-shot, Wendy Brown offers a more sophisticated caution against the dangers of *ressentiment*.She argues that identity politics has its own genealogy in liberal capitalism that relentlessly reinforces the "wounded attachments" it claims to sever: "Politicized identity thus enunciates itself, makes claims for itself, only by entrenching, restating, dramatizing, and inscribing its pain in politics; it can hold out no future - for itself or others - that triumphs over this pain".

What political alternatives does this model imply? Proponents of identity politics have suggested that poststructuralism is politically impotent, capable only of deconstruction and never of action.Yet there are political projects motivated by poststructuralist theses. For example, Judith Butler's famous articulation of *performativity* as a way of understanding subject-development suggests to her and others the possibility of disarticulating seamless performances to subvert the meanings with which they are invested.Drag can constitute such a disarticulation, although other critics have suggested other examples; Adrian Piper's conceptual art seeks to disrupt the presumed self-identity of race by showing how it is actively interpreted and reconstituted, never determinate and self-evident.

Identity Politics in the 21st Century

The continuing intellectual crisis surrounding identity politics paradoxically marks its importance to contemporary political philosophy and practice. Both flexible and extensible, identity political tropes continue to influence new political claims: an extensive literature approaches disability, for example, as a set of experiences of social injustice that sediment self-understandings among the disabled and motivate a politics of disability that refuses the legacy of charity to insist that the dominant culture change its exclusionary social practices rather than represent itself as generously accommodating the "special" demands of the disabled.On less well traversed political philosophical ground: can identity politics be extended to children, for example, as the emergent children's rights movement implies? Identity politics has limits, too: is it too person-centered? How can identity politics also be an environmental politics? Perhaps most important for philosophers, any idea of identity itself appears to be in a period of rapid evolution.

Changing technologies are having a profound impact on our philosophical understandings of who we are. Attempts to decode human genetics and possibly shape the genetic make-up of future persons, to clone human beings, or to xeno-transplant animal organs, and so on, all raise deep philosophical questions about the kind of thing a person is. We are capable of changing our bodies in ways that dramatically change our identities, including through sex change or cosmetic surgeries, with immediate consequences for the kinds of identities I have been discussing in this essay. As more and more people form political alliances using disembodied communications technologies, the kinds of identities that matter seem also to shift.Behaviors, beliefs, and self-understandings are increasingly pathologized as syndromes and disorders, including through the identification of new "types" of person. At the same time, familiar mechanisms of oppression are further entrenching the very identities that may be fragmenting in some western, wealthy contexts. Global capitalism appears to be widening the gap between the over- and less-developed countries, and working to further marginalize women, ethnic or indigenous minorities, and the disabled in the so-called Third and Fourth Worlds. This mass of shifts and contradictions might be thought to mark the end of the era of identity politics. Whatever limits are inherent to identity political formations, however, the unfashionableness of the phrase itself belies the deep implication of questions of power and legitimate government with demands for self-determination that are unlikely to fade away.

5

Mobilizing Feminists

Social Movements and Political Activism

Social movements raise serious questions outside normal government channels, often concerning subjects that are not being treated as topics of public concern.Such movements may be viewed along a continuum from unconventional, almost spontaneous, sometimes illegal activity to movement groups that seek more conventional political and legal change. Social movement organizations are the acting components of the movement, which may help turn grievances into programs.It is the hypothesis of this chapter that while American women's liberation groups have moved closer to an accommodation both to the political system and to the more "reformist" wing of the movement, largely because of an emphasis on coalition politics and pragmatic achievements (goals), no such tendencies are evident in the British movement. Rather, there has been little institutional transformation since the movement's inception in Britain, although constant activity is maintained and proliferation and fragmentation occur owing to conflicts regarding strategies and ideology.

Feminist theory about the role of women in politics and society may be analyzed in several ways. One is to differentiate between "reformist" and "radical" feminists. Reformist feminists seek equality through freedomthey do not seek to overturn the prevailing system, although they may be in conflict with those elements of it that they see as oppressive and hostile to women's self-determination. Thus, the stated goal of NOW is "to bring women into full participation into the mainstream of American society in a truly equal partnership with men".In contrast, "radical" feminists perceive society as rooted in inequality, based on patriarchy, or male domination, and often on racism and capitalism as well. In this perspective, the only way to alter women's oppression is to transform the ideology and institutions of existing society.A somewhat different approach to the disparate views within feminism may be found in the distinction between "radical revolutionary" and "socialist" feminism. Socialist feminists, rooted more firmly within Marxist theory, insist on the primacy of the class struggle and seek to redefine those aspects of Marxism that seem inadequate to alter women's oppression to meet the needs of contemporary feminists. Socialist feminists wish to develop a strategy to jointly attack male domination and capitalism and thus restructure male-female relationships.

A second group, the "radical" feminists see the source of societal inequality in the institution of male domination, or "patriarchy," usually rooted in biological differences and roles. Both the family and the state are seen to embody systematic male power and domination. In this view, alliances with men are not possible, since men are always oppressors and society cannot be reformed. Women must form "separatist" groups, shun relations with men, and seek an end to male domination.Revolutionary feminists have forcefully restated many traditional radical feminist positions, especially hostility to men.Their major points of attack are marriage, the family, control of reproduction, and violence against women.

Although in both the United States and Britain elements of these different views exist, in the United Kingdom what we have referred to as "reformist" feminism occupies a far more limited role than in the United States. And, although socialist feminism exists in the United States, it has tended to remain outside the mainstream of the feminist movement, given the historic American antipathy to leftist politics. In turn, because British feminism is linked by reasons of history and ideology to the left and socialism, it has tended to develop more theoretical perspectives on the relationship between these two ideological tendencies. As liberal feminists Betty Freidan and Gloria Steinem have tended to dominate aspects of the American feminist movement, so have the socialist feminists Sheila Rowbotham and Juliet Mitchell been major forces within the British movement. However, two significant differences ought to be noted. First, the contributions of the latter two are less related to movement activism than to an interest in theoretical reinterpretation. Second, Rowbotham and Mitchell are not viewed as "spokeswomen" for or by the British movement, which does not recognize movement "stars" in any role at all. Radical feminism, sparked by such writers as Shulamith Firestone and Kate Millett, had its origins in the United States, although it has now gained considerable support among British women's liberationists.

For some observers, "revolutionary feminism" has eclipsed other significant strands within the British movement. An article in the New Statesman deplored the tendency toward "political lesbianism" in the United Kingdom, suggesting that many feminists had entered a social and sexual stage that denigrated engagement with existing structures that could lead to change. The author decried a new prescriptive definition of feminism that limited options and rendered the British movement no longer open to all women who recognized the oppression of women as a social group and sought change. Whether a new and more exclusive era in British feminism has truly dawned is difficult to determine; but such commentary does suggest a vast chasm between socialist and some radical feminists in the United Kingdom.

A final element within feminism is "cultural" feminism. It may be animated by either socialist or radical feminism, but its major concern is less political than it is personal: that is, it seeks to change life-styles and modes of behavior.

It is only a partial exaggeration to suggest that the American civil rights movement played a role in the creation of second-wave American feminism comparable to that of the socialist left in Britain.

Historical Background

The recent history of British and American feminist development reveals disparate organizational tendencies and styles. In the United States the New Left and the civil rights movement, each stressing different aspects of political equality, gave rise to the younger, or more "radical," branch of the feminist movement. As women activists in these protest movements became aware of their secondary status, based on gender, they began to develop new, female-based groupings. Early on, these groups stressed consciousness-raising as a technique to develop greater self-and group awareness and, like their British counterparts, created localized, participatory projects, including day care, rape crisis centers, and shelters for battered women, bookstores, and self-help health clinics. A second group of feminist activists formed around the national and state commissions on the status of women. These commissions created a focus and forum for a different set of women, older and of a more professional and media-oriented bent, to begin to contemplate the need for a feminist pressure group. Their efforts were given additional impetus after the passage of the Civil Rights Act of 1964, which was passed with the inclusion of Title VII, prohibiting sex discrimination in employment.The climate of expectations created by these two governmentally based actions, and the subsequent failure of the agency created by the Civil Rights Act, the EEOC, to enforce Title VII, led to the creation of NOW. Additional groups finally joined the Washington feminist lobby, including the Women's Equity Action League (WEAL), which initially rejected NOW's seemingly "radical" position on abortion rights; the National Women's Political Caucus (NWPC), focusing on recruiting and electing more women to political office and on legislative pressure; numerous groups concerned with single issues; and litigation groups.

The British Feminist Movement

The British suffrage movement early demonstrated tendencies that persist in British feminism today. One was an early link between the Labour Party and constitutional feminists.Another was militancyperhaps related to the example of Irish nationalism, perhaps born of rage and disappointment when apparently close-at-hand victory failed. Antisuffrage leaders and the Liberal Party served to isolate the movement and make it more sectarian and rigid.However, although suffragists were interested in engaging public power in order to gain the vote, contemporary feminist advocates in Britain are not so sure.

As in the United States, the contemporary British feminist movement received its impetus from radical and New Left politics, especially the CND and anti-Vietnam campaigns.In addition, working-class women in the 1960s organized as well: at Hull in 1968 for better conditions for their fishermen husbands and at Ford's auto machine works in Dagenham, where the demands for equal pay and equal work resulted in the creation of the short-lived Joint Action Committee for Women's Rights. This early effort at feminist militancy among working-class women seemed promising, but it has not proved as yet to be a significant element in British feminism, although in 198485 a new working-class women's movement, Women Against Pit Closures, emerged during the yearlong strike by the National Union of Miners (NUM).

The revived movement in the United States provided the immediate spark for many women liberation activity, which early on developed strength among socialist and university women. A London-based women's liberation workshop coordinated over 70-odd local groups and published a journal, Shrew.A national women's liberation movement held its first conference at Oxford in 1970. The demands that emerged from the conference 24-hour child care, equal pay and education, free contraception, and abortion on demandreflected a practical orientation, new to some movement activists.

Like the "younger," more radical branch of the American movement, the British movement lacked a coordinating structure other than national, regional, or issue-oriented conferences. The British movement developed numerous factions; one chart listed at least 14 different "tendencies" within the movement.Conflicts within the movementlargely between radical and socialist feministshave since 1978 prevented the holding of a national conference. The conflicts have centered largely on the scrapping of the six demands listed in earlier chapter in favor of the seventh demand against male violence. Spare Rib, a monthly journalistic publication produced by a feminist collective, and the London-based Women's Research and Resources Center (WRRC) today provide the only comprehensive foci relating to different elements within the movement. (A Women's Place, also in London, is similarly run by a collective of women and operates a bookshop and reference facility, as well as publishing a weekly newsletter.) The once significant Women's Information, Reference and Enquiry Service (WIRES) have been severely circumscribed.

Despite the absence of a focal point, feminist activities in the United Kingdom continue energetically. Spare Rib and other publications advertise a host of feminist activities, and numerous groups are listed under "Women's Liberation" in the London and regional phone books. However, unlike the mass-membership equal rights focus of the visible American movement, the major locus of activity is the small group, which, eschewing formal rules and leadership, prefers to arrive at decisions by consensus. The movement's character is also defined by the proliferation of small groups, each with a single-issue orientation. Even more "traditional" women's groups, such as Women in the Media and the National Housewives Register, operate on the basis of principles of participatory democracy and minimization of hierarchy and rigid structure.It is possible that British women's experience with bureaucracyin labor and leftist politics and, in the public sphere, in such areas as national healthhas contributed to dislike of centralized, hierarchical power. However, though other British promotional groups began with a similarly diffuse structure, some, including the CPAG, have moved toward traditional interest-group organization. Often allied with feminist groups, the CPAG has developed a staff-dominated structure and a small membership as well, become more interested in fund-raising, and sought to develop a parliamentary lobby. These activities are in marked contrast to the deliberately antihierarchical structure maintained by feminist groups.

Feminists have developed legal groups, such as Rights of Women, day nurseries, shelters for battered women, and proabortion groups. National coordinating structures have evolved to focus on specific issues such as abortion and domestic violence, but their scope is limited. Women's Aid was established in London in 1972 by Erin Pizzey to counter domestic violence and, somewhat unique in British feminist experience, was able to attract government and charitable funding.Perhaps because it requires fewer resources than child care, domestic violence became a women's issue suitable for limited external support.The Women's Aid movement broke away from its founder on ideological grounds and has proliferatedwith 99 groups and 200 refugees in 1980.

Member organizations operate on feminist principles, with an emphasis on autonomy and self-determination for women.Local women support the National Women's Aid Federation (NWAF) through adherence to its aims and attendance at meetings.Within the national and half-dozen regional offices, jobs rotate every two to three years to provide varied experiences for all and prevent domination by one person. Activists share in all work and there is no status distinction among the new staff members. Fund-raising is virtually nonexistent because of fear of creating strong central power, although resources from the national Department of Health and Social Services (DHSS) help pay staff salaries. While in the mid 1980s the London office of the NWAF was forced to close because of lack of funding, a newly modified collective structure has resumed national leadership in Bristol, England, as of 1988.

The NWAF's past activities helped create legislative reforms that gave increased protection to women against violent mates and imposed obligations on local authorities to rehouse victimized women. The NWAF also campaigned for more serious intervention by local police authorities.(Women Against Rape, formed in 1976, has had some comparable success in raising consciousness and was in part responsible for the passage of the Sexual Offenses Act of 1976 making the rape victim's past sexual history irrelevant.)

A second organization that has developed a national structure is the National Abortion Campaign (NAC), launched in the spring of 1975 to defend the 1967 Abortion Act. It has a loosely organized mass base and operates from a socialist feminist perspective and on principles of participatory democracy.The nonhierarchical, decentralized structure linking local groups claims a coalition of 400 organizations, with membership open to all who support its aims.In contrast to the operation of abortion rights groups in the United States, half the groups involved in NAC are trade union-related and receive some funding from the unions. Local groups are completely autonomous, deciding their own policy and method of campaigning. They have no elected officials or delegated structure. National policy is decided at the NAC annual conference and meetings are open to all members. An annual general meeting provides a forum for discussion of issues, although there is no mechanism for the resolution of conflicts on issues such as the role of racism and the broadening of the group's agenda to include types of reproductive freedom other than abortion. (In 1983, an organizational split between those who sought focus on abortion as a single issue and advocates of broader reproductive rights divided NAC.) A national office provides backup resources and coordinates; a steering committee handles daily work. The staff is limited in policy-making authority, leaving most decision-making to annual and regional meetings. Volunteers are heavily relied on, particularly in the absence of funds to pay workers.

The contrast with most American pro-abortion groups is marked: U.S. organizations, such as the National Abortion Rights Action League (NARAL) and Planned Parenthood, tend to be professionalized, hierarchical in structure, and reliant on although not necessarily directly responsible toa dues-paying, mass-membership constituency. Such groups may fit the model of reliance on a "conscience constituency" in which contributors supply movement resources without direct material benefit. Effective policy-making is in the hands of the full-time staff, as in the "funded social movement organizations" described by McCarthy and Zald (1977). Abortion rights groups lobby extensively to prevent progressive weakening of abortion legislation and, in marked contrast to the British experience, where courts have virtually no role in this policy area, have been active in litigating to preserve and strengthen abortion rights. NAC's strategy is largely extraparliamentary, emphasizing proselytizing through demonstrations and picketing, influencing Parliament by showing M.P.'s that grass-roots support for abortion rights exists.

In the United Kingdom, even groups with a national focus are ambivalent about campaigning and the legislative process, although in fact the NWAF and NAC have intervened effectively in the political system. In 1975, NAC mobilized 20,000 supporters to defeat James White's antiabortion bill. It has collaborated with other sections of the pro-abortion lobby, including the Abortion Law Reform Association (ALRA), and with Labour Party women. NAC supporters have been active in unions and have gained support from the Trades Union Congress (TUC) for their efforts.In July 1981, they held their first meeting with representatives from the trade union movement and Labour Party constituency parties in an effort to gain commitments for positive legislation on abortion. (After this meeting, a first attempt to enact legislation making abortion facilities mandatory under the NHS was introduced, and although it failed, it gained some media attention, perhaps setting the stage for further efforts [Spare Rib,Sept. 1981:106].) Because NAC's members are socialist feminists, they have close ties to the Labour Party and trade union movement, particularly the National Union of Public Employees.

The potential of this alliance was evident in 1979 when a mass demonstration, with major participation by the TUC, helped stop the Corrie bill, which threatened to reduce access to legal abortions. This was the largest union demonstration ever held in Britain for a noneconomic issue, and it demonstrated the mobilization potential inherent in the feminist movement. However, at the NAC National Congress in September 1983, a split developed over the organization's need to cover other areas of women's reproductive rights, including contraception and sterilization. A new group, the Women's Reproductive Rights Group, was formed as a result of this disagreement, further contributing to the proliferation of women's liberation groups.

A second effort related to women's liberation, though not strictly part of it, has been the mobilization of Greenham Common women in protest against a cruise missile installation in Britain. Organized around feminist principles, and exclusively populated by women, it has numbered some 30,000 women in rotating order. Utilizing principles of nonviolence, even when arrested and subject to police harassment and eviction attempts, these women have helped mobilize national consciousness about peace issues based on feminist ideology.

Other feminist groups, such as Rights of Women (ROW), exist in the field of law and have been active for the past decade. Their goal has been to provide legal advice to the women's movement, formulate legal policy, and campaign on issues of concern to women. They have produced informational material, discussion documents, parliamentary briefings, and responses to government publications in areas such as violence against women, rights of lesbians, and family law. Nonetheless, the movement lacks a professional campaigning body of women lawyers, partly owing to funding problems.Another promotional group, the NCCL, has had a women's officer active since 1975 and has played an important role in movement politics.

A movement comparable to the liberal feminist structure in the United States does not really exist in the United Kingdom. Nonetheless, while never dominant in the British feminist movement, there are groups that seek to play a centrist, coordinating role. Among these are the Fawcett Society and Women in the Media. The Fawcett Society remains a small group of only about 375 members, its efforts to develop a membership base in northeast England having failed. Women in the Media, organized in 1970, have engaged in active campaigning for equal pay and for legislation against sex discrimination. Other groups that do not identify with women's liberation but do support many feminist demands and efforts to achieve them are current manifestations of more traditional women's activities. Among them are the WI, with a membership base of 400,000; the TG, with 217,000; the British Federation of University Women, with 14,000; and the NCW, with 5,000.While these groups often support women's rights, by and large they eschew relationships with socialist and radical feminists.

Several new developments in Britain represent steps toward coalition building among different ideological groups in the women's community. In London in November 1980, a Women's Action Day involved some 67 organizations from a variety of women's perspectives and sought to discuss and develop common policies. A "women's agenda" was issued, dealing with issues of equal opportunity in law, education, work, politics, finances, the family, health, and the media. Groups represented included unions, NAC and ROW, traditional women's groups such as the NCW, and elements of the Liberal and Labour parties. With a grant from the EOC, the Women's Action Group (WAG) created a Lobby Pack with questions to be put to candidates for by-elections and parliamentary election.Aided by funds from the Greater London Council (GLC), a number of feminist groups purchased a new building to share cooperatively in London. The EOC and NCCL have also provided opportunities for discussion of specific feminist issues through conferences and forums and helped link trade unionists with other feminist activities. The GLC Women's Committee and other local women's committees have also sought to end centrifugal politics by involving a variety of women's groups as policy participants and recipients. In 1986 a campaign to defend children's benefits against restrictive cuts by the Thatcher government engendered a national effort. Included within the alliance, consisting of over 60 organizations, were the National Federation of Women's Institutes, Women's Aid Federation, Fawcett Society, and Mother's Union. The future significance of such cooperative efforts remains unclear.

A fairly new political advocacy groupthe 300 Grouphas sought to increase the number of women in the House of Commons.Like its American counterpart, the NWPC, it aims to recruit and train women candidates for political office. It has sought to build a dues-paying base, in 1982 having a membership of 3,000 and dues of £12 annually.Now under new leadership, the 300 Group has a central staff and offices, indicating its ability to endure and grow even though it continues to encounter hostility from traditional party groups that resent external intrusion and from feminists who dislike its relatively centralized entrepreneurial style. Nonetheless, it has trained well over 1,500 women and helped them gain an interest and confidence in politics.

The focus of most British feminist groups, however, is interaction emphasizing value and life-style changes. Consciousness-raising is an important element, and values such as self-confidence, skill attainment, and self-esteem are promoted.The democratic character of the movement provides flexibility and permits accommodation of all types of grass-roots activity, incorporating diverse elements. As Mansbridge has pointed out, small size allows intense interaction, and continued face-to-face contact may prevent elitism. Yet, the group process, rather than attainment of group ends, may develop as a major focus.Conformity to the group may be encouraged. The absence of recordkeeping and repetition of old issues may retard group development.An ahistorical perspective may cause repetition of past mistakes. Decision-making may be slowed and the real administrative and political skills of some may be underutilized or ignored.Individuals may become preoccupied with their own liberation and fail to seek more universal women's goals. And local, single-issue-oriented activity may reduce possibilities for national impact and comprehensive, as opposed to ad hoc, solutions to problems.

This analysis is consistent with Freeman's critique of movement structurelessness in the United States, in which she argues that the movement provided no coordinated or structured means of fitting local activity into other, existing projects. As she suggests, the consequence is that new groups form and dissolve at an accelerating rate, creating a great deal of consciousness and very little concerted action, failing to consolidate old gains while moving into new areas.

Finally, unaccountability to a constituency may create irresponsibility and unrealistic expectations. Inability to agree on goals and pool resources weakens opportunities for creation of alliances.If, as suggested here, the women's movement in Britain is a "deliberately dispersed collection of groups, campaigns and political tendencies with no single ideology," the absence of coalitional structures prevents organization around multiple issues in a continuing fashion.The politics of personal experience, inward-looking and seeking redemptive life-styles, has often eclipsed the overtly "political." Women's liberation politics is fragmented centered on single issues, and without networks in which different views may find expression and audience. The British emphasis on personal politics has often, though not always, resulted in reluctance to engage in the politics of the state.Although feminist politics may serve as a model for other leftist groups in its emphasis on autonomy, flexibility, and democracy, the lack of a coordinating mechanism and national political presence presents a continuing challenge.

American Women's Liberation

The structure of grass-roots, radical feminism in the United States is similar to that in Britain. However, even within this wing of feminist politics, recent developments have suggested somewhat different tendencies. For example, in shelters for battered women and in rape crisis centers, which emphasize the feminist ideology discussed earlier, professionals have often combined with feminist influences to provide services, negotiate with bureaucracies, write funding proposals, and develop more enduring organizational structures.While conflicts over the importance of service, self-determination, and politics continue to exist, there can be little doubt that such elements as networking, lobbying, and emphasis on legal changes are more evident in the American movement.

Activists have mobilized around state legislation and legal changeand have often been less reluctant to engage with political and bureaucratic forces and to seek legitimacy than is true for their British counterparts. Structures have been modified as specialization has created more hierarchical organizations, including staffs and boards.Schechter concludes that the need for government support has forced activists to modify practices and informal procedures. In some instances, "modified collectives" have sought a compromise between external imperatives and feminist principles.From local coalitions, statewide and then federal efforts have been generated. There has been willingness to engage political authorities at all levels in order to gain resources and reform legal procedures.

Coalitions reflect a variety of influencesincluding traditional groups,professional and service providers, radical feminists, and equal rights feminists from groups such as NOWand emphasize the sharing of resources, access, and skills.To aid battered women, a National Coalition against Domestic Violence (NCADV) was created, which lobbied for passage of a Domestic Violence Act, built a large network of contacts, sought to build a dues-paying membership base, and wrote proposals to raise money from the federal government and private foundations. The coalition continues to monitor relevant public policy, disseminate information to state and local groups, and seek to retain a nonhierarchical, multiracial approach.

In contrast to the British experience, change-oriented feminists have often been able to rely on government "insiders" to put forward issues and build government support for movement concerns.Hence, leadership and structure, engagement with political forces at all levels, and the need for coalition have been treated differently in the United States than in the United Kingdom. But, as an instance of congruence, women's liberation groups in both countries have tended to focus on single issues and do not necessarily coalesce with other movement activists in multiple-issue alignments. However, while in the United States a grass-roots women's movement still exists, it is less visible than formerly and has to a greater degree joined forces with the more "middle-class" reformist sector of the original movement.

In the United States, then, though a grass-roots movement continues to exist, having successfully helped shape a new policy agenda based on the alternative services it created at the state and local levels, the character of the movement has changed considerably. In addition to the pull toward coalitions and political engagement we have described, to some degree overlapping memberships and joint activities have altered this segment of the movement's role. These linkages have been strengthened by campaigns to save abortion rights and pass the ERA, which have tended to unite feminists of all ideologies.

In addition, NOW, although founded as a feminist pressure group from the top down, has sought to move further in the direction of feminist principles than might earlier have been expected. First, it has sought to break down traditional organizational roles, combining staff and elected positions and thus creating a more participatory structural setting. Second, it has moved to adopt more controversial issue orientations, in addition to its continued interest in equal rights.

The organization first endorsed abortion on demand, at that time (1970) and still a controversial political and moral issue. It also acknowledged, in an even more controversial act, that sexual self-determination lesbianism was a legitimate part of the women's movement. It has continued to examine alternative life-styles and support alternate forms of sexuality, even as it ages in political terms, indicating that it has hardly become more conservative with time.

Finally, galvanized by growing evidence of the costs and consequences of the "feminization of poverty," NOW has joined with other feminist groups and has moved to a more radical view of ways to eradicate poverty, although it clearly remains within the American tradition. And as the major feminist mass-membership group, NOW, though not always successful, has sometimes been able to act as an umbrella group for different interests within the feminist movement.As the most prominent feminist organization, NOW has to some degree eclipsed the more radical elements of the movement, because, given the American political system, its actions are more visible while its demands are viewed as both newsworthy and mildly radical.

Though in many ways a traditional interest group involved in electoral politics and campaign endorsements, litigation, and lobbying, NOW's major significance for the movement continues to lie in its ability to focus public attention on key movement demands. It is able to do this through demonstrations, access to the media, and other social movement techniques.

But NOW does not operate alone in the political arena. Because the structure of American feminism has become specialized along issue and functional lines, groups such as NARAL in the area of abortion, WEAL on economic reform, and other organizations play a major role as well. In the area of domestic violence, the NCADV has become a leading voice. It may be argued that through the process, noted earlier, of coalition building and group mergers the movement has lost its radical edge and become limited by a turn toward more conventional politics. But the "legitimization" of American feminism as an interest group of political significanceat the same time as the movement has deepened its commitment to key feminist issuessuggests that considerable progress has been made from a feminist perspective.

The movement was strengthened by the creation of two types of women's groups: single-issue and multi-issue, or umbrella, groups. Single-issue groups dealing with abortion or domestic violence concentrate their resources and energy on one topic, keeping the issue before the public.Multi-issue organizations may have a broader range of contacts, a larger support base, and the ability to create coalitions.

NOW and other feminist-oriented groups gained additional membership and support from contributors, especially during 198082, in response to conservative threats symbolized by the Reagan election of 1980 and the defeat of the ERA in 1982. Membership in NOW increased to 250,000 in 1983 but had decreased to 156,000 by 1986.During this period, in addition to strengthening relations with the more radical sector of the feminist movement, NOW built stronger links to traditional women's groups, including the League of Women Voters, American Association of University Women, General Federation of Women's Clubs, and National Federation of Business and Professional Women. Although some of these older, established women's groups had early on shared resources and opportunities for access with their feminist sisters, as the movement moved into its second decade, they too became constituents of feminist-sponsored, issue-based coalitions on key economic and other issues.

Finally, congressional and administrative staff members, primarily women, have played a key role in advancing women's issues. They help build support for feminist-sponsored policy, alert lobbyists about proposed, potentially negative changes, and provide the type of information only "insiders" can have.

While both in the United States and Britain a variety of theoretical and practical approaches to feminism constitute movement politics, in America the pressure to build coalitions and seek reform through more or less traditional interest-group politics has been notable. As we have suggested, networking across ideological lines is still rare in the United Kingdom, although it is a concept gaining support from many feminist activists.

Traditional women's groups do have a mass constituency base in the United Kingdom, but they are usually reluctant to join forces with those perceived, with reinforcement by media coverage, as being lesbian and antimale. The close relationship that has developedin terms of resource sharing, political access, and even consensus on goalsbetween the so-called traditional women's groups and their reformist and radical feminist allies in the United States has no analogue in the political culture of Britain. The failure to seek advancement of women in existing political structures and the emphasis on sectarian politics have denied British feminists the mainstream voice their American sisters have been able to articulate.

At the same time, the British movement has continued to be distinguished by its diversity and its capacity to celebrate difference and spontaneity.

6

The Role of Women in Parties and Unions

As noted in earlier chapter, the resurgence of feminism in the latter half of this century has been characterized by the development of at least two wings of feminist organization. One wing, the autonomous feminists described in earlier chapter, has been more concerned with creating alternatives than with exerting political influence, particularly in Britain.The other wing has tended to emphasize rights and legal change and to operate within the decision-making process via traditional parties and unions or through a new set of lobbying-oriented interest groups. In this chapter, we explore two different approaches to legal and political change as manifested by British and American feminists, each constrained by the context of movement politics.

Parties: Britain

Despite the striking absence in British feminism of a counterpart to the dues-paying, mass-membership orientation of American feminism represented by such organizations as NOW, one way contend that in the British political system, such mass-based feminist groups are not necessary or even desirable. It may be argued that the functional equivalent of liberal feminism exists in Britain because, as suggested in earlier chapter, British feminists have historically been organized and influential as pressure groups within existing institutions, namely political parties and trade unions. Despite concern about co-optation and ideological dilution by male-dominated structures, feminists, especially on the left, have sought to develop alliances with these institutions to further their political goals. Nonetheless, this chapter suggests that increased activism by feminists has not ended a pattern of women's participation in these institutions that has been marked by "marginalization" and isolation from power. We thus share the view that existing political structures give little priority to feminists' interests; rather than seeking to solidify feminist strength and advancing women's interests, they have aided in their dissipation and fragmentation.

We will examine the role of women within party organizations in three ways: the role of women's groups within the parties, the role of women within the party hierarchy, and the party's approach to promoting women as candidates for political office. Underlying this chapter's perspective is the view that as Britain is becoming a more administrative state, the importance of feminist influence within groups whose major impact is on the legislative process may, in any case, be seriously debated.

Although women compose at least half the membership of the Labour and Conservative parties,their role within party structures appears to be circumscribed. Women in parties and unions are organized into separate advisory groups having few powers and little ability to gain acceptance for resolutions they have passed. In addition, they are limited to reserve or set-aside seats on key decision-making bodies. In the main, the more significant a policy-making body is, the fewer women it has on it. Somewhat surprisingly, the Labour Party though closer to feminists on some policy issues and in ideological terms, has had no better a record on representation and power sharing than its Conservative opposition. Women are poorly represented within the party's annual conference and are allotted five seats of 29 on the party's National Executive Committee (NEC), the dominant administrative and policy-making body. (Since 1960 only two women have been selected for the NEC by the constituencyor localsection of the party;

none have been elected by the trade unions.) The principle of setting aside women's places on executive bodies is a well-established one in parties and unions, as we shall see. Because trade unions are dominant in the Labour Party and unions cast their vote in block fashion, in practice the set-aside women's seats are union controlled.Hence, most women selected for the NEC are not independent feminists.

The Women's Section of the Labour Party is constituency based. Like other women's groups in similar institutions, it holds annual meetings and passes resolutions.Resolutions are forwarded to the NEC, which may or may not choose to consider them. In essence; then, the women's organization is powerless to affect policy and has no direct representation at the party's annual conference.

Unlike the Conservative Party, the Labour Party is a confederal organization, with a vast array of women's groups.In recent years, women's Labour groups have grown and proliferatedfrom the Women's Action Committee, to a Women's Rights Study group established with M.P. Jo Richardson as chair. A group called Fightback for Women's Rights is active at the party's fringes. It has been especially vigorous in pressing for more channels to the Labour Party hierarchyadvocating that five resolutions be sent to the party's annual conference by the Women's Section and that women members be elected to the NEC directly by the Women's Conference. Fightback and WAC both espouse an end to all-male parliamentary shortlists.A Woman's Charter has been developed and promoted by WAC.

A measure of the expanded interest in women's activities was the upsurge in the number of women's delegatesfrom 320 in 1980 to 650 in 1981at the annual Women's Conference. This increase indicated an intensified resolve to use the conference as a forum from which to articulate concerns and press demands on the party hierarchy. In recent years, there has been growing evidence of serious debate on key feminist issues.At the 1982 party conference, party feminists sought to establish a more significant policy-making role. Their resolutions called for the right both to elect the women members of the NEC directly and to send to the conference five resolutions that would be automatically considered. Surprisingly, the Women's Conference defeated an effort to make selection of women on candidate shortlists mandatory.

The Labour Party hierarchy has responded to feminist pressure by appointing a national women's officer and, more recently, designating a shadow minister for women's affairs,formerly M.P. Joan Lestor and now M.P. Jo Richardson. A women's subcommittee of the NEC has been created to formulate policy on women's issues. Its members are also members of a National Women's Committee elected by women at regional conferences around the country, thus providing a direct link between the NEC and grass-roots women. A National Women's Charter drawn up by the NEC in 1982 calls for greater women's representation at all party levels and for day-care services for women attending all party meetings.Joyce Gould, the national women's officer, has sought to promote more female candidacies for office. As of the mid-1980s, the NEC recommended, though it did not mandate, at least one woman on each shortlist. Constituency parties were permitted to establish women's sections without prior approval from the party hierarchy.

The extent of feminist participation within the Labour Party is impressive and often channels socialist feminist energy into party activities, but because of the party's disarray at present, any victory may be a pyrrhic one. In addition, there is some suspicion that several groups seeking dominance within the party may be using the feminist issue to build their own power basewith little actual regard for feminist concerns.

And although the Labour Party committed itself to supporting abortion and contraception rights, measures against rape and wife battering, and equal pay for work of equal value, and to ending job segregation, promoting positive action, and strengthening the Sex Discrimination Act, it has yet to make these policies central campaign issues.Rather, as with women in general, such policies are isolated as women's issues and even treated as ethical matters on which M.P.'s need not be bound to party policy. Hence, it may be premature to contend that British women are emerging from a decade of isolation and an exclusive grass-roots focus to help unite the left and the Labour Party.In fact, though the party's feminist activity in recent years has expanded, it is not a new development. Nor is it clear that, at national-level party politics, major claims for feminist influence are supported by the evidence.

In the Conservative Party, women's participation in local politics is significant but has not altered the pattern of "marginalization" we have suggested. While women are better represented at the party's annual conference, this body lacks the policy-making powers of its Labour Party counterpart.Women constitute about 20 per cent of the membership of the Executive Committee of the National Union, which is the highest point in the party hierarchy, although its policy-making and administrative powers are limited by the primacy of parliamentary leadership, consigning it to more of an advisory role. As of 1982, 50 of the 200 members were women, 19 of these being in statutory or mandated seats.At least one analyst has contended that although Conservative women are better represented than their Labour sisters, they have only limited impact at party conferences because they are not very vocal.

As in the Labour Party, there is a women's national advisory organization with its own annual conference, now called the Conservative Women's National Committee. This committee often discusses women's issues in the guise of such concerns as education.Another group affiliated with the Conservative Party, the British section of the European Union of Women, is active on behalf of women's issues as well and was instrumental in stopping cuts in Social Security proposed by the Thatcher government.This group has pressed for a party rule to include at least one woman candidate on shortlists and for mandated interviews of women by candidate selection committees. It also recommended in 1982 that women's groups within the party undertake candidate education and training.

Prime Minister Margaret Thatcher's leading political role in the party has not altered the position of women in her party at all. She has consciously distanced herself from women's interests and has neither appointed other women to key positions nor advanced policies of concern to women. (The Vice Chair, Emma Nicholson was charged of encouraging more women to join the party in the Parliament appointed after the 1979 election). Although Thatcher's campaign in 1979 stressed her image as a housewife and mother, she has made it clear that she does not view women's issues as a cause for concern. (In 1986, however, Thatcher announced that women must be shortlisted for all public appointments and that an explanation must be provided for failure to comply [Economist, Nov. 1, 1986:53]).

Thatcher has openly suggested that women with children should leave the labor force, and her government has steadily reduced nursery and child-care provisions, maternity and child-care benefits, and women's work rights.It is difficult to disagree with Richard Rose, who has written that of the four women in the British cabinet from 1964 to 1969, in no instance was their political stature derived from their sex or from their expression of feminist views. Both Thatcher's critics and supporters see her sex as largely irrelevant and her political views as significant.

As the only woman in her cabinet, Margaret Thatcher demonstrates that high positions for women are an exception.Nonetheless, Thatcher is assessed favorably for leadership qualities, for standing up for Britain, for ability to communicate, and for crisis management, suggesting that as a role model her position may augur well for future women in British politics.However, as an indication that many women find Thatcher's policies wanting and may tend to reject them, the 1983 election saw a move toward the Alliancethe Social Democrat-Liberal partnershipand away from the major parties among women voters.

Finally, with regard to candidates standing for election, women have continually been underrepresented in both major parties. They have also been consistently underselected by constituencies; even when they are chosen, they are selected disproportionately for unwinnable or marginal seats.

Although in 1983, for the first time over 10 per cent of the party's candidates were female, a third higher than in 1979, it has been argued that with regard to selection women are worse off today than they were a century ago.As of 1983, only 3.5 per cent of M.P.'s were women, in contrast to 5.1 per cent of representatives in the U.S. Congress.By 1987, however, partially reflecting the effort by parties to reach out to women voters in a hard-fought campaign, over 6 per cent of the M.P.'s selected were women.

In the Labour Party the "A" list is union-dominated. In 1972, two of 100 candidates nominated were women; in 1977, three of 103; and in 1983, seven of 153. The TUC's increasing sympathy for women's concerns may aid in the future expansion of women's role in the Labour Party, but there is little evidence that much change has occurred as yet. The limited support extended by unions to women denies them the crucial access to monetary and other resources enjoyed by men. In 1982, Labour with 11 women M.P.'s had just 25 women on a list of 250 candidates.By 1983, Labour had increased its female representation on candidate lists to 15 percent, resulting in 12.5 per cent female candidates, of whom just 10 were elected.As of 1987, of 85, or 16 per cent, female candidates nominated, 21 were elected.

In 1982 the Conservative Party had just eight women M.P.'s.In the past, according to Hills,the Conservative Party may have attracted more women candidates than the Labour Party,but that did not seem to be the case in 1982. A centralized party office keeps a list of approved candidates. In 1982, of 600 names on the list, only 10 percent were women. The Conservatives shortlisted 10 percent female candidates, with 6.3 percent (or 40) selected, resulting in an increase to 13 female M.P.'s.In 1987 the party nominated 36 women, or 7 percent,with 17 being elected. The new Social Democratic Party (SDP) has recruited women discontented with the other parties' attitudes and practices, and its National Steering Committee has adopted two of three women-sponsored resolutions. These resolutions mandate that women be included on every shortlist and that four of the eight members on the party's National Steering Committee be women. A mail ballot to party members resulted in the defeat of a resolution requiring equal representation by sex to the party's central decision-making body, the Council for Social Democracy. Despite this defeat, the SDP has gone a bit further than its better-established partisan colleagues in meeting some feminist demands for sharing power and issue concerns. Together with the Liberals, the SDP has disseminated endorsements of far-reaching policy changes related to women, including better child care provisions, strengthening of antidiscrimination legislation, parental leave, and rights for part-time workers.The SDP and its Alliance partner, the Liberals, also sought to increase female representation in 1982. The SDP nominated 17 per cent women to its shortlists, resulting in 14.4 per cent female candidates of whom, however, none won! In 1986 the Alliance nominated 100 women, although only two were elected. The Alliance and the Labour Party, apparently competing for the women's vote, thus nominated increasing numbers of women. The SDP threat, though not yet translated into electoral power, may have galvanized Labour in particular to adopt a more "feminist" perspective in the most recent election.

Summary of British Women's Role in Parties

Each party seems to be firmly committed to the continuation of separate women's committees. These committees are endorsed by feminists as an important forum through which demands may be articulated and attention focused on women's issues. In each case, feminist party activists would like to see women's groups play a stronger consultative role. Dahlerup and Gulli have suggested that separate women's organizations within parties have five purposes: 1) to get women to support the party, 2) to recruit women members to the party, 3) to activate women and train them for top party posts, 4) to influence party policy, and 5) to create linkages to women in other groups. Apparently few, if any, of these aims have been achieved by women's organizations in British parties.We will examine the degree to which separate Swedish women's organizations within four of the five major parties have affected nominations, party policy, and recruitment to leadership roles.

It seems that only limited benefits have accrued to British women as a result of separatist organization in parties. In 1973 the merits of retaining a separate women's conference were debated at the Labour Party Conference meeting, and its continued existence was endorsed as a mechanism to provide encouragement and training for female activists, as well as to promote solidarity.However, women remain underrepresented in policy-making and leadership roles at all levels. In any event, parties appear to provide less of a link to policy-making in a system, such as the British one, increasingly controlled by bureaucratic functionaries. In addition, the hierarchical, mass-based structure of party groups in the United Kingdom is antithetical to the ideals of women's liberation, and so the relationship between many women and party activism is at best ambivalent.

While women in parties have called for mandated positive action with regard to candidate selectionas most obstacles to women's selection appear to exist at the local levellittle change has occurred. In response to pressure, the parties have moved toward expressions of greater concern for the nomination of women, but they have not insisted on equality of representation in the final selection process or in any other aspect of party politics. The ability of the 300 Group to attract over 1,500 women for training sessions for political activism points to the continuing gap between rhetoric and reality in much of British party politics. As an all-party group that defies traditional British political dictates, its endurance and continuing appeal say a great deal.

Parties: United States

Political parties are less central to the political process in the United States than in Britain, and feminist interest groups such as the NWPC, NOW, and other groups have played an important role in recruiting women for political office, providing training and some campaign support, and actively campaigning for key political issues such as abortion rights and the ERA. In the United States, the tradition of separate women's groups and the principle of numerical reservation of seats for women in the party hierarchy within the parties have largely been viewed as anachronistic. However, in the Democratic Party, women moved to mandate equal representation of male and female convention delegates via the 1972 McGovern-Fraser guidelines. The 1972 Democratic Convention had 40 percent female delegates, while the Republican Convention had 30 percent.Since then, women's task forces in both parties have pressed for women's concerns within the parties and the provision of some funding and training for women candidates.After the numbers of women delegates to conventions fell somewhat in 1976, the Democratic Party in 1978-80 moved to equalize convention representation by men and women and to provide support for such key feminist concerns as the ERA, election of more women to state and local offices, and even abortion rights. At the same time, the Reaganite Republican Party moved further to the right and away from commitment to feminist concerns. Nonetheless, in 1984, 48 percent of Republican delegates were women, as were about half of the Democratic delegates, an apparent response in both parties to Democratic-inspired rules reforms.

The increasing significance of feminist interest groups in the Democratic Party has been particularly striking during the past decade. Jo Freeman has pointed to the different political cultures that dominate the Republican and Democratic parties. In the Republican Party, power flows from the top down and delegates' relationship to party leaders and loyalty to the party itself tend to be significant. In contrast, in the Democratic Party, constituencies are seen as the party's building blocks, and power flows from the bottom up.These cultural distinctions help explain the important role feminist groups have been able to gain in the Democratic Party. In the Republican Party a Woman's Division was created in 1983, joining the National Federation of Republican Women, but its major functions were to mobilize, recruit, and publicize party accomplishments rather than to work as an advocacy group within the party. In fact, in the Republican Party, feminists are viewed as having competing loyalties and have been eliminated from leadership and administrative roles.Instead, right-winger Phyllis Schlafly has become the major policy arbiter on women's issues.

In the Democratic Party, because of the different structure and mechanism for representation, feminist groups came to have a major role. Building initially on the turmoil surrounding the 1968 convention, which opened the Democratic Party to reform, feminists gained one vice chair for their ranks. In 1976, disturbed by the falloff in female representation, feminist groups, especially the NWPC, together with the Women's Caucus of the Democratic National Committee and NOW, fought for a 50-50 rule guaranteeing equal representation to women and men. The Carter campaign, initially hostile to this idea, eventually acquiesced. Apparently Carter operatives felt that their refusal to support these feminist concerns would lead to a pro-Kennedy move. By 1980, over 20 percent of the Democratic delegates were members of NOW or of the NWPC.They gained support for a proposal to deny Democratic Party funds to any candidate who did not support the ERA. NARAL, like the NWPC, had its own floor operation and lobbied successfully for the addition of another minority plank to the platformone supporting government funding for abortions for poor women.

Therefore, by 1984, feminists had demonstrated their political clout. NOW met with five of the Democratic presidential candidates and pressed them on their support for women's issues, female appointments, and willingness to select a female vice presidential candidate. NOW Vice President Mary Jane Collins was appointed to the platform-drafting committee and given the leading role on matters of concern to NOW.A coalition of women's groups presented a list of acceptable female vice presidential candidates to Walter Mondale.After the nomination of Geraldine Ferraro, a committed feminist, the feminist coalition had little to do at the convention itself. At the time of this writing, it is not clear how Republican efforts to label feminism as an electoral liabilitybecause of its identification as a "special interest" and because of the failure to deliver a "gender gap" vote on behalf of Ferrarowill affect feminist access to power at future Democratic Party conventions.

Despite real gains in representation and support for women's issues, the role of convention politics in the American policy-making process is limited and marginal at best. In addition, numerous women seeking political office at all levels in the United States have by-passed traditional centers of candidate support and sought other routes to elective and appointive office. This contention is confirmed by a recent study of female candidates appointed to political office in state government: party-related factors were important for less than a third, with only 15 percent indicating that efforts by state and national party leaders had been very important.Younger women perceived party leaders as having played virtually no role in their appointments and, in contrast to some of their older female colleagues, had almost no history of party activism or campaign activity.Crucial to women candidates is a network of women's political organizations, which provide financial aid, research and information, and financial campaign assistance, and generally encourage women's active participation in the political process. Especially prominent in this regard are the Women's Campaign Fund (WCF) and NWPC.

In the United States, once a candidate is elected to political office, partisanship is only one influence that defines his or her political behavior. In Britain, only the 300 Group, an all-party organization that trains and recruits women who wish to run for political office, is analogous to the American model.

In the United Kingdom it can no longer be claimed that the women's vote is more "conservative" than men's nor that women are more conservative in their political attitudes, but neither can it be claimed that they are more left-wing. To the degree that a "gender gap" is emerging in Britain it does not represent the result of a feminist organizing effort. What it does seem to represent is a slight movement away from the two major parties, neither of which has met feminist aspirations effectively.

In the United States, what had appeared to be a significant "gender gap" in 1980, involving female rejection of Reaganite social policy and, in particular, opposition to defense spending and support for domestic spending, was reduced in 1984 to 8 per cent in the presidential race, although still providing evidence that fewer women supported Reagan.Nonetheless, despite the feminist movement's role in gaining a place for Ferraro on the ticket and efforts to mobilize against Reaganite conservatism, at the national level this strategy was not effective in attracting a majority of women voters. Feminist efforts in congressional elections and the women's vote at state and local levels in 1984 and 1986 resulted in greater evidence for the existence of a gender gap.

Unions: Britain

An early link between trade unions and the "new feminism" was evident in Britain in the 1970s. The NCCL held a conference in 1974 that brought together some 550 representatives of women's groups and labor, which was followed by the London Trade's Council's issuance of a ten-point Working Women's Charter drawn up by Communist Party feminists.Nonetheless, what appeared to be a promising relationship has not developed into a set of positive, concrete developments for feminist activists. In contrast to the United States, where about 15 per cent of women are union members and women compose about 30 per cent of union membership, in Britain about 31 per cent of women are union members and they account for about 40 per cent of union membership. Swedish women, reflecting the national trends, are among the most highly unionized in the world, despite their extensive part-time status.

In Britain, as well as the United States, the number of women unionizing has increased dramatically in the last decade. Of 12 million British TUC members in 1980, about 4 million were women.Female union membership increased from 1961 to 1980 by 111 per cent, while male membership increased by only 17.6 per cent.

While many socialist and nonaligned feminists have organized autonomously in their local communities and sought to develop specific feminist projects and activitiesshelters for battered women, day-care facilities, self-help clinics, and the likeother socialist feminists have sought to forge links with trade unions in order to reach out to working-class women. Nonetheless, because of the largely middle-class composition of the movement, the separatist ideas that some union women find abhorrent, and the lack of time that plagues many working-class women, it has often been difficult for the women's movement to make headway with its working-class sisters.It is unusual in Britain for campaigning organizations such as feminist groups to have links to trade union politics; particularly at the local level, there is suspicion of women's liberation.But there has been an increase in exchange of ideas between union and other feminist women, facilitated by such groups as NAC and the NCCL, which have ties to both.

Table: 6.1

Representation of Women in Unions and the Labour Party

Union*	Female Members	NEC	Full-Time Officers	TUC	Labour Party Delegates
TGWU	15.5	0/39	7/500	4/82	1/40
GMWU	34	0/40	13/243	4/74	4/63
AEUW	13.5	7 nonvoting seats/66	1 district secretary	1/37	NA
USDAW	62	3/16	None	5/38	5/34
NUTGW	90	5/15	8/43	12/17	NA
NUPE	66	8/26	6/125	9/32	6/18
NALGO	50	14/69	11/165	11/72	NA**
NUT	72	4/44	17/110	4/34	NA
CPSA	73	12/28	4/NA	10/36	NA
ASTMS	17.5	2/24	6/63	4/31	5/28
TASS	15	NA	NA	4/18	2/17
APEX	56	1/15	1 national, 1 area/of 51	4/15	1/6

Source: women's fightback, march 1982:67.*tgwu transport and general workers uniongmwu general and municipal workers unionaeuw amalgamated union of engineering workersusdaw union of shop, distributive, and allied workersnutgw national union of tailors and garment workersnupe national union of public employees not available. Nalgo national and local government officers' associationnut national union of teacherscpsa civil and public services associationastms association of scientific, technical, and managerial stafftass technical and supervisory section [of engineers' union]apex association of professional, executive, clerical, and computer staff.

Efforts to politicize newly organized women workers have met with some success, and socialist feminists have gained support for some key issues from the trade unions. But, in the main, women have virtually no power in unions and have been unable to alter existing patterns of low pay and job segregation. Women lack representation in key union committees, among full-time officers, and at the local shop level as stewards and district committee members.

A 1980 survey by Coote and Kellner (1981) showed that while 38 percent of union members surveyed were women, only 11 percent of the executive members, fewer than 6 percent of the full-time officials, and fewer than 15 percent of delegates to the TUC in these unions were women. Of 1,600 trade union officials, only 90 were women in 1983.

At the 1981 TUC annual meeting, 116 of 1,188 delegates were women, and at the 1983 meeting, 121 of 1,155.Although a number of unions have a majority of women workers, men remain in control of top positions in individual unions and the TUC. For example, the National Union of Education, with 70 percent female membership, had only four women members on the Executive Committee of 44 in 1980. Several major unions, including the two largest, the Transport and General Workers Union have not a single female executive member among them. (Table 6.1) Feminists have sought greater influence in two ways:

One approach, as in parties, has been to advocate "positive action/positive discrimination," retaining or establishing set-aside or statutory seats on executive committees and seeking other types of special representation, through advisory committees, women's conferences, and the like. In some instances, such efforts do not represent a "new approach"; in the TUC, the Women's Advisory Committee and annual women's conference date back to the 1920s and 1930s, respectively.In 1920 the Women's Trade Union League (WTUL), a women's labor union, merged with the TUC in return for two protected seats on the TUC Executive Committee.

At the same time, another militant women's union, the National Federation of Women Workers, merged with what is now the TGWU. (In short order, the number of women officials fell from 16 to one. It has been an uphill struggle to regain strength ever since. In the late 1920s the TUC Women's Conference was created, essentially establishing a group without power. As is true for parties, advisory committees have a solely consultative role and depend on the sympathy of general councils and other policy-making bodies for acceptance. The TUC Women's Action Committee has ten members appointed by the General Council and eight appointed by the Women's Conference; hence, like similar party-related bodies, it is not truly representative of women activists.In 1981 the TUC, to which most British unions are affiliated, responded to a Women's Conference demand by increasing the number of statutory delegate places reserved for women on the TUC Executive Committee from two to five.

However, among the white-collar unions, whose female membership is growing especially rapidly, there have been efforts to create special opportunities for women. Some unions have appointed a national women's officer.Others have introduced the practice of setting aside executive council seats for women. Still others, including the GMWU and the Association of Scientific, Technical, and Managerial Staff (ASTMS), have established women's advisory committees or set up equal opportunities groups or women's rights groups at the district level. Even consciousness-raising and special-training sessions for women have been introduced into several unionsincluding the GMWU, TASS, and the TUC. But, in the main, what has distinguished these efforts has been their "from the top down" quality.

In Britain, unlike the situation in Italy and, to a degree, in France, consciousness-raising and feminist groups did not emerge in the workplace.Except in a few instances (as in NALGO and the ASTMS, where several local women's groups were established, and in unions providing women-run courses "for women only"), most women's committees and efforts are institutionalized, segregating their concerns and removing them from grass-roots feminism.The lack of a tradition of autonomous women's labor organizations, like those in other European countries and in the United States,has lessened the impact of these efforts. The tensions created by efforts to develop autonomy yet gain influence have not seriously been addressed by trade union feminists in Britain.

The second approach feminists in unions have taken to increase their influence is their drive to gain union support for feminist-related issues. Even in the 1960s, prior to the activization of feminism, the TUC had lobbied for the Equal Pay Act. Later, prompted in part by the 1974 Working Women's Charterthe London-based effort to promote a minimum set of feminist demands in trade unionsthe TUC set about revamping its own charter, "Aims for Women at Work." The feminist campaign for child care found expression in the TUC's Charter for Under Fives (1978), calling for comprehensive and universal child care and flextime. The TUC has recognized the "outdated" concept of the family wage and has called for positive action in employment and education. A 1979 TUC ten-point "Charter for Equality" for trade union women advocated special efforts to include women on decision-making bodies and supported child care and awareness-training programs to aid in increasing women's union participation. In addition, the TUC has held conferences on women's issues, established guidelines for positive action in employment, and taken an active role in supporting amendments to the Equal Pay and Sex Discrimination acts.

A dramatic instance of union support for feminist issues came in a massive demonstrationa joint TUC-feminist march in 1979to protest the possibility of restrictive antiabortion legislation, then pending in the House of Commons in the Corrie Bill. This demonstration marked a unique expression of union support that moved beyond the rhetorical level to practical action.

In 1983, partially owing to pressure from the Labour Party Women's Action Committee, the biennial conference of the largest union in the country, the TGWU, supported a series of resolutions on positive action, including "a call for the extension and formal constitution of effective womens' organizations" in the union and in the Labour Party. It also instructed the union's Labour delegation to support proposals designed to improve women's access to and participation in the party.This action represented a victory because trade union feminists mobilized the delegates in opposition to the proposed platform, voted down a compromise proposal, and successfully pushed for a strong program of positive action.

Nonetheless, with regard to key feminist demands equal job opportunity for women and an end to pay discrimination only limited progress has been made. As suggested earlier, male dominance still exists in the unions at all levels, from regional councils to the shop floor to the industry-wide negotiating teams. In crucial negotiations with employers and with the federal government, bargaining priorities related to women have been neglected. The gap between stated policy in resolutions and its implementation in agreements and at the local and plant levels remains a key hurdle for union women.Hence, while unions have provided rhetorical support for "social issues" of concern to working women,their impact has been minimal on economic and industrial matters such as pay and maternity leaves. It is those matters over which men still retain firm control and discretion, limiting possibilities for the implementation of the numerous resolutions passed in union conferences. To a large degree, women's interests are viewed as secondary to the larger concern for social and economic issues. The resulting subordination of feminist demands leaves male bastions of power and sexism untouched.The indifference with which unions treat women is reflected in a survey that found clear hostility to unions among women factory workers. They articulated the view that unions cared only for men and pointed to the exclusion from unions of part-time workers who are disproportionately female.Policies such as affirmative action have been met with hostility and suspicion owing to high unemployment and concern for male jobs.

Several conclusions appear in order. The first is that, in the main, trade unions are unwilling to extend their purported support of feminist concerns to meaningful action in concrete areas. While they have endorsed and supported legislation related to women, they have usually not translated such support to other arenas of power. Although most unions are affiliated to the Labour Party, and effectively control its policies through their majority of votes, they have neither pressed for greater representation for women nor supported other efforts that increase women's power in the party. Nor have their representatives on public bodies, such as the EOC, been advocates on behalf of women's concerns. Hence, there is a need to move beyond the current stage of rhetorical support to a broadened perception of feminist issues in the unions themselves and in the larger society. As Labourite Audrey Wise has said, the aim of feminists is to feminize general issues of policy and generalize issues that are currently defined as women's issues. Given the analysis presented here, it is difficult to justify Hewlett's contention that the most effective women's groups in Britain are in parties and unionsnot in separate feminist organizations. In addition, though women's committees, equal opportunity officers, and the like exist in most unions, their failure thus far to alter power relations and policy priorities leads to the conclusion, to be explored later, that autonomous women's groups, which organize outside the union structure, may have the best opportunity to produce meaningful change.

Unions: United States

Women compose 16 per cent of the unionized labor force in the United States. If employee associations are included, the number rises to 30 per cent. As in Britain, the percentage of women currently unionizing is greater than that of men, although total membership in unions is declining precipitously. Like their British counterparts, few American women appear in leadership ranks, one exception being the National Education Association (NEA), a predominantly female union in which they constitute a majority of the board.

In the International Ladies Garment Workers Union (ILGWU), where they also compose over three-fourths of the membership, they hold 25 per cent of the board positions. In public sector unions, such as the American Federation of State, County, and Municipal Employees,which is 40 per cent female, women's increasing membership and their participation in union activities have resulted in more of them running for office and becoming shop stewards.In 1982, 33 per cent of local presidents were womenup from 25 per cent seven years before. In 1982, women also held 45 per cent of local union offices.

Within the last few years, a woman was elected international vice president of the Service Employees International Union (SEIU), which has estimated 45 percent women members, while two women were elected to the international board of the AFSCME. The SEIU held a conference in 1981 to discuss women's issues such as organizational roles, leadership, and collective bargaining; and several unions, particularly SEIU and AFSCME, have been active in fighting in the courts for women's concerns such as pregnancy disability insurance and comparable worth.

In general, women hold an increasing number of local-level union positions as stewards and officersthough there are still many more female secretaries than presidents. More women have been elected to high office and more resolutions passed on women's recruitment and promotion. Nonetheless, women do not hold top leadership positions in any unions and make up only a small minority of executive board members.In 1978; women held 31 of 655 elective or appointed offices in unions affiliated with the AFL-CIO and 109 of 662 positions in unaffiliated unions and employee associations. They constituted 7.2 per cent of national executive board members in AFL-CIO affiliates and 35.3 per cent of board members in employee associations where female membership is over twice that in traditional unions.

Table: 6.2

Female Membership and Leadership in Labor Organizations with 250,000 or More Women Members, 1978

Organization	Women Members	Percent Female	Women Officers and Board Members	Percent Female
National Education Association	1,219,500	75	5	55
International Brotherhood of Teamsters	480,974	25	0	0
United Food and Commercial Workers	480,105	39	2	3
American Federation of State, County and Municipal Employee	408,000	40	1	3
Amalgamated Clothing and Textile Workers' Union	130,660	66	6	15
Service Employees International Union	312,500	50	7	15
International Brotherhood of Electrical Workers	303,518	30	0	0
American Federation of Teachers	300,000	60	8	25
International Ladies Garment Workers Union	278,704	80	2	7
Communication Workers of America	259,112	51	0	0

Source: Coalition of Labor Union Women 1980

Women's caucuses and committees have been created in a number of unions, and feminist activity has spurred a new interest in union activism among many women workers. Women in the ILGWU and the American Postal Workers

Union (APWU) organized to gain support at union conventions for such issues as affirmative action.Elsewhere, women's divisions have pressed for increased child-care and flextime provisions. As in Britain, the class separation between the larger feminist movement and the working-class women involved in union politics has resulted in considerable distance between these two groups. Nonetheless, despite a reluctance of union women to identify with "women's lib," they have adapted consciousness-raising and other innovative feminist techniques and have been especially interested in issues of gender equality in the labor force.Efforts to organize around women's issues within unions have most often come from women themselves rather than from union leaders.

However, an aversion to the creation of special interests within unions, as well as the persistence of "male culture," has prevented women from gaining access to substantial internal power in unions, although as in Britain, the trade union movement has become an important ally of the women's movement in the political process. In the United States this support has gone beyond lobbying for legislation to active coalition participation in the Leadership Conference for Civil Rights and similar groups, in which the two movements have in many instances developed a joint agenda for policy. Such coalitional activity has been especially valuable with regard to the legal process and intervention in the administrative sector.

It has become evident that women compose a large segment of unorganized workers and, more importantly, are likelier than males to join unions. Evidence also indicates that unions win more representational elections when they stress women's issues.Unions have therefore become more receptive to such issues, as they assess their options in a situation of crisis and decline.

However, the American tradition of feminist autonomy from established groups is evident in relationships with the trade union movement as well as with parties.

Feminists have organized withinbut also outside the labor movement. As in Britain, a tradition of women's worker groups, such as the WTUL, gave rise to networks of women at the perimeter of the organized trade union movement.But while some groups, such as the Coalition of Labor Union Women (CLUW), operate within the traditional labor structure, an alternate approach to organizing, untested in Britain, continues to exist outside the American unions.

CLUW

In 1974, after a set of legal challenges to force unions to comply with provisions of antidiscrimination measures, the leading arm of the American labor movement, the AFL-CIO, helped establish a women's caucus within its ranks CLUW. Like women's groups within British unions, CLUW has pressed for greater sensitivity to women's concerns, increased representation in leadership circles, and an end to job discrimination. CLUW has created a women's base and forum for networking within the labor movement, and the result has been more representation of women in union offices and the creation of women's departments and committees in some unions. CLUW has taken the union structure as a given, with the goal of advancing women's interests as workers and unionists within it. Membership in CLUW is limited to those who were already both union members and activists in the trade union movement along traditional lines.Thus, CLUW functions as a means to network within union circles, creating pressure to act on women's demands. In the main, the group has served as a mechanism to promote women into leadership ranks; its chapters rarely include the union rank and file.At present, CLUW's membership comprises only about 1 percent of union women members, themselves a minority of union workers. As currently constituted, the group serves best as an internal union "watchdog," effective at leadership levels and only nominally attentive to the unorganized and the rank and file.

Like its British counterparts, the CLUW has largely met with an uneven response. Progress in increasing the representation of women in leadership ranks has been slow, but one visible result of CLUW's efforts was the selection of Joyce Miller in 1980 as the first woman on the AFL-CIO's executive council. Although union support has been generated for such issues as the ERA and the Pregnancy Discrimination Act and for coalitions formed to promote them, there has been limited progress in gaining support for matters like affirmative action. With 16,000 members and 72 local chapters, CLUW operates within the constraints of labor union politics and has avoided confrontation with the union hierarchy.

A Second Route to Organizing Women Workers

In the United States a second tradition of organizing labor women has developed, owing in part to the ambivalence of many professional Americans toward the organized labor movement and perhaps also to the absence of a vigorous socialist presence. This alternate route involves independent organizations of working women, primarily white-collar workersgroups like Wider Opportunities for Women (WOW), Working Women, and Union WAGE. Unlike unions that concentrate on collective bargaining, these groups seek to enforce antidiscrimination and affirmative action legislation, demonstrate against employers, and engage in educational efforts to promote safety, organization, and job rights.As unions have perceived the growing strength of autonomous groups of women workers, they have sought to establish links with them, such as the relationship recently forged between Working Women and the SEIU, which created a new union, District 925, to organize women.

In the 1970s, a younger group of feminist activists, who had roots in the New Left and the seminal women's liberation movement but who were also critical of labor politics, organized among previously uninvolved office workers. The group Working Women, formerly called 9 to 5, was a particularly successful result. Rather than dealing directly with unionization, this group concentrated on consciousness-raising and public dramatization of issues involving union organizations as well as on developing participatory democracy.After 1975, Working Women moved closer to the organized union movement when Local 925 was organized in conjunction with the SEIU. The new "union" was charged with organizing office workers all over the country and, although a part of the SEIU structure, drew staff direction from Working Women and retained autonomy within the union structure.Working Women has continued as a separate entity outside the union as well. In addition to concentrating on unionization, it has focused on other issues of concern to women, including age discrimination and bank and insurance company relations with women workers. The group's emphasis on participation by all members continues and visible public actions, involving media attention, are utilized.In its emphasis on developing specifically female organizational forms and concerns, Working Women seems to be almost a direct descendant of the WTUL.

The dilemma for autonomous groups is how to maintain independence while at the same time influencing the larger union structure. If the Working Women experiment proves successful, it may point the way to the creation of a uniquely feminist worker's presence, with influence in the union and access to its resources and power.

Another approach to women's employment is WOW, which grew from a locally focused volunteer organization stressing part time work to a national nonprofit organization with several staff members. WOW has sought to combine service and advocacy, providing training programs and job placement in nontraditional occupations. Through monitoring, coalition building, and advocacy, as well as publicizing and documenting job inequity, WOW and other groups have sought to reach women who are not union members and are outside the traditional labor market.The independent tradition continues and autonomous groups of working women, together with groups such as WOW and Catalyst, have been active in finding jobs for women in all levels of the economic ladder and in fighting job discrimination.

Local Women's Committees: "Municipal Feminism" A New Direction in British Politics

Recent efforts at the local level of British politics suggest that in some instances it may be possible for feminist women to work closely with Labour councils and local authorities. New developments in numerous British urban areas have interacted effectively with the decentralized structure of British feminism. Since 1969, a variety of multifaced action groups have developed in many British urban centers, focusing on feminist collectives, rape crisis centers and shelters for battered women, health clinics, black women's groups, and groups of women in law, the media, and other professions.Feminists have turned to local council governments for funding, access, and space to maintain their activities; and, fearing hierarchy and male co-optation, they have tended to prefer local-level dialogues to those at the national level.

Since 1982, aided in part by the increased number of local councilors who are women, several local councils have created women's committees to promote representation of women and women's interests.Such committees have been established by the Greater London Council (GLC), numerous London boroughs, including Camden, Islington, Southwark, and Hackney, and by 22 other British urban centers.Virtually all these constituencies are under Labour Party domination. In some communities, support for women's committees came from local councilors, while in others the initiative for commission establishment emanated from the women's movement itself. In Leeds, for example, a local conference that drew together Labour Party and SDP women, trade union members, and local women's groups resulted in the formation of a women's Subcommittee of the Policy and Resources Committee.This body strengthened the work already begun by the Women's Equal Employment Group, which had been established in 1982 by trade union and other local women. By 1984, the Leeds council had trebled childcare funding.

The greatest resources were those of the GLC, which in 1984 devoted nearly £8 million to funding local women's groups and projects.The GLC Women's Committee sought to involve a wide spectrum of women by holding open meetings and coopting women to represent such groups as lesbians, the disabled, and trade unionists.Funding was given to Greenham Common women for day care and to a female transportation service, as well as to day care and health facilitiesall to a generally hostile press reception.A major thrust of the GLC Women's Committee was to foster multiaction centers for women, thus bringing some order to the centrifugal politics we have described, perhaps building on the women's action centers that already existed in many British cities.At the GLC, efforts were made to emphasize participatory democracy and openness through public meetings, which received enthusiastic response and enjoyed large attendance.Meetings were open to all interested women and tasks were rotated, in accordance with feminist theory. Despite media emphasis on funding of "radical" projects, child-care subsidies in fact, accounted for the bulk of GLC funding efforts.

The GLC budget for grants to women increased from £300,000 in 1982 to over £7 million in 1984.Between April and December 1983 alone, 227 projects were funded for a total of £4.5 million, an unusually large infusion of funds for previously impoverished feminist groups.Nonetheless, the portion allocated to women still was only a fraction of the total GLC 198384 budget of £824 millionless than 1 percent, in fact.However, by 1986, the fourth and final year of the GLC Women's Committee's budget existence, its budget had grown to £90 million.In this committee, as in other women's committees, local councilors retained the right to outvote and override the interest of the feminist consultants a situation that has led some observers to suggest that in this instance women's groups are relatively autonomous but lack effective power.However, the GLC did provide a meeting place at County Hall for a wide variety of women's activities and purchased a building for the specific use of two feminist groups, A Women's Place and the Women's Research and Resources Center.In addition, the GLC Women's Committee played a campaigning or mobilizing role, aiding efforts related to working women, child care, and Greenham Common.

Women's committees established in the London boroughs of Camden and Islington have had varying degrees of success and funding. The Camden group, with strong support from local Labour councilors, has devoted considerable funding to women's efforts. A Woman's Bus has traveled the community to focus discussions and provide information and advice, circumventing the media by going directly to local women.However, in Islington, as of 1984, the Women's Unit was all but defunded and defunct.

The women's committees have been unique in creating new structures that bring women into the political process. They have aimed at breaking down traditional hierarchical processes and, through innovative systems of publicity and participation, tried to seek out women who are not normally part of the political process. They have also attempted to broaden the framework of service provision from a feminist perspective. Some feminists, especially those wary of Labour Party practices in the past, fear that such efforts may co-opt the movement.In fact, however, these committees may act as a bridge between the movement and both labor and governmental structures, if they are successful.

A major drawback to these promising efforts has been the attack of the Conservative government on both the GLC and local London council governments'. The GLC itself was dissolved in 1986 by the Thatcher government. Although the trend toward local-level support for women's efforts in Britain is still too new to measure, these efforts are notable in providing linkages between traditional, socialist, and radical feminist groups and in seeking to reach out to the vast number of British women who have heretofore been unaffected by the feminist movement. Can local-level priorities be reorganized and feminists given real power rather than just their customary advisory role? Can a modus vivendi be reached between feminist democracy and traditional hierarchical government structures? These questions are as yet unresolved.

This chapter has assessed two different approaches to feminist political organizing: the British one, in which movement activity has been contained within the existing parties and unions, and the American one, in which gender-based groups have sought to interact with a weaker party and union system. It seems evident that the British model of organizing women's groups within parties and unions has had only limited impact on representation and policy. Whether, as Coote and Campbell have recently argued, the new forces of radical activism in the Labour Party are sufficient to "break down some of the barriers that had stood between the women's movement and parliamentary politics in the 1970's" is not clear from the analysis presented here.

In the United States, independent groups such as NOW, the NWPC, and NARAL have gained a significant voice in the Democratic Party, pressing their views effectively on a still predominantly male leadership. The role of feminist movements as constituents in electoral politics appears to be clearer from the American case; although in Britain there have been some efforts to mobilize them in order to create new alignments of political power.

Unions in both countries present an ambiguous picture, although in the United States the innovative model created by 9 to 5, emanating from an independent feminist base, has suggested new alternatives for workers and organizers. In Britain a new model of feminist activism, at the local level, has seemed to represent a fresh, more "political phase" of the movement where it has felt most at home. The effect of the abolition of the GLC, which had the most resources and influence of all local committees and working parties, is still undetermined.

We will explore the rather different Swedish model of integration into existing structures. But first, we examine the role of feminists in policy-making in Britain and the United States.

7

Feminism in Government
Advocacy and Policy-making

We can test the impact feminists have made on national politics by analyzing public policy issues by exploring 1) agenda setting the role of feminist groups in initiating and structuring public policy 2) the influence of these groups on legislative and executive decision-making, and 3) the implementation of the policies enacted. Central to this analysis is an examination of the role played by feminist groups in any or all of these crucial steps in the policy-making process. Implicit in our discussion will be the question: Have the policies enacted made a difference?

In this chapter we analyze the role of two apparently similar bodies: the Equal Opportunities Commission in the United States. In addition, we examine the structure of the policy-making process in both countries by focusing on abortion and sex discrimination politics. Finally, we assess the role of British and American feminist groups in affecting policy outcomes by looking closely at the politics of domestic violence, an issue first brought to public consciousness in Britain. We will extend the analysis to Sweden.

Women are poorly represented in British political life. In 1982, only 23 women served in Parliament, although a record 210 stood for election.By 1987 a higher number 40 out of 221 candidateshad gained seats. In addition to the female Prime Minister, Margaret Thatcher, there are three other women ministers in the present Conservative government, but they do not hold cabinet rank. Of 97 senior judges, only two are women. While women increasingly qualified as barristers and solicitors during the 1970s and 1980s, in England and Wales they composed only 3 per cent of the Queens Counsels, from whom judges in the High Court and above are chosen.In 1983 only 4 percent of High Court judges were women. No women were represented among the higher-level appeals judges. In the senior civil service, in 1986, fewer than 4 per cent of high administrative officers were women. In 1983, while women composed 47.1 per cent of Home civil servants, there were no female permanent secretaries.Few women are nominated to, or serve on, government committees, councils, or other public bodies. And, at the local level, in the mid-1970s there were only two chief women's officers out of 500.But more women are becoming local councilorsin 1982 they numbered 18.4 per cent. However, as we noted earlier, the overwhelming structure of power in Britain is predominantly male.

Government-based Advocacy of Women's Issues in Britain

The Economic Opportunities Commission

During the 1960s and early '70s, pressure arose in Parliament for the creation of a quasi-independent body to "act as an amalgam of recipient and investigator complaints relating to sex discrimination, conciliator where possible and prosecutor in the courts where this failed".The result was the creation of the Equal Opportunities Commission to enforce the Equal Pay Act and Sex Discrimination Act.The EOC was given law enforcement powers, research and investigative capacity, and jurisdiction over a number of policy areas related to women. Excluded from EOC jurisdiction were the social security, pensions, taxes, and nationality.

It was hoped that the EOC would be a vigorous voice on behalf of women and would play a strong enforcement role. In practice, the EOC has not developed as robust a defender of equal rights as many hoped, although it does provide a forum and base for feminist-related issues, one of the few that exists in a system essentially closed to change-oriented groups.

The EOC is a quango, or quasi-judicial/legislative entity, and as such is not strictly accountable to the House of Commons or the executive branch. The agency therefore apparently has a degree of independence. In the United States, by contrast, appointments to commissions and agencies dealing specifically with women's issuesthe Equal Employment Opportunities Commission (EEOC), Commission on Civil Rights, and Office of Civil Rights are politicized, and feminist groups are consulted and vocal about their preferences.

As a quango, in fact the EOC relies on funding from the Home Office and is dependent on government departments. It also lacks the supportive constituency necessary for a successful confrontationist stance.It is therefore reliant on informal government contacts and, as a result, lacks a public image and awareness. Perhaps mindful of the restrictive role to which the Commission for Racial Equality was limited when it sought to build a stronger relationship with ethnic groups and develop a constituency, the EOC has been more cautious.

In addition, a history of tripartism limits the role of women both at the EOC and within the judicial process. Secrecy pervades the appointments process and access is limited, except for established groups. Nominations to the agency are made by reference to lists of "The Great and the Good," on which few, if any, women are found; interests represented include those of party, region, and, especially, business and labor. Recommendations of women clearly identified with feminism were rejected until the late 1970s.Until recently, when two women with a feminist orientation were appointed, the commission reflected little input from women per se. In the main, female trade union representatives on the EOC have been more responsive to labor than to women's concerns.Meehan points out that when in one instance a TUC representative on the EOC dissented from the union position on protective legislation, she was met with punitive action by the TUC, including denial of reappointment to the EOC and removal from her senior position in the TUC. Leadership roles on the commission have been given primarily to majority party representatives.

In addition to the lack of access to appointments and the policy-making process, the role of the EOC is limited by the neocorporatist structure of the legal system. British employment suits are first heard in industrial tribunals rather than in courts. Tribunals are comprised of representatives of industry and labor and are seen as part of the collective bargaining process.In this process, there is limited representation for complainants by unions or groups similar to the American Civil Liberties Union provide some legal aid, there are no pro bono, public interest, law-related groups that play an advocacy role on behalf of the disadvantaged. Trade unions, which could aid complainants in bringing suits, usually do not. In addition, tribunal personnel are overworked and undertrained and lack an understanding of sex discrimination issues. The number of cases heard and upheld by tribunals is discouraging to feminist aspirations.Tribunals do not create case law; therefore their rulings result in a plethora of ad hoc decisions. The British judiciary is naturally conservative, and not surprisingly, has shown itself to be far from progressive on issues of sex discrimination. Of the cases that have been won, at least two important ones have been on appeal to the European Court.

Among them was a case of indirect discrimination brought by Belinda Price. She alleged that the Civil Service Commission's requirement of an upper-age limit of 28 for executive officers discriminated against women as childbearers and rearers during their twenties. Because of the limited legal advocacy structure and the tradition of bureaucratic neutrality, outside pressure and monitoring of compliance with the law are absent in the United Kingdom.In contrast to the United States, where the existence of policy networks is a key part of the process of influence, in Britain women have not developed similar networks for reasons of ideology and institutional structure. Hence, there has been little or no organization per se to bolster the enforcement of sex discrimination laws.

The style of the 15-person EOC itself has been to limit emphasis on enforcement and sanctions and to concentrate on research and publicity. It has sought to avoid confrontation in favor of consultation and persuasion and has been involved in few, if any; dramatic cases.It has conducted several protracted informal investigations into equal pay and employment issueswith limited outcomes. The House of Lords has prevented the EOC from mounting formal investigations into the general workings of organizations.As a result, the EOC has sought to influence government at higher levels, by submitting proposals and evidence to the House of Commons and relevant agencies, including royal commissions and agencies concerned with manpower services and education.It has provided legal assistance and advice to individuals and brought several cases to the European Court. Perhaps most significantly, it has played a major role in educating public opinion on sex discrimination issues.It has helped create consciousness of the need for change and has demonstrated the extent of discrimination. The EOC has issued films as well as pamphlets and other documents, held conferences, and played a key role in funding projects, even those of women's groups considered "radical." Among them have been grants to the Women's Action Group, the Women's Health Information Center, the NCCL, Asian women's groups, Women's Aid, the Women's Therapy Center, Sisterwrite,the Women's Research and Resource Center, and unions. In a system where funding opportunities are limited, the EOC is a new and important source of financial support for emerging feminist groups.

The EOC may also play a role in building relationships among disparate groups concerned with women's issues. An example is the commission's large annual conference, to which 70 to 80 women's organizations are invited, thus providing a rare forum and meeting place for a wide variety of feminist activists. Additional factors limiting the effectiveness of the EOC are its location in Manchester and the absence of regional offices as well as the high turnover rate among its chief executives four different heads during its first five years of existence.

The commission has had difficulty in maintaining traditional bureaucratic neutrality among a staff with feminist inclinations. The result has been tensions between commissioners and staffunlike the situation in its American counterpart, the EEOC, whose staff and groups frequently consult and may be mutually supportive.The election of a more sympathetic government would undoubtedly help, considering that the Conservative government cuts forced the EOC to reduce its staff from 400 to 148.Some British feminists fear that having created a body with extensive purported power, although far less in actual terms, the commission may actually impede further action regarding sex equality.The creation of a feminist alliance that transcends ideological, party, and class bias and that could provide legitimacy for feminist-related concerns may be the only way to strengthen the EOC.The EOC itself has concluded that little further progress can be made without "substantial amendment".

The Women's National Commission

A second government-based potential advocacy group in Britain is even more limited by constraints than the EOC. The Women's National Commission (WNC) is a government-founded and sponsored organization that was established in 1969. It has two co-chairs, one government appointed and one elected by the commission itself. The WNC's mission is "to ensure by all possible means that the informed opinion of women is given due weight in government".The commission has a requisite size of 50 organizations, which must be national bodies with a large and active membership. Current members include women's sections of unions and parties.

The WNC develops working groups to examine issues and has produced papers, often in response to government Green and White papers. While superficially resembling such American federal agencies as the Women's Bureau in the Department of Labor and the commissions on the status of women, the WNC shares some of their weaknesses and then some! The WNC is constrained in its criticism of government because of its close ties to the incumbent administration. In addition, the scope of its membership is limited by the requirement that member groups must have been in existence a number of years and must have a national presence and membership. These ground rules militate against inclusion of mostif not allwomen's liberation groups that have no say; hence, the WNC lacks true representativeness of women's interests.Even such small London-based groups as the Fawcett Society are excluded by this policy, although nonmember groups are occasionally invited to participate in the WNC's deliberations on an ad hoc basis. In addition, the group's charter lacks a provision for changing its organizational membership.

The WNC is run by the general secretary and one staff member, limiting its role greatly. Moreover, the group's power, like many others discussed here, is strictly advisory. The group exists on a budget that makes up 3 percent of the EOC's resources.Hence, while the WNC remains as a symbol of women's influence and a potential advocate for women's concerns, which no government will abolish for symbolic reasons; it represents a classic case of institutional powerlessness.

Government-based Advocacy of Women in the United States

In the United States by 1980 the number of women state legislators tripled in 12 years to over 14 per cent, although they constituted only 5.1 per cent of Congress.In the 1980s women mayors governed several of America's largest cities, including Houston, Chicago, and San Francisco, and the number of municipal officials who were women tripled to 13 per cent.Especially under the Carter administration, women's fortunes in the administrative sector improved dramatically. The number of women in top policy-making jobs subject to presidential appointment increased from a pre-Carter 14 per cent to 33 per cent in 1979. In cabinet and subcabinet positions, women's representation improved from 4 to 8 percent. Carter also appointed an unprecedented number of women as federal judges, bringing female representation on the federal bench to 6.6 percent. Under Ronald Reagan's administration after 1980, however, these numbers dropped significantly to 4.4 percent of judicial nominations and 9 percent of senior federal appointments.By 1987, Reagan appointments of women to top positions had reached 15 percent, although, despite their gender, many could be classified as antifeminists.

In the United States, as in the United Kingdom, the activities of agencies addressing sex discrimination, especially the EEOC, have been limited by an insufficient budget and bureaucratic ineptitude.Enforcement has been primarily left to individuals who face serious obstacles in pursuing sex discrimination cases.

In the United States the Women's Bureau was for some 40 years the focal point for women in government. Its role was hampered to some degree by its advocacy of protective legislation for women and its accompanying antipathy to the ERA.Nonetheless, after it abandoned its endorsement of protection and came to support the ERA; it became both a resource and an advocacy agency on behalf of women's concerns. It has helped provide resources and a forum for a variety of women's concerns. However, though at one time it was the only federal agency charged with looking after women's welfare, it has been joined by the federal commissions on the status of women, the Civil Rights Commission, and the EEOC. The significance of these bodies has varied with the particular administrative viewpoints and with the type of leadership provided at a given time.

The EEOC was created pursuant to the passage of Title VII of the Civil Rights Act of 1964. As Vicki Randall has pointed out, it initially had fewer formal enforcement powers than its British counterpart, the EOC. Nonetheless, it emerged as a relatively important tool through which major policy advances in equal employment might be made, although its effectiveness has varied with the commitment of different administrations to it. The initial EEOC had power only to seek voluntary compliance with the Civil Rights Act; it could not litigate, although it could file amicus curiae briefs. After 1972, largely owing to pressure from the organized feminist movement and from commissioners sympathetic to the movement, its enforcement powers were strengthened.

For the EEOC, enforcement involves the resolution of individual charges and the elimination of "patterns and practices" of discrimination.Executive Order 11375 amends the earlier Executive Order 11246 to include sex discriminatory employment practices among those prohibited to employers under contract to the federal government. Although the enforcing agency, the Office of Federal Contract Compliance Programs (OFCCP), has not been vigorous in enforcing policy, a 1969 order spelled out in detail what affirmative action would entail, in terms of goals, timetables, and monitoring progress. Under pressure from WEAL, the executive orders were applied to women in higher education as well.

Despite the unevenness of the enforcement process, nondiscrimination efforts have been aided in the United States by a variety of factors unavailable to the British feminist movement. Nonetheless, during most of the 1970s, major questions were raised by critics about the EEOC's administrative efficiency and the seriousness of its commitment to end discrimination. The backlog of unresolved cases seemed particularly indicative of inadequate efforts. But in 1977, Eleanor Holmes Norton, a new chair appointed by the Carter administration, instituted a complete overhaul of the commission in order to rationalize its structure and procedures. Even prior to that, though, the commission had demonstrated its ability to litigate effectively on behalf of individuals. Through issuance of guidelines and briefs, it was able in large measure to shape the nature of judicial response to the issues raised. Particularly noteworthy was the 1973 settlement with the American Telephone and Telegraph Company (AT&T), the largest such award ever made under civil rights legislation.Hundreds of briefs were filed on behalf of individuals and also in class action suits. In 1977 alone, 35 class action suits were resolved.

A major factor in the EEOC's ability to change law was the establishment of a policy network that aided in the appointment of sympathetic staff and commissioners, consulted with the commission, and produced additional legislation to strengthen the functioning of the agency. A Washington women's policy network brought legislators, bureaucrats, staff, and feminist advocates together on a variety of issues. The emergence of the women's movement aided in expanding federal policies, and because the bureaucratic process in the United States is recognized as more explicitly "political" than that of Britain, the effectiveness and persistence of the Washington women's lobby helped to influence appointments, press for continuing antidiscrimination legislation,and monitor agency enforcement.The appointment of an outspoken black woman leader to head the EEOC in 1977 was made in consultation with civil rights and women's groups. "With its amicus curiae briefs, strict guidelines and its power to litigate after 1974, the EEOC is thought to have become, in the 1970's, a strong and successful proponent of women's rights".

Under the Reagan administration, funding for civil rights enforcement dropped, now constituting only 0.07 percent of the federal budget. The ability of federal agencies to conduct compliance reviews, investigate complaints, and attack discrimination in a systematic fashion has been severely curtailed.Like the British EOC, the EEOC has experienced cutbacks in staff and budget, with clerical staff and legal positions most affected. These reductions in turn have slowed the production of documentation needed to prosecute cases. Litigation activities have also been curtailed owing to reduced funding, with little money available for witnesses, special studies, and data processing.Staff at the OFCCP has also been cut back, resulting in a backlog of individual complaints.New regulations further curtail coverage and may discourage the bringing of systemic discrimination suits. For the first time, an administration has intervened as a "friend of the Court" against women and minorities in "reverse discrimination" suits, although the Supreme Court has generally upheld affirmative action in recent cases.Women have not yet lost most of the equal employment gains of the last two decades, although they have been forced to expend enormous energy and scarce resources just to maintain the status quo. But the resignation under protest of government officials such as Joseph Cooper, responsible for compliance with affirmative action guidelines, has helped highlight the administration's failure to vigorously enforce the law.

The Contrast between U.S. and British Advocacy

To the degree that the EEOC has been a more effective force for change than its British counterpartalthough its role depends in large measure on the sympathetic support of both the executive and judicial branchesseveral points of contrast appear significant. First, the federal courts in the United States have upheld and reinforced numerous claims pursued under Title VII. Second, American courts are more available to make and interpret policy and may provide another access route to policy change. Third, class action suits may result in more sweeping and effective remedies, and the growing litigation sector among women's groups has used its limited resources to aid in bringing such suits before the courts.

A final area of contrast is the policy toward affirmative action. Atkins and Hoggett suggest that four factors present in the United States regarding this policy are absent in the United Kingdom: 1) the public availability of requisite statistics, 2) the imposition of high damages in discrimination cases, 3) the powerful position of the EEOC in conciliating and monitoring out-of-court settlements, and 4) the willingness and power of the courts to uphold positive action orders. As we shall see, similar constraints limit the effectiveness of Sweden's machinery for equal opportunities. An additional factor limiting the impact of the British EOC may be that its power is separated from that of the Commission on Racial Equality (CRE) and its racial and ethnic base, so that joint efforts, such as those facilitated in the United States by the Civil Rights Commission and EEOC, are not feasible in Britain. A possible opening for more effective policy-making by the EOC may lie in its emerging relationship with the EEC, via the European Commission, European Parliament, and European Court of Justice.(In 1984, for example, the EOC finally met its obligations as stated in an EEC directive of 1975, amending the Equal Pay Act to cover equal pay for equal valueor comparable worth, in American terminology.) But despite this potential support for a stronger EOC role, it is difficult to see the emergence of a greatly altered commission unless a more cohesive and politicized feminist movement can effectively intervene at the administrative level.

The absence of an organized British feminist movement, coupled with an institutional setting that makes monitoring of implementation far more difficult than it is in the United States, helps explain in part the considerably different outcomes in the two nations.In the United Kingdom the ensuing separation between the so-called neutral bureaucracy and feminist activists has both reflected and reinforced the absence of a feminist lobby. In the United States, equal opportunity policies have had a greater impact than in Britain because they have been in effect longer and have been accompanied by more aggressive enforcement of antidiscrimination policies.

Women in Power: Mobilizing Power in the Legislative Arena

Britain

Women as elected political officials may provide support for feminist issues. Consistent with our analysis of the EOC and the EEOC, British women M.P.'s have been reluctant allies of the women's movement, while their American counterparts have developed a bit more cohesion on certain issues of interest to the feminist community. The women in Parliament who became concerned with abortion apparently did so only after a decision was visited on them by their male colleagues.Once limiting bills were introduced in 1974-75; the M.P.'s were galvanized into action and helped organize support in committees and through petitions, marches, and the like. (In contrast, the Sex Discrimination Act was given qualified support by women M.P.'s because many of them saw it largely as publicity concocted for International Women's Year. But whatever the momentum created around the abortion issue, parliamentary women have no very clear and "certainly no very enduring sense of themselves as a group".The presence of Margaret Thatcher as the lone woman in her cabinet merely reinforces the view that there are "exceptional women" who occasionally achieve power and who rule in "splendid isolation" from their female colleagues. In the House of Commons, women do not see themselves as having any "esprit de corps." Most Labour women may have a degree of camaraderie and unity of purpose about some, though not all, issues. The existence of separate Lady Member's Sitting Rooms by party has developed in recent years, accentuating partisan differences between women M.P.'s. In the House of Lords as well, party is a greater influence on behavior than is sex. Women peers are not united by a feminist ideology, nor have they provided any feminist input in Parliament.

In contrast, in the United States a congressional Caucus for Women's Issues founded in 1977 claimed a bipartisan membership of 127,including a majority of men.The group acts as a lobbying organization, with a bipartisan leadership and an all-female executive committee. The caucus aids in gaining electoral support for members and provides information to its constituents through a newsletter; Update.It prepares news releases and promotes legislation through meetings with administration officials and through media advocacy efforts. The caucus may be weakened by its somewhat partisan cast, and its failure to solicit support from all women members.

However, though women legislators in the United States do not necessarily or even usually behave as a bloc, studies have found that women are consistently more liberal, particularly on issues concerning women and consumer protection.Republican women and men in Congress exhibit contrasting behavior on such issues as abortion rights, child benefits, and the ERA.Women legislators also appear to favor decreased military expenditures and arms control, regardless of party affiliation. In this context it may prove especially significant that the caucus supports legislation such as that contained in the Economic Equity Act (EEA). The group has served as a source of information and consensus building.

THE POLICY PROCESS

Britain

Pym suggests that few promotional pressure groups have a meaningful impact on the policy-making process in the United Kingdom, although she views the case of abortion reform as having been almost unique. Most legislation relating to women has been submitted as a private member's bill, and depends on tacit to overt government support for passage. The House of Lords and appointed select committees have often played a key role in mobilizing support for "women's" legislation. Many feminists in Britain are skeptical about the ability of equal rights campaigns and legislation to alter the balance of power between men and women.Hence the passage of the Equal Pay Act owed more to the parties, the TUC, and also the EEC than it did to the women's movement. Women's groups have played an auxiliarybut not central rolein creating support for legislative enactments.

The EPA was enacted under the aegis of a Labour government committed after 1964 to the principle of equal pay for equal work.After consultation with the CBI and TUC, it was agreed that the act passed in 1970 would take effect in 1975. Randall attributes the support of the TUC for equal pay legislation not to its concern for feminism but to its fear that lower women's wages would undercut those of men. Lorwin and Boston point out that until the late 1960s, unions preferred to deal with matters of equal pay through wage negotiations rather than through the legislative process.

The EPA provided that machinery for complaints would be the same as that for other industrial disputes: efforts to reach a settlement via the Advisory Conciliation and Arbitration Service (ACAS), recourse to industrial tribunals, and, as a last resort, employee appeals tribunals. The passage of the act did not end the demand for sex discrimination legislation. Private member's bills were introduced after 1967 by Joyce Butler. A 1972 bill introduced by Willie Hamilton provided the basis for a bill placed by Baroness Nancy Seear before the House of Lords. It was then referred to a Select Committee; a similar Select Committee was established in the House of Commons. The Conservative Party then in power announced support for an equal opportunities commission and some form of legislation.The ensuing Labour government in 1974 pledged support for strong sex discrimination legislation. The SDA was passed in 1975, providing for expanded scope and enforcement and a more powerful EOC.

The legislative process involved in the sex discrimination bill suggests that there was little opposition to the idea of some kind of legislative action on the issue. "The most admirable feature of the debate was the generally sympathetic attitude of the opposition," at least as far as the principle of the bill was concerned; the bill survived the parliamentary legislative process virtually intact.It may be argued that activity of women in the two major parties created both a pressure and political climate in which legislation was thought necessary. However, there was, in fact, little influence by feminists or female politicians in Parliament.The Labour government in power in 1974 did endorse the idea of an enforcement body with strong powers as opposed to an organization that, as envisioned by the Conservatives, would be largely devoted to campaigning. Among parliamentary groups, the NCCL, the TUC, the Fawcett Society, and Women in the Media, as well as a short-lived Women's Lobby, pressed avidly for legislation. At the other extreme, the act's passage was greeted with total hostility by segments of the feminist community, who described it as "fraudulent," "hypocrisy," "a sellout," and "miserable tokenism" and conducted a National Day of Action against the bill, chaining themselves to the railings outside Parliament.Their opposition was based on the loopholes in the act, its presumed middle-class bias, and the weakness of the EOC. They viewed the SDA as a cheap concession, aimed at staving off more meaningful and expensive demands for economic and family equality.In the end, however, it appears that "lobbying was relatively weak and what mattered was M.P.s' willingness to pay [the bill] attention".As was the case with equal credit legislation in the United States, M.P.'s may have perceived the bill's proposals as a bow to a growing "women's vote," somewhat in anticipation of organized demands.Other reasons for the easy passage were Britain's pending entry into the Common Marketand the EEC directives requiring equal pay and job equalityand, as in the United States, the relationship between action against race discrimination and action against sex discrimination.

A third law, the Employment Protection Act of 1975, was supported vigorously by the TUC.The act gave women, for the first time, statutory protection against the loss of jobs due to pregnancy and childbirth. Women now had a statutory right to paid maternity leave, protection from unfair dismissal during pregnancy, and the right to regain their jobs up to 29 weeks of giving birth.However, in practice, the rights defined are so narrow that only a minority of women qualify; the majority cannot meet criteria regarding length of service and hours worked per week. No more than one woman in ten who leaves work to have a baby returns.Only some 5 percent of women in manual work who took maternity leave and wished to return to their job have been able to do so.

The record nonetheless demonstrates that the 1970s in Britain marked legislative acceptance of the principle of equality in several different areas. How well has the legislation worked in practice?

We have suggested that the role of women's groups in facilitating the passage of legislation was an auxiliary rather than central one. Their participation has been even more minimal in the implementation process. As suggested earlier in this chapter, the EOC, which was set up under the Sex Discrimination Act, has been limited in its role, and, reflecting the systemic constraints within which it operates, has acted cautiously. Neither unions nor feminist groups have pressured vigorously for increased action, either at the EOC or in places of employment.The EOC has used its power of formal investigation and its power to issue nondiscrimination notices "judiciously." In 1979 it issued its first nondiscrimination notice on equal pay to the Electrolux factory at Luton.A lawsuit involving "indirect" discrimination was successfully won in Price v. Civil Service.The SDA leaves untouched existing protective labor legislation, except to require the EOC to report on it.Hedged with "genuine occupation qualifications" based on sexual distinctions, it fails to provide any obligation to establish positive action programs.It is difficult to escape the view that the EOC was not given adequate legal machinery to enforce nondiscrimination on any significant scale.And, as suggested earlier, the EOC has been cautious about using those powers it does have, preferring to devote its major resources to research and publicity.

In the British system, the individual is responsible for bringing cases before the appropriate authorities, and there is the assumption of an equal balance of power between the employee and employer. The onus is on the woman to prove that discrimination has occurred. There is no right to obtain all documentation related to the case for the complaint. And individuals who can prove they have been discriminated against can obtain financial compensation but cannot regain their jobs.The burden of proof is on the victim. Since 1976, between 50 and 70 percent of EPA and SDA cases have failed to reach a tribunal. This situation has been largely due to the intervention of the Advisory Conciliation and Arbitration Service, which, as the conciliation service for all industrial complaints, may intervene when there is a prospect of success or when either side requests its assistance. The majority of cases are "settled" at this level or withdrawn.

The number of cases heard and upheld under both acts is discouraging to feminist aspirations. In recent years the number of cases brought to the EOC under the SDA has remained at a relatively low 250 annually, but EPA cases dropped from 1,742 in 1976 to 54 in 1981, which indicates that the EPA in particular has had limited impact because women have become disillusioned with its ability to change their economic circumstances.

In most instances, under the SDA only a handful of cases heard by tribunals result in a positive finding for women. Of the cases that are conciliated, most are "settled," often for token sums, while a large and puzzling number are withdrawn with no settlement.The number of applications, never high, has almost steadily fallen, and from 1977 to 1978 almost one-third of the applicants were men.

Table: 7.1

Industrial Tribunal Statistics, 197681, on Equal Pay Act and Sex Discrimination Act			
Applications to Tribunals Where Action Has Been Completed			
Year	EPA	SDA	Total
1976	1,742	243	1,985
1977	751	229	980
1978	343	171	514
1979	263	178	441
1980	91	180	271
1981	54	256	310
Outcome of Cases Heard			
1981			
Total heard	50.0		34.8
Dismissed	38.9		28.5
Upheld	11.1		6.3
1980			
Total heard	28.6		38.3
Dismissed	24.2		30.6
Upheld	4.4		7.8
Source: Equal Opportunities Commission 1982: Appendix 3, p. 32.			

Amendments to the EPA and SDA might strengthen their significance by clarifying the meaning of "work of equal value," allowing for greater use of "positive action," and permitting the institution of class action suits. Such amendments are supported both by the EOC and the TUC Women's Advisory Committee.Efforts to reformulate the legislation have also been endorsed by the EEC. In 1982, the

European Court of Justice struck down the EPA, saying that Britain has failed to broaden its definition of equal work to conform to the EOC's requirement of equal pay for work of equal value. When the Conservative government declined to comply with the ruling, Jo Richardson in 1983 introduced a private member's Sex Equality Bill, which would extend the definition of equal pay and bring under its aegis the growing number of female part-time workers.The bill was defeated, but it could serve as a model for future legislation if a Labourled government in conjunction with feminist campaigners pressed for its passage at a later time. As noted earlier, in 1984, after nine years, the government finally complied with the 1975 EEC directive that mandated equal pay for equal value. The ensuing amendment to the EPA resulted in several hundred new complaints over the next two years.

By 1980 a new Employment Act had eroded the maternity rights awarded to women in 1975. The act qualifies the right to maternity leave by limiting it to women who work 16 or more hours and have had two years of continuous service with their firm. Part-time workers rights are qualified even more. The size of the firm is now also taken into account in the act; exemptions are given to firms with fewer than six employees. Notification requirements of intent to return to work are made more stringent. Finally, employers are no longer required to provide identical work to returning employees; rather they may offer "suitable alternative work".The act also makes it more difficult for women to claim unfair dismissal.

Under these circumstances, the implementation of equality acts and subsequent legislative process have undoubtedly been a distinct disappointment to women's aspirations. In the absence of a sympathetic judiciary, committed at least in principle to equal rights, and of a government agency with strong powers devoted to antidiscrimination concerns, much of the legislation enacted remains inadequate. Feminist campaigning groups such as the ROW, the NCCL, and the Women's Liberation Campaign for Financial and Legal Independence have pressed for legislative change and the extension of principles of equality in terms of focus and scope.Nonetheless, it is difficult to disagree with the view that "only the organization of women for women" can help reverse existing labor market inequalities.This course would involve the creation of policy networks, at this time lacking in the fragmented feminist political culture of Britain.

What of legislation dealing with social and moral issues? Cases in point are abortion reform and policies toward battered women. Abortion reform was brought before Parliament as a private member's bill, although lobbying by the Abortion Law Reform Association (ALRA) was important in gaining the bill's passage. Pym and others have argued that this is one of the few instances in which a promotional group has successfully "penetrated" the legislative process. Marsh and Chambers also contend that "interest group activity on abortion is unparalleled. There are more interest groups concerned with this topic and they are more politicized than on any other social issue." Randall concludes that, as in the case of sex discrimination legislation, developments within Parliament were crucial in facilitating the measure's passage. Again, the House of Lords played a key role when Lord Silkins' bill provided an important precedent. In the House of Commons, the sympathetic Labour government gave the bill extra time, while the pro-abortion vote on a Third Reading came primarily from a Labour majority that was reform oriented, young, and middle-class (other moral reform issues that gained support during this period were eased divorce and censorship rules, abolition of the death penalty, and legislation decriminalizing homosexuality).

Because the issue was "unwhipped," it reflected something other than a straight "party" vote. At the same time there was a strong relationship between Labour Party membership and a pro-abortion vote. (In the United States, similar trends regarding abortion are evident in the stance of liberals and conservatives and in congressional voting. David Steel, who introduced the bill, proved an able parliamentarian who consulted widely and made concessions to the medical profession to gain support.Opposition forces were not well organized, while the "benevolent neutrality" of the Labour Government supported the reform effort.

The act that was finally passed authorized abortion up to 28 weeks of pregnancy in cases where two registered doctors agreed that the life of the mother or other children would be at risk, or that the baby was likely to be born handicapped. At the time of passage, numerous feminists opposed the act as inadequate because it failed to establish the principle of "abortion on demand," and they decried the definition of abortion as a medical rather than a woman's right. However, since the act's passage, the women's movement has been actively involved in efforts to defend it against restrictive provisions and limitations of its scope.

In the aftermath of the act's passage in 1967, as in the United States after the 1973 Supreme Court decision legalizing abortion, groups formed either to oppose or preserve the legislation. These efforts have been described as "a near classic case of parliamentary lobbyingpossibly unrivalled in the post-war era".By the mid-1970s, ALRA had been more or less eclipsed by the National Abortion Campaign (NAC), the women's liberation group described. NAC was less committed to parliamentary lobbying than to politicizing public opinion on abortion-related issues. Its strategy was largely extraparliamentary, emphasizing proselytizing through demonstrations and picketing.As radical socialist feminists, NAC members also maintained close ties with the Labour Party and trade unions. This relationship produced TUC support for defeat of the anti-abortion Corrie Bill in 1979. In March 1981, NAC and other groups were surprised when, in the absence of parliamentary debates, the DHSS issued new forms concerning abortion that contained no nonmedical grounds for termination of pregnancy.

NAC and other groups have thus far been able to prevent any prosecutions for noncompliance with this administrative edict. In 1981 as well, a bill to make NHS facilities mandatory for abortion was introduced in Parliament, failing by 215 to 139 votes, but nonetheless indicating considerable support for this initiative.An important factor in stopping antichoice restrictions was the Coordinating Committee in Defense of the 1967 Abortion Act, founded in 1976. By 1980, with 50 member organizations, this unique organization had developed a strong defensive posture, unifying such diverse groups as ALRA, medical groups, unions, and the Labour Abortion Rights Campaign (LARC).Labour Party women, including M.P.'s Jo Richardson and Oonagh McDonald as well as Chief Women's Officer Joyce Gould, helped greatly in defending abortion reform in Parliament. Vallance argues that abortion reform produced a rare example of collective action by Labour women in the House. In addition; opposition forces were not well organized. The anti-abortion movement in the United Kingdom has lacked unity and mass support, in contrast to the strong pro-abortion organization in Parliament coordinated with extraparliamentary forces.

As in the United States, the feminist viewpoint has been incorporated in the liberal perspective.Nonetheless, party affiliation is a better predictor of abortion policy-making in Britain, and because of the importance of Parliament in decisionmaking on this issue, and attention has focused on that body. In the United States many more levels of government have been involved in abortion policy-making, including the courts, whose role has been central, as well as state and even urban legislative bodies.

A final case of women-related social legislation to be considered is policy toward battered women and the concept of state-aid and public concern for battered women originated in the United Kingdom in 1972. By 1975, the National Women's Aid Federation (NWAF) had been formed to act as a communications and support network. In 1976, the Domestic Violence and Matrimonial Proceedings Act were passed in Parliament. As in the case of abortion, it was introduced as a private member's bill by Labourite Jo Richardson and enjoyed (some) support from the Labour government.The NWAF and the NCCL aided in building support for the act's passage. The issue was first raised during deliberations by a Select Committee in the House of Commons, at which testimony was presented by women's aid organizers and women victims of domestic violence. The committee found existing criminal and civil laws weak and recommended change. (As in the United States, police had frequently refused to intervene in what the state viewed as "domestic disputes," and appropriate legal remedies were often not available.) The act that was passed in 1976 was a modest effort that sought to strengthen procedures by which a woman could obtain a court injunction to restrain a violent husband or cohabitee.

The 1976 act offers valuable protection in the county courts, permitting exclusion and nonmolestation injunctions without recourse to other judicial proceedings.The 1978 Domestic Proceedings and Magistrates Court Act extended similar protection to that which existed in county courts, but for married women only. The 1977 Housing Act obliged local authorities to provide abused women with alternative accommodations.

However, according to McCann and others, since the enactment of the new laws, the judiciary has favored a limited interpretation of them, largely returning the position of abused wives to their pre-1976 role. The police response has indicated a similar reluctance to utilize the powers inherent in the new legislation. Funding, criminal justice reform, and therapy for victims of violence play a lesser role in the United Kingdom than the United States.

There is absolute discretion with regard to a "power of arrest" attached to injunctions; the Home Office has limited powers of arrest to only three months.No national government funds have been committed thus far to provide financial aid for shelters or victim's related costs; local refuges are funded by local authorities. Although Women's Aid has never seen legislation as particularly important in altering power relations between men and women, the group did campaign not only for the 1976 act but also for the Housing Act of 1977, which gave priority to women and children for access to housing if they left home because of violence.

This brief survey of legislative enactments pertaining to feminist concerns leads to the conclusion that feminists have been able to influence public policy primarily as an auxiliary resource for parliamentary actors who are responsible for initiating and passing the legislation. As our analysis has demonstrated, most legislation in the United Kingdom came about through pressure, not from feminists, but rather from parties and unions, frequently through the vehicle of private members' bills in, Parliament and often with considerable support in the House of Lords.

As we have indicated, legislative support for measures involving women's equality and welfare has left parties and unions free to pursue issues of equality in the workplace and in their own decision-making bodies at their own pace and on their own terms, leaving basic structures of power and male dominance largely untouched.Further, it appears that in Britain implementation of policies enacted regarding equal rights has often been more difficult to secure than the legislation itself. Given the nature of the administrative process outlined earlier, there is virtually no mechanism for interested groups to ensure compliance with enacted policy. This analysis suggests that the impact of policy aimed at women's concerns in Britain has been less than impressive, while at the same time legislation may serve as a convenient symbol muting further demands for political change.

The United States

In the United States an Equal Pay Act was enacted in 1963, with little conflict. As suggested earlier, after the Civil Rights Act of 1964, other women's rights legislation was passed with greater input from feminist groups. In addition, in the implementation process, feminist groups have been vigorous, often acting to strengthen legislation through administrative intervention or judicial proceedings.

Easy passage of legislation on equal rights in regard to education and credit in the 1970s may be attributed to the presence of a policy network in Washington after the ERA. Coalitions of women's groups specialized for specific policy areas lobbied both behind the scenes and overtly to promote legislative efforts and prevent the erosion of legislative gains once secured.The absence of strong party input on equal rights issues and the vulnerability of representatives to pressure from organized constituents created an atmosphere different from that in the United Kingdom. In addition, as we pointed out earlier, the politicization of the bureaucracy led to continued activity by organized feminist groups and their allies at the administrative level to ensure continued commitment to statutory aims.

To a greater degree than in Britain, feminists have continued to present legislative initiatives even during the 1980s, in a less hospitable political atmosphere, achieving some degree of success with portions of the Economic Equity Act. In Britain, efforts to interact with the political process have been more defensive and reactive.

As in Britain, the activity of grass-roots groups engendered a changed public consciousness regarding domestic violence, the result being the creation of over 700 local shelters. But unlike the case in Britain, grass-roots women "forged alliances with Congress, the administration and national women's organizations".Although federal legislation was initially defeated and finally resulted in only modest funding, the effort to pass a federal law generated the coalescence of a new policy network. And although federal legislation fell short of feminist goals, in several important ways the movement to gain public support for the policy area succeeded. First, although it was short-lived, a federal agency, the Office on Domestic Violence (ODV), was created in the Department of Health, Education and Welfare during the Carter administration, and it helped focus attention on wife abuse as a serious political concern. Second, federally based lobbying efforts galvanized the movement against domestic violence. Third, legislation was passed at the state and local levels that provided, as in Britain, for increased responsiveness by the legal process, but, in addition, other policy initiatives were undertaken that increased support for victims of domestic violence.

In 1977, in the wake of the 1975 establishment of NOW, hundreds of interested representatives from all over the country attended a meeting of the Task Force on Domestic Violence in Milwaukee. This gathering led to the creation of a new group, the National Coalition Against Domestic Violence (NCADV), which began to mobilize on a national basis and press for legislation. The issue was further highlighted by the International Women's Year convention in 1977 and by hearings conducted by the U.S. Commission on Civil Rights. In response to pressure from feminist groups, the Carter administration created the ODV, with the mission of disseminating information and funding technical assistance and demonstration projects. Another federal agency, the Law Enforcement Assistance Program (LEAA), had been supporting and funding direct service and mediation programs for domestic violence victims since the mid- 1970s.

In 1977, legislation to combat domestic violence was introduced in Congress. Female members of Congress, as well as such congressmen as Democrat George Miller of California, endorsed federal funding of community-based shelters.The bill failed to pass in 1978 largely because of concern over procedural issues in the legislative process. Further objections were raised, as they would be with increasing frequency, to the concept of federal intervention in domestic life and the creation of yet another federal social program.

The bill was reintroduced the following year, in the 96th Congress, with support from an extremely broad coalition of supporters, including feminist and traditional women's groups, the police, prosecutors, religious groups, the National Football League, and the Junior League.By this time, the NCADV had established headquarters in the capital and comprised some 350 groups and 25 state coalitions. Although the group had developed a national lobbying presence, it continued to support the concept of community control of shelters by affected women in accordance with feminist principles of participatory democracy. Support for the bill was also forthcoming from female members of the congressional staff and feminists in the bureaucracy, particularly from the ODV and a large number of co-sponsors in Congress itself.

The bill passed the House by a vote of 292 to 106, with all congresswomen voting in favor of ita key reason for the victory being "the work both by the sponsors with their colleagues and by shelter providers and other groups in their home districts".As passed, the bill would have provided for $65 million over a three-year period to supply "seed money" for local shelters. A similar bill was approved in the Senate, but by this time it had become the object of a concerted attack by right-wing forces. The bill passed the Senate narrowly, and a House-Senate Conference Committee was convened to resolve the differences in the two bills. The conference report passed the House easily, but a massive lobbying campaign by the "New Right" continued to oppose the bill's passage in the Senate. The Senate did not take up the bill until after the election of 1980, when a major shift in power took place. Under threat of a filibuster, and lacking sufficient votes to invoke cloture, the bill was never brought to the floor again and died. The failure of the legislation to pass meant the death of the ODV as well, although some of its functions were merged into the National Center on Child Abuse and Neglect.

This significant defeat at the national level was accompanied by numerous cutbacks in federal aid to victim-related programs. In 1984, Congress appropriated $6 million for shelter funding, in a more modest version of earlier legislation.In subsequent years such funding has continued, and several additional federal programs now also provide support for victims of wife battering.

Given the nature of the federal system, however, prospects for change at the state level have appeared much brighter. In recent years three-quarters of the states have altered their policies regarding battered women, usually providing some funding for shelters and improved access to a more responsive legal system.By 1981, 49 states and the District of Columbia had passed some form of reform legislation to combat domestic violence.Most states have created new civil and criminal remedies for abused victims. States and numerous cities have specified in detail the duties of police who respond to domestic violence calls mandated better recordkeeping, and often created special training programs for police and judicial personnel and Police departments in more and more cities yearly report an increasing number of arrests for domestic violence.

In addition, and most importantly in the short run, states have provided funds for shelters and other victim-related services, including job training, child care, and legal and psychological counseling for abused women.Some states have raised additional revenue for their programs through surcharges on marriage licenses and divorce filing papers. Significantly, the policies leading to such improvements have been promoted largely under the aegis of state coalitions against domestic violence, which have lobbied for change in conjunction with a wide group of coalition supporters and carefully cultivated legislative support. These groups have continued to monitor the implementation of policies after their passage. It seems accurate to conclude that in the United States the scope and significance of legislation on domestic violence has been greater than in Britain, largely owing to the existence of a feminist lobby and a newly created policy network focusing on wife abuse.

While in both countries the grass-roots orientation of the battered-women issue has been maintained, resources have been more readily available in the United States, thanks to lobbying and legislative pressure. Even grass-roots American activists have moved in the direction of coalitions, greater organizational strength, and more avowed politicization than their British counterparts.

A similar point is made by Jennifer Temkin in her analysis of law reform for rape in Britain and the United States. American women's groups lobbied tirelessly for reform and developed liaisons with media representatives and politicians of all political persuasions. They engendered public interest and support through newsletters and other efforts, creating laws that resulted in a larger number of arrests and convictions in cases of sexual assault and improving the treatment of victims within the legal process. In contrast, similarly radical law reforms in Britain "in the mid-1980's -128;| is as remote a prospect as ever".

In the absence of a cohesive and powerful women's lobby, as well as the general absence of women from corridors of power, recommendations by the House of Lords were modified to permit judges to consider the victim's sexual history and to extend efforts to gain anonymity for the victim and for the defendant as well. A 1984 Criminal Law Revision Committee similarly permitted rape to be viewed within a narrow perspective, providing for little change, particularly in comparison with U.S. legislation.

Political Opposition to Feminism in the United States and Britain

In both the United States and Britain the past decade has seen the ascendancy of conservative political administrations that have sought to reprivatize political issues, particularly those affecting the family and dependent women. There can be little doubt that the policies articulated by both British and American conservatives have a disproportionately negative policy impact, both on public sector employment and on availability of necessary public services especially important for dependent women.To what degree does the emergence of a New Right suggest negative future outcomes for feminist aspirations?

Recent politics in both countries have been marked by attacks on the role of the state in the economy and by the reassertion of traditional values regarding the family and the role of women.In the United States some of the same forces that led to the emergence of feminism as a social movement have led to its antithesis, the New Right and the anti-abortion "pro-family" movement. Galvanized in part by the Supreme Court decision in Roe v. Wade helped create one sector of the feminist movement, antifeminists mobilized to oppose the ruling. They have viewed the expansion of government activism as threatening to traditional values and have organized effectively to combat what they regard as pernicious social tendencies. Aided by reforms in campaign financing and the relative decline in political parties, they have organized effectively to lobby at the congressional and administrative level and to seek to achieve change via the electoral process.

The New Right has been extremely adept at using direct mail to raise large sums of money, at grass-roots lobbying and indirect lobbying, and at influencing politics primarily through efforts to affect the outcomes of elections.In the United States, one arm of the New Right has linked antifeminism to a religious base,which has provided powerful support for religious conservatives. The other arm includes such groups as Phyllis Schlafly's Eagle Forum, dedicated to restoring women to their traditional role in the family and in society, and the anti-abortion "Right to Life" movement. These forces were able to converge effectively with the Reaganite Republican Party in the 1970s and 1980s, gaining a significant role both in the party and in the Reagan administration.

It is probable that one source of the greater opposition to U.S. than to British feminism is the American women's movement's greater visibility and impact. Hence, antifeminism may constitute a larger segment of New Right politics in this country, although at the same time it remains only one interest group within the current Republican orbit. Other groups include some elements of the eastern establishment, cold warriors, and economic conservatives. The somewhat uneasy coalition erected during Reagan's reign may prove to be too fragile to endure. It appears, however, that in the United States both the women's movement and the New Right are strong, and it is by no means clear that feminism has been routed. Support for Reagan's personal leadership has apparently not meant a significant shift to the right among the American public; rather, judgments about Reagan's leadership qualities and personality and about the state of the economy appear to have been most significant in aiding his electoral victories.Nor have candidates backed by the right wing continued to sustain the electoral momentum they seemingly had in the late seventies and early eighties.

There is little evidence that the election of either 1980 or 1984 constituted a conservative mandate or that the two major symbolic issues of the New Rightabortion and the ERAhad any impact on the outcome of the vote.Nor does it appear that the outcomes of most House and Senate races are attributable to New Right efforts. The power of this new coalition in shaping mass attitudes and political behavior does not seem particularly great. Nor has public opinion regarding abortion and the ERA shifted to the right.Single-issue voting by members of the New Right does not seem to have a major impact on outcomes either.

Regarding abortion, for example, an NBC News exit poll in 1984 found that two-thirds of the electorate endorsed the legalization of abortion, with the decision "left to the woman and her physician," while only a quarter did not. Soon after the election, an ABC News poll found the share of Americans supporting the relatively radical position that women should have a right to abortion on demand, "no matter what the reason," actually increased over Reagan's first term, rising from 40 per cent in 1981 to 52 per cent in 1985, while the percentage opposing abortion on demand declined from 59 to 46 per cent. According to a Los Angeles Times poll, only 23 per cent of the electorate supported a constitutional amendment prohibiting abortion, and only 32 per cent of those who voted for Reagan endorsed his policy on abortion. Louis Harris reports that Americans support passage of the ERA by 60 to 34 per cent. And few Americans are enthusiastic about Jerry Falwell, the most prominent leader of the religious right. A 1984 Los Angeles Times exit poll found that only 16 per cent of the voters approved of the minister.

Recent trends in public attitudes toward affirmative action merit special notice because of the Reagan administration's sustained attack on affirmative action and repeated insistence on the public's impatience with such "special interests" as women and minorities. In 1978, Louis Harris reported that only 45 per cent of the public agreed that "if there are no affirmative action programs helping women and minorities in employment and education, then these groups will continue to fail to get their share of jobs and higher education, thereby continuing past discrimination in the future"; 36 percent disagreed. By September of 1985, 71 per cent agreed and 27 per cent disagreed. Those favoring a "federal law requiring affirmative action programs for women and minorities in employment and education, provided there are no rigid quotas," numbered 67 per cent by 1984, and those opposed, 18 per cent; by 1985, support had risen to 75 per cent.Here, too, the trends in public opinion have been directly opposite to the trends in public policy.

Partially as a consequence of Reagan's failure to extend his coattails to other offices, primarily in Congress, his strategy has been to seek only marginal policy changes, regardless of his rhetoric. This approach has tended to moderate the impact of New Right forces on the actual policy process, as compromise and incrementalism dominate the need to operate in the practical world. The prospects for continued Republican ascendancy rely far more on economics than on the conservative social agenda, which lacks broad public support and even endorsement from many coalition members.Although right-wing activisms has had a major impact on administrative appointments and consequently on policymakers as well, the long-term effects on policy remain unclear. What is clear is that while feminists have been forced into a more defensive political role and subject to considerable harassment in the legislative and administrative process, they have not been totally defeated. The fragmentation of American politics, both at the federal level and in state and local initiatives, as well as the degree to which feminism has been institutionalized as a legitimate interest group continuing to intervene effectively in policy-making, would suggest that all is not lost.

Examining the organization and mobilization of the pro-family movement versus the feminist movement, Conover and Gray found that the feminist network is far better organized at the state level, having almost twice as many organized groups as the.right in the 40 states they surveyed. In general, their analysis suggests that the significance of right wing organizational power is far less than the media and New Right itself would lead one to believe, although in terms of financial resources they are formidable adversaries.

In the United Kingdom, while similar shifts in the postwar consensus regarding the scope and direction of the welfare state exist and have been epitomized in the Thatcher government, several differences appear significant. First, given the importance of the party structure in Britain, the Thatcher government may represent a more coherent and tough-minded partisan bloc than Reagan's somewhat uneasy coalition.Some observers perceive in Mrs. Thatcher's approach a significant break with traditional conservatism as well as with social democracyan approach that has transformed the nature of British policies.There is considerable evidence that the British public, particularly the skilled working class, has swung somewhat to the right, but nonetheless what has been called "authoritarian populism" may not reflect a complete or even significant rejection of the welfare state in Britain.Nevertheless, there is support for some privatization and greater individualism as well as resentment of taxation and waste.

In British politics it is clear that support for the Conservative party manifesto means decreased spending, including reductions in funding for housing and education; cuts in some state benefits and abolition of others as well, including supplementary benefits; reduced levels of public service and reduced subsidies to those services; and the privatization of public assets, including council housing and some industry.Most of these policy areas directly affect women as employees and clients of the state. Both the electorate and popular ideology have shifted to the right regarding abortion, women's rights, and welfare.However, results of a recent poll indicate that the overwhelming majority of British women view abortion as legitimate if the woman's health is endangered, if the child is likely to be born deformed, or if the woman is a rape victim. Abortion is opposed if the child is not wanted or if the woman wishes to abort because she is unmarried.

Anti-abortion views, in the absence of a religious base, have never gained the same political resonance in Britain as in the United States. While Prime Minister Thatcher holds views hostile to women's liberation, including her insistence that women with children remain out of the work force and her policy of defunding such areas as child care and state aid to dependent women, her rhetoric is not specifically antifeminist. However, the concern of her government for family policyparticularly via the all-male family policy group that has taken over important cabinet functions, most notably in the absence of consultation with women's groups implies a tacit antagonism to feminist issues.

In contrast to the situation in the United States, and perhaps because of difficulties encountered by all promotional groups in the political arena, neither the Society for the Unborn Child (SPUC) nor LIFE, another anti-abortion group, has ever been able to gain a foothold in the political arena. Pro-choice groups such as NAC have been more effective in establishing relationships with M.P.'s and mounting campaigns for popular support. SPUC lacks a connection comparable to that of anti-abortion groups in the United States with the Catholic Church, which in any event denounced a SPUC effort in 1983, saying that the "ends don't justify the means".The church itself lacks the numbers and fervor of its American counterpart and seems less avowedly political, particularly with regard to the abortion issue. Rogers reports that wide differences exist between the M.P.'s of different parties on social policy, 83 percent of Labour M.P.'s favoring free child care and 86 percent of Conservatives favoring the view that women be obliged to care for their children. The partisan cast of views on feminism is obvious and points up the possibilities inherent in the election of a more sympathetic government.

Only a future general election will reveal whether the vacuum left by the disarray of left-wing politics, created by the internal disorder of the Labour Party, will be filled either by the SDP or by a reconstituted Labour Party, permitting a different political attitude toward women to prevail.

Assessment

We have examined the policy process in the United States and Britain to determine the relative impact of the feminist movement in each nation. In the United States, while administrative agencies such as the EEOC have not always been effective and their enforcement strength has varied with political commitment, they have played a significant role with regard to nondiscrimination policies. The EEOC has benefited from the existence of a feminist policy network that has not only influenced both policy orientation and political appointments, but has also been instrumental in gaining substantial judicial and public endorsement of principles of affirmative action. Such a supportive network has been lacking in the United Kingdom, where the superficially comparable EOC has been isolated politically in the absence of political and material resources.

In Britain, policy has generally been initiated by private members, and, in the case of sex discrimination, prodded by the EEC. Feminists have played the role of secondary activists, given their ambivalence about political participation in national-level politics and their frequent lack of information regarding the policy process. The absence of policy networks, combined with the highly centralized and closed system described earlier, prevents any significant feminist presence in the implementation process. Nonetheless, we have seen that feminists have intervened successfully in collective action on the abortion issue, where they have continued to maintain a political presence and sustained a sometimes uneasy alliance with such groups as labor unions. Abortion-related efforts point the way to coalition building on other issues, although it is not clear whether similar congruence may be achieved on economic policies. American feminists have engaged in extensive lobbying, networking, and coalition building on a variety of policy issues at the state, local, and national levels of politics, even making some policy inroads during the conservative Reagan era.

New Right opposition to the type of social change represented by feminism has developed in both Britain and the United States, necessitating a reactive and defensive role for feminist groups, as well as lessening their ability to set political priorities. However, Mrs. Thatcher's third electoral victory and British public opinion data indicate an even more substantial right-wing shift in the United Kingdom than in the United States. Given the considerable political and ideological obstacles to feminist political mobilization addressed earlier, the persistence and reinforcement of Conservative Party strength do not augur well for feminist influence in British national politics.

8

The Swedish Political Opportunity Structure

Sweden has often been viewed as the nation in which equality has proceeded further than in any other Western country. Ruggie regards Sweden as the society in which the interests of women workers have been most nearly realized, while Adams and Winston (1969) portray the Swedish approach to the integration of working women into the labor force and political system as in many ways superior to the American approach. Baude has suggested that Sweden has witnessed the development of a new role identity for women. The purpose of this chapter, then, is to examine what has been achieved in Sweden, viewed within the context of the propositions outlined at the outset. What light does the Swedish experience shed on issues of autonomy, the sources of social change, and the impact of feminism as a social movement on political systems?

To a far greater degree than is true for either Britain or the United States, Swedish politics has been dominated by the primacy of party government and the continuity of power. In Sweden, "the individual legislator is elected as one among several representatives from multimember constituencies. He or she is nominated by the party and represents the party more than the special interests of the constituency. Cabinet ministries and administrative agencies are formally separated from each other. In reality, though, there is close cooperation on most matters of policy interpretation and implementation guidelines. Special interests in Sweden are thoroughly organized. They are represented not only on the main vehicles for Swedish policy formulation, the Royal Commissions, but also on the boards of administrative agencies".Moreover, the courts have no balancing power *vis-a -vis* the executive or legislative branches of government. Private interest groups thus cannot use the courts as a means for challenging government policy. In short, the center of gravity in the Swedish polity lies in the cabinet.

The bureaucratic structure in Sweden may appear to be more susceptible to party and other political intervention and possibilities for recruitment to a more open political system seem greater than is the case in Britain. Nonetheless, the political impact of corporatism,or representation of the economic groups,again moderates the extent to which promotional groups may gain representation.

Swedish political parties dominate interest group mobilization and aggregation as well as policy-making to a significant degree. In the highly organized Swedish state, the public sector makes up almost two-thirds of the Gross National Product, and public sector employment involves about 40 percent of the working population.

The Swedish system is recognized as a consensual democracy, or a liberal democratic state characterized by a low level of opposition to the framework of rules and regulations for the resolution of conflict.In such a system, groups tend to be absorbed by the corporatist state; alienated subgroups that resort to violence, protest, or even dissent are rare, as evidenced by the relatively low incidence of strikes and the tradition of voluntary collective agreements between business and labor. The system's apparent openness to popular views is exemplified by the commissions of inquiry that circulate proposals for reform projects for comment from agencies and interest groups.The Riksdag is generally reactive in nature, with most of its business structured by the administration of the government. The effort to resolve conflict with a minimum of controversy is perhaps best typified by the office of the ombudsman to oversee the legality of state administrationan office that dates back to early eighteenth century!

In Swedish politics a distinction is made between policy formulation and day-to-day administration. Ministers establish directives and policies to be executed by agencies. Heads of ministries are politically appointed, and the small ministries function as their staffs. The over 100 agencies are responsible to the government, not to the ministries.A strong tradition of local government gives extensive powers of initiative and action to the municipal councils and to executive committees that govern at the community level.

Swedish politics is characterized by a high degree of continuity. The Social Democratic Party (SDP) has dominated politics for 40 years, relinquishing its hold only in 1976 -128; -147; 82, when a nonsocialist coalition ruled. However, because the five parties that in the main compose the Swedish political system represent only a relatively modest transition from left to right, political compromise is usually possible regardless of electoral outcomes. Swedish politics is also distinguished by a high degree of organizational participation. Nonetheless, most such participation tends to be economically oriented.

There is a relatively low level of political activism other than voting; day-to-day participation and communal activity are limited in a society that relies heavily on state intervention. Women are less participatory than men, although the 1970s saw increased activism in parties, unions, and the like among young women. Whether this trend has survived women's domestic responsibilities and continued into the 1980s is open to question. The society is highly institutionalized, providing limited space for different or extraparliamentary views. To the degree that woman's group exist in Sweden, they tend to be traditional rather than "liberationist" in their orientation.In this political context, promotional groups play only a minor role, and feminism, or women's liberation, is viewed with suspicion by many political actors.The society emphasizes consensus and the absence of conflict; extra-political activity beyond the parliamentary system and public sector is rarely mobilized effectively.As most observers agree that in Sweden everything is "already so established" that new and small groups may have difficulty gaining a hearing and access,it is not surprising that no significant feminist movement has developed.

The search for consensus emphasizes participatory values, but in fact opponents are encouraged to compromise and accept government ideas and limited participation in policy formulation.Public debate is far more limited than that in the United States; the circle of participating groups is determined by the government. Policy formulation is conducted primarily via state commissions that include all parties and "relevant" interest groups; these commissions are the key to power and influence as the Riksdag has increasingly become relatively powerless.Only a small proportion 16 percent of the commission members responsible for policy formation are women.

Because of the emphasis on consensus, there is little room for alternative recommendations.The Riksdag acts on legislation whose passage is already assured. Perhaps even more than in Britain, the parliament's primary legislative function appears to be debate, not decision-making. Informal contacts between governmental leaders and organizations are a vital part of the system; personal contacts between such leaders, who constitute relatively small elite, dominate policy-making.

With regard to values and social change, however, Sweden is among the most "advanced" nations in the world. In 1976, one of every two marriages ended in divorce,and oneparent families were two of every nine, or 18 percent, double the figure in the United Kingdom.Out-of-wedlock births are common and relatively unstigmatized because children of nonmarried parents have rights equal to those of all others. One-third of households involve a single person only,and the percentage of nonmarried cohabitees is the highest in the world21 percent in 1983,whereas it was only 2.5 percent in Britain.

The percentage of women in higher education is almost equal to that of men, in contrast to Britain, although at the postgraduate level their numbers drop significantly.Swedish women tend to refrain from long-term education choices, diminishing their career alternatives.

Work-related norms appear strong for women and men: a survey conducted at the end of the 1970s revealed that only 10 per cent of Swedish women preferred domesticity to a life combining work and home.Labor force participation by women is extremely highin 1980 it was about 80 per cent.Most Swedish women work part-time; only 23 per cent of women worked continuously at full-time jobs from 1978 to 1980. In addition, occupational sex segregation in Sweden is among the highest in the industrialized world. Sweden and Britain demonstrate the highest proportion of sex segregation in OECD countries 82 per cent and 76 per cent, respectively, of women are found in sex-segregated occupations as employees of the welfare state.

The Swedish unemployment rate is comparatively low, for women as well as men. More than half of women are employed by the public sector, primarily in local communities, where they are concentrated in the health and social services.Since 90 per cent of blue-collar workers and 75 per cent of white-collar workers belong to labor unions, women have joined them as well.

Female membership in the Landsorganisationen (LO), Sweden's dominant trade union, increased from 7 per cent in 1945 to 40 percent in the 1980s, but, as in Britain and the United States, the growth in female labor union membership has come primarily in the white-collar sector. Hence, other unions, such as the Central Organization of Salaried Employees (TCO), which represents most salaried workers, and the Swedish Confederation of Professional Organizations, which represents professional groups, have the largest female presence. Women currently comprise over half the membership of the TCO and 35 per cent of the SACO/SR.

Data on full-time, year-round employees in Sweden demonstrate a higher ration of women's pay as a proportion of men's than in either Britain or the United States. Although

Sylvia Hewlett has argued that Sweden is the country with the smallest male/female wage gap, the assertion is true only if the large number of part-time female workers in Sweden is ignored. The percentage of women employed part-time has increased steadily since 1968 from 42 to 52 per cent of employed women. Because so many Swedish women work part-time, the high male/ female wage ratio conveys less than meets the eye. While Swedish men receive 63 percent of the wages, women receive only 37 per cent.Pay differentials are not so great between the sexes at ages 20 to 24, but become accentuated thereafter, especially during the childbearing years for women. In 1980, the average income for men was almost twice that for women.Among women with young children, especially two or more, the proportion of women who work part-time is 60 per cent. Similarly, among women 45 to 64 with no children under 17, the part-time rate is 58 per cent. Only among women who are childless and under 44 does the part-time employment rate drop. As in the United States and Britain, part-time work results not only in male/female wage discrepancies, but also in marginalized relations with trade unions, as well as lack of mobility and of access to bonuses, overtime pay, and other rewards.

Swedish women hold relatively few high positions, especially in the private sector, where in 1978 they held only 0.2 percent of top positions in management,3 per cent of senior executive positions and less than 1 percent of the jobs in public authorities and companies. They held 4 per cent of senior government posts.Both the United States and Britain have a higher percentage of women in top executive positions than does Sweden.

As is the case of Britain and the United States, the effects of recession in recent years have often fallen disproportionately on female workers, who are often public-sector employees with marginal jobs.

The Structure of Politics and Women

The history of early policy regarding women in Sweden demonstrated tendencies still present today is true for other nations. In the 1800s, women in Sweden gained the right to attend school, equal inheritance rights, and the right to conduct business in their own names all in the absence of an organized movement. Similarly, the struggle for women's suffrage was tied to universal suffrage. A National Association for Women's Suffrage, comprised largely of Social Democratic women, existed but pursued its course with a minimum of protest. Subsequently, suffrage came to be included on the agenda of the major political parties, and the struggle was conducted primarily in them. In the main, feminism was incorporated into the structure of political parties, creating a relationship that still persists.

As in Britain, women's unions were established in the late 1800s and early 1900s. In the 1930s and 1940s the female trade unions merged with newly created white-collar federations to form the TCO and the Swedish Confederation of Professional Organizations.

Unlike the case in Britain or the United States, a women's liberation movement has existed in only a minimal way in Sweden. Although a relatively militant Group 8 was created in the 1960s, it has never developed into a strong and coherent feminist movement with major influence in Swedish politics. Most feminists were more concerned with class than with gender, and the struggle for women's liberation was conducted primarily within parties and other political institutions. Militant feminism was unacceptable in a consensus-oriented society. In Sweden, neither alternative political structures nor consciousness-raising for individualsboth so important in the development of the British and American movementswere ever viewed as significant except among a few activists.

However, the women's liberation movement in Sweden ought not to be entirely discounted. Founded in 1968, Group 8 had about 1,000 members. It was responsible for creating a sense of political activism, especially during the 1970s. Although feminism is generally viewed as "un-Swedish," the activists did influence people's attitudes through media coverage and the subsequent hiring of feminist columnists and writers by the two major newspapers, Dagens Nyheter and Svenska Dagbladet.The movement sponsored women's houses in several Swedish cities and operated on the basis of small decentralized groupsnever more than ten members.Although the Group 8 barely exists today, a magazine, Kvinnobull-etinen,is published monthly, with a circulation of 3,000 to 4,000.

In comparison with the situation in Britain and the United States, cultural and theoretical feminism have never become a strong force in Sweden, nor have new approaches to service delivery for women, such as rape crisis centers, ever gained adherents. Nonetheless, as we shall see, there has been political activity regarding rape and a movement to create shelters for female victims of domestic violence.

Consider this interesting commentary on the current status of the women's liberation movement: When this interviewer asked her numerous interviewees about the existence of a women's center in the Stockholm area, she was repeatedly told, "I think there is one but I don't know where." In fact, a women's center and bookstore/informational center, Kvinnocentrum, has existed in the center of Stockholm, operated by two women, since 1975. Several other "women's houses" in the Stockholm area combine shelters with other feminist-oriented activities.

But the most successful tend to be the least overtly "women's liberationist" and are funded by the local municipality and dominant party organizations. Nonetheless, annually, on March 8, numerous women's groups come together to celebrate International Women's Day. A study in Orebro found that the ideas of the women's liberation movement have had an impact on local legislators by increasing the number of women politicians, making them aware of the importance of gender-based concerns, and helping them structure the content of political debateif not the political agendain a more feminist way.

Another approach to feminism is demonstrated by the Fredrika Bremer League, a women's rights organization created in 1884. In 1985 it claimed a membership of 6,000 in local chapters seeking to increase the representation of women in party leadership and public life as well as engaging in networking.The league played a particularly vigorous role during 1976 -128; -147;82 when Birgitta Wistrand, a forceful and dynamic leader, was its president.

Despite the relatively limited influence of the league, it has apparently seemed threatening to many Swedes, including ministers of government and LO leaders who accused Birgitta Wistrand of being too aggressive and working for the "wrong" type of woman. Other Swedes portray the league as "bourgeois" and "bluestocking," in an effort to pejoratively place it beyond the acceptable political pale. In Swedish, unlike American society and politics, individual change is viewed as less important than structural and societal change.

Although traditional women's organizations "have demonstrated a higher level of activity vis-Ã -vis the authorities than the new women's movement," the 1981 disbanding of the Swedish National council of Women's Organizations suggests a relatively limited base of activities for such groups in Sweden. The council had only ten member groups during its existence, a smaller number than in any other Nordic country.

Parties and Unions

In examining the role of Swedish women in political parties and unions, it seems inescapable that they have been more effective working via the parties than working in the unions. Although the structure of women's activities within the parties differs and women's issues are undoubtedly not in the forefront of party leaders' concerns, both in the Social Democratic Party and in the more centrist parties since then, women have achieved a degree of influence. As in Britain, women's sections in the parties have usually played a secondary role. However, in Sweden the entire major parties support increased women's representation.

Table 8.1 shows that representation of women at various levels of party organization has grown dramatically. Nonetheless, virtually all the women party leaders interviewed felt that the concerns of women are often ignored and viewed as secondary by male party leaders. Women leaders of the SDP perceived the Liberal and Center parties as more interested in women than their own, dominant party.The LO, linked historically to the Social Democrats, was seen as having a far more important role in the party than the women's organization. The members of the VPK, though lacking a women's section, often express views most sympathetic to a feminist perspective, particularly as reflected in 1985 data.

Table: 8.1

Representation of Women in Swedish Political Parties, 1982

	Members			Congress		
Party	Total	Women	%	Total	Women	%
Center	140,941	10,993	8	285	91	32
Liberal	47,556	21,535	45	220	95	43
Conservative	155,550	63,000	41	200	70	35*
Social Democratic	1,205,064	363,706	30	350	119	34*
Communist	17,793	6.714	38	313	112	36

Representative Assembly			Executive Board			Working Committee		
Total	Women	%	Total	Women	%	Total	Women	%
90	26	29	17	4	24	7	2	29
			27	12	44	19	7	38
96	22	23	30	9	30	8	2	25
			27	8	30	10	3	30
			35	2	34		2	29

Source: Haavio-Mannila et al. 1985

Dahlerup's objectives for women's party organizations include cooperation with corresponding parties abroad. Although that may be an important goal, we will expand this idea to include collaboration among domestic political parties. Greater cooperation among the women in the five major Swedish parties in national politics has been evident. In an innovative effort in 1979, women from these parties joined together to demand increased representation. Other efforts followed in the 1980s and discussions across party lines have continued.Such efforts at cross-party discussions have no parallel in the more divisive and ideological politics of Britain.

Meetings have been held in the Riksdag, occasionally resulting in joint policy on issues relatively insignificant to the respective parties.Joint demonstrations have also been directed toward reforms related to women, sometimes generated via women's leagues within the parties themselves.

In the SDP the National Federation of Social Democratic women (SSKF) founded in the 1880s, played a crucial role in bringing the issue of sex equality to the fore in the 1960s. A study group formed in 1960 produced a set of policy proposals regarding day care and sex role equality that was later incorporated into the 1969 party programs. More recently, the SSKF has generated internal debate and formulated programs related to women's concerns. Particularly in the 1970s, Social Democratic women were prominent in raising issues concerning the future of nuclear power in Sweden. But, partly as a result of dissension among younger feminists, the membership of the SSKF fell from 68,000 in the 1960s to 45,000 in 1974.The federation is affiliated to the party, giving it only consultative status.In the SDP, sexual equality is subordinated to class equality.Although the SDP has called for increased representation for women at all levels, neither abortion nor affirmative action has ever become an important policy issue.The SDP has demonstrated an ability to suck up all new movements of opinion and incorporate them into the party apparatus, and feminism has been no exception.

All parliamentary parties adhere to the 60/40 principle: neither sex is to have more than 60 per cent nor less than 40 per cent of representation within party ranks. Nonetheless, some parties have been especially active in recruiting and nominating women; since the 1970s the Center Party has consistently returned the most women to the Riksdag.

The Center Party has the largest women's organization in Sweden, with a membership of almost 75,000. When the former foreign minister, Karin Soder, was elected head of the party in 1986, she became the first woman president of a Swedish political party. Members of the women's organization have seats on the Center board. Most recently, the group has advocated a policy requiring every nominating list to contain the names of women. In the last election, at least one-third of the districts complied.

In 1972, the Liberal Party translated its concern for women's equality into a demand for greater female representation, requiring that a minimum of 40 percent women be on all district boards and in all party bodies. The Federation of Liberal Women, founded in 1936, has a membership of over 20,000 and has been most successful in gaining representation of women by setting a goal of at least 40 percent representation at all levels of the party.As of 1986, this goal had all but been achieved, with 39 percent female representation in the Riksdag, 33 percent on the Stockholm City Council, and 38 percent at the county level.The Left Party Communists (VPK) do not have a women's section but rather a women's committee, which issued a women's program in 1979 and whose members are sympathetic to women's liberation.

The Moderate Party women's association, established in 1920, has its own membership and its members are also members of the party. With a membership of 67,000, it has moved away from a previous policy in which all women party members were automatically members of the women's section.According to party leaders, the new policy has led to an increase in membership.The representation of women within the party at all levels has reached about 30 percent, except at the top level of the working committee, where their numbers are few. Most of the women's sections of parties stress the training and recruitment of women as candidates, as well as the significance of women's issues, such as day care and family and labor market policy.

It appears that at least several of Dahlerup's five objectives of separate women's organizations in parties have been achieved in Swedish parties. Among these are activation of women, recruitment for top posts, and pursuance of women's policies within the party. Swedish parties, particularly in contrast to the British ones have reacted relatively rapidly to women's demands for increased representation and can therefore, be described as fairly democratic. Kerstin Peanberg of the Social Democratic Women's Federation, for example, feels strongly that in the absence of the federation, there would be no national day-care policy in Sweden. While some women's sections have few powers, several derive their own support from dues as well as relying on party support, thus providing a degree of autonomy. Women politicians have often, though not always, emerged from the women's sections. One study found, for example, that 40 percent of Swedish M.P.'s used the organizational channel provided by women's organizations to advance politically.Women say that issues they first brought up in the women's organization of a party are subsequently raised at meetings of the party itself. More than half the women who have become active party members have been drawn from women's party groupings. Particularly in Stockholm, women's party organizations have mobilized to fight prostitution and pornography.

Throughout the 1960s and 1970s, the Center Party was the most active recruiter of women councilors, but in the 1980s local representation has been similar for all parties. Because the Conservative and Liberal parties had higher female membership than the dominant SDP in 1985, although they are smaller parties, doubt is cast on the conventional wisdom that leftist parties are necessarily more sympathetic to feminist concerns. As in the United Kingdom, women still tend to be nominated for marginal seats. However, the party list system gives women a greater opportunity to gain representation than the single-member district system, especially if women are placed high on the list.

Women in Sweden have gained an unusually high degree of representation in the political system. A tremendous increase in electoral representation occurred in the 1970s, and by 1985 women constituted 31 percent of the Riksdag.At the county and municipal levels women's representation has also surged since 1970; they now make up over 33 percent of county councils and 30 percent of municipal councils. Women's representation in high governmental positions has climbed, too;

since 1982 five women have served in the 21-member cabinet.

Nonetheless, women still remain relatively isolated from leadership positions in the Riksdag and, even more importantly, in the crucial administrative sector.Moreover, they tend to be concentrated in areas associated with women's traditional societal role. Women's participation in administrative policy-making echelons is low on public commissions, which prepare policies to present to the Riksdag and play a key decision-making role. In 1983 -128; -147; 84 there were only 16.8 percent women on such commissions, although this represents a 10 percent increase from the early 1970s. At the policy-making administrative level, 10 percent of the high-level appointees were women.

Women appear to be absent from most leadership roles and their public visibility is often limited as well.While 28 percent of standing committee memberships in the Riksdag, where the most important work tends to be done, are held by women, they are best represented in committees dealing with social welfare, insurance, and cultural affairs. Women are allotted fewer influential appointments and are particularly weak in nonelected bureaucratic roles. A recent report found that the higher up in the administrative hierarchy, the fewer women present. Even when women tend to be given responsibility in areas of traditional concerns such as education and social welfare policy, they tend to have peripheral rather than central decision-making positions.And, once in office, women in government have tended to support party loyalties rather than gender concerns, in keeping with the structure we have outlined. Female party leaders' attitudes resemble party dictates more than feminist views, diverging as much as or more than men's attitudes on women-related issues.

In local-level politics, which are particularly important in determining the scope and direction of funding priorities such as day care, city councilors who have nominal authority are less significant than the heads of administrative committees. The local policy-making structure is a four-fold one, ranging from municipal council members to members of municipal executives, to members of local administrative committees, to heads of administrative committees. Women's representation on committees rose from 1 percent in 1971 to 5 percent in 1977, although the increase was largely in committees dealing with "reproductive" rather than "productive" sectors. Thus, the pattern of isolation from power in all but limited areas is reflected in local, as well as national, politics.

Unions

Given the corporatist approach that characterizes Swedish policy-making, unions occupy a particularly significant political role. As is true for parties, unions have put their support behind equality-oriented goals, although, as is the Swedish norm, such support is forthcoming in the absence of feminist demands or a special role for women's groups.The Swedish "sex equality" ideology that came to dominate political debate in the 1960s was bent on removing barriers that prevented women from becoming full-fledged members of the labor force.Unions viewed women as an alternative preferable to continued use of immigrant labor.Women's policy has usually been subsumed under family and labor market concerns; in the 1960s the LO transformed its women's council into a Council for Family Affairs composed of six women and five men.The TCO in 1970 also adopted a family policy program to facilitate work force participation by both parents, through day care, parental leagues, and nontraditional training and education for women. The LO's policy of "wage solidarity",aimed at closing the gap between higher- and lower-paid categories of workers, benefited women, most of whom were in lower-paid jobs, although women were not singled out as a special group for treatment.

Yet, despite union support for women's equality in the labor force and although Swedish women constitute about 40 percent of LO membership, they are under-represented in leadership roles.There are only a handful of women on the National Executive Committee of the LO and few on legislative bodies and collective bargaining units of the national unions, including those with a majority of women members, although some efforts at improved representation have occurred in the last decade.Like its American and British counterparts, the white-collar TCO seems to have a greater sensitivity to women's concerns than do blue-collar unions. In 1980, women made up 57 percent of the membership and 23 percent of the Executive Board, while at the district level; their executive representation was about 20 percent. As in England, women's committees have been formed, training courses established, and equality officers appointed, but these have been created from the top down and do not represent an independent feminist force.Although Cook and Till Ritz (1981) suggest that there have been outspoken efforts in white-collar unions to set up women's committees, study and consciousness-raising groups, and even local-level women's caucuses, this researcher found little evidence of such activism. Equality officers lack support and resources; most do not even devote full time to their "equality" role. Among the labor unions making up the LO in 1986, only the metal workers had a full-time equality officer.Gender-based activism seems rare in Swedish trade unions.

As a consequence and as an example of the failure to articulate a feminist perspective, there has been virtually no effort to use the Co-determination Act passed in 1977, which gives employees greater influence over the organization and content of their jobs, at the local level on behalf of women's concerns. Local unions have continued to discourage active participation by women and failed to advance women's issues through the negotiating system.The framing of discussion about women in the guise of "equality" and "family policy" often results in failure to discuss women's issues in sexual power terms.There are in unions no autonomous women's groups that might negotiate or monitor collective agreements, nor does the union leadership seem receptive to fostering such groups.

This situation has led Hernes and other observers to the view that the organizations most crucial in decision-making and strategic influencethat is, those that are economically basedare even less responsive to women's power and access than electorally based ones. In such contexts, women are often powerless "policy-takers" instead of policymakers. Unlike Swedish men, Swedish women have no basis for political organization in the labor sector.The corporate channel is thus the least participative, and the most hierarchical, oligarchical, and elitist.

Table: 8.2

Percentage of Women in Swedish Blue-Collar Trade Unions (LO) and Trade Union Offices, 1983

Union	Women Members	Congressional Delegates	National Executive	Central Negotiating Board	Regional Executives
Garment workers	68.9	52.4	28.6	23.3	49.1
Sheet metal workers	None	None	None	None	None
Building workers	1.6	0.4	None	None	0.2
Electricians		0.4	None	None	None
Factory workers	30.5	13.8	13.8	7.3	12.0
Maintenance workers	54.5	21.7	9.5	27.3	28.4
Hairdressers	93.9	87.8	94.7	71.4	83.3
Social insurance and insurance agents	71.6	37.9	30.8	20.0	39.2
Graphic industry employees	29.5	9.3	11.1	3.3	18.9
Miners	10.5	5.0	None	None	6.0
Retail and commercial employees	76.5	58.4	50.0	49.7	55.5
Hotel and restaurant workers	78.6	74.0	52.0	56.0	67.1
Municipal workers	79.2	46.2	53.8	32.3	40.8
Agricultural workers	27.7	15.0	15.8	8.7	NA*
Food employees	39.6	20.3	4.5	11.7	17.3
Metal workers	17.4	3.3	2.2	1.8	NA
Musicians	25.0	9.2	10.5	6.7	18.0
Painters	1.1	None	None	None	None
Pulp and paper workers	17.8	6.0	3.2	11.1	10.3
Seamen	12.7	9.8	30.8	7.1	NA
Forest workers	8.5	7.4	NA	4.2	1.2
State employees	27.0	10.7	12.0	9.4	15.5
Transport workers	13.1	10.2	6.2	NA	7.6
Wood industry workers	15.7	7.2	2.9	2.4	5.3
Total	41.7	21.3	18.5	20.2	20.2

Source: Based on data in Landsorganisationen 1984.
*Not available.

Given the resistance to change in the still male-dominated union structures, unions are not likely to be the major route for access to power for Swedish women.While unions support equality in the labor market, they tend to view "class differences as greater than the differences between the sexes".Under these circumstances, it is not difficult to see that recognition of women's interests in party structures may have only a limited parallel in unions.Although women have gradually been increasing their role in union offices over the past two decades, in the powerful LO with strong links to the dominant Social Democratic Party, there has been little evidence of changed attitudes toward power and policy.

Table: 8.3

Women as Percentage of Members and Elected Officials in Swedish Trade Union Confederations, 1977, 1980, and 1986

	LO			TCO			SACO/SR		
	1977	1980	1986	1977	1980	1986	1977	1980	1986
Members	36	40	43	46	57	57	31	35	39
Convention delegates	18	25 (1981)	NA*	20	32	NA	24	NA	NA
General council	9	NA	14	16	NA	33	15	NA	29
Executive board	0	0	7	20	23	18	30	NA	20
National union presidents	0	0	NA	8	NA	15	8	NA	28

Source: JA SAF/PTK. Siffror om MÃ¤n och Kvinnor,Stockholm: 1987, p. 267; Qvist, Acker, and Lorwin 1984:277; and Central Statistics, Kvinno-och Mansvarlden, Stockholm: 1986, p. 177.

Not available.

Policies

Equal Opportunity

From the 1960s on, prompted by Eva Moberg's pamphlet "The Conditional Emancipation of Women," a sex-role debate was engendered and all political parties came to support equality-related policies in Sweden. As already noted, Swedish policy regarding women has been viewed as aimed at alleviating labor shortages by bringing women into the work force, with welfare and other policies directed toward this end rather than toward women's needs and concerns per se.

Eduards and her colleagues have suggested that the equality focus had a second source: economic issues so long at the core of party activity were now removed from the hands of the parties and elected representatives and placed in the administrative sector. This shift resulted in a changed relationship to societal groups and a diffusion of party divisions, giving the parties more opportunity to create a new ideological profile. Women were correctly perceived as a new source of members and voters, and the thrust toward equality policy followed accordingly. As in Britain and the United States, changing patterns of electoral politics sometimes resulted in partisan efforts to mobilize a new coalition that included women's groups.

The Swedish need for an increase in labor force participation led to a recognition of women as a large, virtually untapped labor source.The 1960s saw the beginning of special courses and other measures designed to induce and facilitate increased labor force participation by women as well as a debate on sex roles. First to be introduced were income tax reforms that lowered the burden on married working women by providing for separate taxation of spouses and reducing the marginal tax rate. In 1972 an Advisory Council to the Prime Minister on Equality Between Men and Women was appointed to enhance "free personal development" and alter sex roles and responsibilities.According to Kelman, the unusual placement of this agency in the office of the prime minister meant enhanced possibilities for close political control. In general, the council provided for experimental efforts to place women in nontraditional jobs, to shorten the workday to six hours and allow two shifts, and to provide "equality grants" for companies that train women for jobs traditionally occupied by men.A Parliamentary Committee on Equality, appointed in 1976, continued to work on integrative policies. Thus, by the 1970s, the public discussion had turned from "sex roles" to "equality" policy.

The LO had supported efforts to reform income tax laws, day care, and parental leave.But, as in Britain, on issues of wages, hiring, and promotion the unions were reluctant to abandon their collective bargaining efforts in the interest of legislative rule-making. Strong opposition from labor and employers was overcome only when a nonsocialist government gained power. In 1976 the government enacted the first antisex discrimination act, creating an equality ombudsman and calling for affirmative action, increased representation by women on public bodies, and efforts to increase recruitment of women in male-dominated positions.The 1976 Equality Ordinance provided for the appointment of an Equal Opportunities Commission and a full-time equality ombudsman who has the right to resolve complaints.

A 1979 Act on Equality Between Men and Women prohibited sex discrimination and required employees to work actively for equality. The act's coverage is confined to groups not covered by collective agreements, which take precedence.The concept of affirmative action does not really exist operationally in Sweden because there is no timetable set for compliance with the act and because the equality ombudsman cannot override collective agreements and enforce compliance.There are no statutory sanctions if employers do not comply with the legislative enactments (of the three countries examined, only in the United States have financial sanctions been employed successfully to enforce equality laws).Since 1983 a national Equality Council, comprised of party representatives, women's organizations, unions, and employers, has superseded the earlier Advisory Council.

In 1977, the LO and the TCO signed equality agreements with the Swedish Employers Confederation (SAF) covering all workers in the private work force. The agreement banned all discrimination and called for equality-related measures. Cases to be settled were to go to the tripartite Labour Court. In the three years between the signing of equality agreements and 1980 when an amended version went into effect, no cases went to the Labour Court under the LO-SAF agreement. It is doubtful that the absence of complaints signifies the absence of problems; rather, the concern about producing conflict, the lack of a feminist presence, and the unfamiliarity of this approach may limit its effectiveness.

In a society where a tradition of special women's groups has not existed since 1900, unions appear to be reluctant to act once a complaint has been made. They are especially remiss in taking action on job recruitment, let alone wages and salaries. Originally opposed to the idea of legislation to deal with sex equality, they have never been very enthusiastic about aiding the process of compliance.

The "equality grants" have not proven successful. Since 1980, only 693 trainees have been placed in jobs, just 1.5 percent of all trainees.Given the small incentive, or subsidy, of 20 SEK for each trainee and the narrow range of possible occupations covered, the lack of compliance is not surprising. Another measure, part of Sweden's regional policy, which mandated gender-based quotas in new firms or industries in Sweden's outlying areas, met with mixed results during 1974 -128; -147;79.

Numerous unions have set up equality committees, special training forces, and other groups directed particularly at women. Nonetheless, the results of private-sector efforts seem disappointing: in four years of subsidies to firms to hire women for male-dominated occupations, only about 1,000, or one-tenth of 1 percent, of the female labor force were hired.Under the Social Democratic government that returned to power in 1982, a Ministry for Equality and Immigration was established in the Department of Labour. Among the directives given to this new agency: change the conditions for women, change the roles of men, influence policy, and aid immigrant women.The ministry has thus far sought to spend its rather substantial budget to promote courses for young girls to broaden their choices in order to break the pronounced pattern of occupational segregation in all areas of life. There has been little evaluation research done to assess "success," because "they are not sure how to go about it".As for the mandate to change men's attitudes, thus far no conclusions have been reached on how to implement it.

The equality ombudsman, Inga Britt Tornell, has received enthusiastic support from many Swedish women for her forthright activism. However, with a staff of only seven, the tasks for the ombudsman appear formidable. The tasks are 1) taking complaints to the Labour Court, 2) supervising employers, and 3) molding public opinion.The ombudsman's office has been particularly effective with regard to the last task: four times a year it issues a report, Jamsides, and it has released over 20,000 copies of an excellent statistical and factual compendium on women in Sweden entitled Side by Side.The ombudsman has even tackled the issue of women priests in the' Swedish Church, albeit unsuccessfully. The ombudsman may issue injunctions only on employment discrimination initiated by individuals, employee organizations, or by the ombudsman office itself. The office responds to about 150 complaints per year. Numerous observers, including the deputy ombudsman, point to the difficulty of getting women to make complaints in a culture that does not value aggressive individualists. Issues of equal pay for work of equal value have thus far not moved beyond the discussion stage. The commission's work is somewhat constrained by the fact that it does not have the right to request documentation in discrimination cases in the private sector.

Only several hundred cases have come before the ombudsman, and just nine cases were taken by her to the Labour Court through 1984. The four settled at that time resulted in financial compensation, but no requirement was made for remedial action by the employer with regard to either the individual involved or the discriminatory practice.Several observers have concluded that the law establishing the ombudsman's office has few teeth and is not very effective. As Karin Andersson, the former chair of the Swedish Equality Committee, commented, "It is difficult to struggle for something on which, formally, everyone agrees".In this context, Swedish equality agencies may be seen more as channeling pressure regarding discrimination than responding to it.

Social Policies

No account of public policy regarding women in Sweden would be complete without a discussion of related social policies. In 1976 an abortion act was passed that gives women the right to abortion on request up to the eighteenth week of pregnancy, largely a ratification of practices already common. (After the twelfth week a special investigation is held to judge the risks; after the eighteenth week the abortion may be granted only by the Board of Health.) This policy was not widely perceived as a women's issue; rather, debate centered on the social and economic costs of unwanted children.

As early as 1945, Swedish women were entitled to six months' maternity leavewithout pay. In 1974 the well-known parental insurance law was passed that gave fathers as well as mothers the right to paid leave of absence following birth of a child. The benefit was roughly equivalent to 90 percent of lost income for seven months. In 1978, the period for parental leave was extended to nine months. In practice, women still use the parental leave provisions most frequently. In 1976 the number of fathers exercising their right to stay home was 10 percent; the number has never been higher than 12 percent. Men may also take 15 days of leave at the time of a child's birth. Either parent may also take paid sick leave of up to 60 days a year to care for a sick child. Men who take such leave do so only for a few days, whereas women are more likely to extend their periods of absence.

Day care, long a concern of the LO in the interest of increasing female labor force participation, was endorsed by the Riksdag in the 1970s. Efforts to increase, by 1980, the number of places available for children during and after school care were intended to further the goal of providing publicly supported day care for the children of all parents who work through a system of state subsidies.The actual increase fell short of the goal. A new goal of 100 percent of day-care places has been set for 1991.

No plan for implementing this new stage of expansion to meet demand has yet been presented. At the time of this writing, the number of day-care places still lags far behind the necessary numbers, especially considering the high number of women in the labor force; about 60 percent of the children from one to five are housed in community-supported family day-care homes or public day-care centers.Nonetheless, available day-care places have risen rapidly since 1966, when the policy was initiated, and programs are well staffed and regulated, in contrast to their British and American counterparts.

The Swedish tradition of public education is unlike that of most of Western Europe and of the United States in that children do not begin school until the age of seven, and even at that time school hours are limited. This situation exacerbates the problem of finding day-care places for a larger population. Children from ages seven to 12 who require after-school care are usually unable to obtain it.Because the extent of day care in a given community depends largely on local initiatives, the variance between rural and urban availability may be great.

Since 1979, parents of children under eight may work a six-hour day, at a reduced salary; they may remain at home full-time with a child up to one and a half years old. Child minders are available for sick children (although they may exist more in principle than in reality, as one professional woman remarked that they are often available only after the children are well) and even on weekends, a particularly thoughtful aspect of the Swedish social policy for single parents. Single-parent families are given higher maintenance subsidies than two parent families; unlike the situation in the United States, there are few social or economic stigmas attached to divorce or out-of-wedlock births.

The state makes direct payments to all families with children in the form of generous child allowances, housing subsidies, and advance payments on maintenance allowances.This last form of aid means that in effect the state has taken over the burden of child support from absent fathers and shores up single-parent families.

Other Women-related Policies

Rape has not been publicly perceived as a major problem in Sweden, a nation in which crimes of violence seem rare. This attitude has been one explanation for the absence of a rape crisis movement in Sweden. Nonetheless, the incidence of rape annually is about 10,000 reported cases, the number having risen steeply with a greater willingness to file charges.In 1976 the women's organizations of all the major parties as well as numerous other women's groups protested a proposed change in the rape law that would have permitted the courts to take into account the previous sexual behavior of the victim. The outcry and pressure of this all-party women's effort were sufficiently strong to lead to the creation of a new commission to rewrite the law. As of 1984, a new law was passed entitling women suffering assault to have someone with them during legal proceedings. The prior sexual behavior of the victim is not to be taken into account, nor is the victim's relationship to the offender. Legal aid for victims is now possible in some cases and is likely to be expanded in the future.

The issue of domestic violence attracted belated but intense interest in Sweden primarily in the 1980s. In 1978, the first Woman's House under the auspices of a feminist group in Gateborg, combining a shelter with other activities, was opened. Elsewhere, as in Orebro, the community was responsible for funding a crisis center. It appears that more avowedly feminist groups have sometimes had difficulty obtaining funding from their local councils; nonetheless, about a hundred shelters exist today in Sweden.Because Sweden lacks both a philanthropic and a voluntary action tradition and citizens expect the state to assume responsibility for all social services and needs, the likelihood of an independent shelter movement enduring is limited. Funding is sometimes forthcoming at the municipal level, and the National Organization for Women's Shelters (RUKS) has been established. This new organization is entitled to special funding of about 100,000 SEK annually from a special government fund created for women's groups.Wife beating has been open to public prosecution only since 1982. At that time the law was amended so that the victimized woman herself did not have to prefer charges against the man or plead in court. Domestic assault had formerly been indictable only by information, meaning that no charges could be filed unless the woman herself reported them. The change means that a neighbor or police officer can prefer charges, the upshot being an increase in the number of complaints filed. Although the shelter movement initially was feminist in impetus, and marks a rare case of public acceptance, as in the United States today its influences are mixed.Shelter employees are paid and view their work as a job just like any other. National action on battered women has been followed by a report undertaken by the Social Services Department of the government. However, statistics on the actual incidence of domestic violence are exceedingly difficult to obtain. The treatment of offending males seems to have taken a somewhat different turn in Sweden than in the United Kingdom and, especially, the United States. In the main, punishment, other than short jail sentences, is often eschewed in favor of providing therapeutic treatment for men. A men's shelter has even been formed in Gateborg to provide support for troubled men. Hence, the Swedish approach stresses rehabilitation rather than punitive treatment, with offenders also seen as "victims".As of March 1985, the Swedish government decided to award grants to encourage shelters to develop their activities further.

Assessment

In Sweden, women's organizations have little impact either on public authorities or on public policy per se. Gender is not seen as an explicitly deliberate or legitimate dimension of politics in Scandinavia despite the presence of a large number of women in legislative politics.

Swedish women appear to have many of the demands of their feminist sisters elsewhere taken care of by the state and political system, yet their concerns seem to be almost obscured by the efforts to reach equality that are, in the main, not the result of their own efforts. In 1973, Rita Liljjestrom wrote that if women are to achieve collective liberation, they "need to rally around a community of values, around a program which roots them in shared experiences, and which gives them political identity for 'sisterhood' and an alternative value system to keep them from being devoured by equality under the terms set by the male value system." This course has not been followed in Sweden, nor has there been a public dialogue on women's issues conducted by women on their terms. As Baude (1979), among others, points out, women's liberation and feminism have been viewed as confrontational and "anti-Swedish."

There is limited room for experimentation and grass-roots efforts in a society in which all is encompassed by the state. Hence, issues like rape, wife battering, and other aspects of male power, violence, and domination have only begun to be raised in this society so devoted to the establishment of equality in a sex-neutral fashion. Nonetheless, even when grass-roots level efforts are made for examples, to develop female-operated refuges for battered womenthey are soon incorporated by the state. As Cheri Register puts it:

> When conflicts have arisen in Sweden and demands are put forth by different groups, they must be swallowed quickly by the all-encompassing Social Democracy. Social Democracy must show without delay that it is also capable of coping with the new demands emanating from women. In other words, the special interests of women have been subordinated to the general good, the definition of which still lies in the hands of men -128;¦. Reforms can also be considered as a preventive measureone which is necessary to divert more radical demands and conflicts which could lead to a more serious split.

In this type of system, significant issues regarding male-female relations and power are rarely seriously discussed as topics of public debate. Autonomous women's organizations are viewed as suspect, and women are deterred from shaping policy on their own terms. While today some activity around single-issue feminist concerns exists, there is little evidence of the past dynamic efforts made by women, especially in political parties in the 1960s and 1970s.

There can be no doubt that Sweden's social support system, especially for single-female heads of families and for all women in the labor force, is superior and perhaps without equal in the Western world. (The one exception is day care, which is still inadequate and lags far behind the near-universal Ã©coles maternelles system provided by the French government, which seeks to respond to the educational and personal needs of each child.) Nevertheless, it should be recalled that welfare, however progressive, is not synonymous with power and the ability to shape one's own status." Qualitative" gender issues, unrelated to economic concerns, have been neglected in a system that defines equality almost exclusively in economic terms.

Because the rhetoric of equality has been widely accepted in Sweden, it is difficult to move beyond it to new approaches. Women are objects of state welfare policies that they have had only a limited role in shaping. There is need for greater scope for the articulation of women's interests, which may result in a more truly egalitarian society. However, it is especially difficult to organize effectively in a society in which everything has been organized and in which the expectation that society will care for all needs animates most social endeavor.Against this backdrop, efforts by women at the grass roots to stress some feminist concerns have been noteworthy, though often short-lived. The emphasis on the need for organization is, of course, particularly incongruent with feminist notions of participation and structure, making the route of radical feminism especially problematic in Sweden.

Sweden's most unique contribution is the effort to change women's status by addressing inequality for men and women alike. An equal-opportunities mentality pervades society and policy-making; the emphasis on sex neutrality coupled with cooperation has produced a system in which women's issues are no longer perceived as a problem and are almost wholly integrated into family and social policy.Nonetheless, thus far equality has been defined exclusively in male terms. As most Swedish women interviewed for this study agreed, gender-neutral policies in a society still highly stratified by gender end up by benefiting the already powerfulthat is, males. That Swedish women have far outnumbered men in the degree to which they wish to use ad hoc political activity suggests how poorly they feel themselves to be integrated into the political structure. This is one area of Swedish politics in which women constitute a plurality! We are left with the view that "society does not change just because laws do", that rule-making may be insufficient in the absence of grass-roots organizations to aid in carrying out the rules. Even policy on sex neutrality has been framed in the guise of recommendation, not dictates, making compliance exceedingly difficult.

Although Swedish policies are held up as models for women in other nations, they have also demonstrated the intransigence of problems of sexual inequality and the possible limits of a system structured so totally around consensus. The labor market remains highly segregated, with women concentrated in low-paying, low-status jobs to an ever greater degree than in other nations.Income differentials, though narrowed, remain significant, and close to 50 percent of Swedish women are primarily part-time workers in the labor force. The acceptance of part-time work by most women locks them into traditional family roles and creates few opportunities for pursuit of serious careers, especially in terms of training and promotion.

The problem appears to lie in the failure to address the sexual division of labor in the home and in the workplace, partially because women's issues have rarely been raised as a concern apart from economic and labor market considerations. The division of labor reflected in the home, in a society still wed to many traditional values regarding sexual roles, is reflected in the larger political and economic society as well, as the marginal position of women in these sectors suggests. Sex segregation continues to exist not only in the labor force but also in the political roles to which women are limited, thus preventing them from advancing into meaningful careers. The anti-individualist rhetoric of Swedish socialism has in this instance kept women in their place.

The Swedish experience suggests that even benevolent state efforts to integrate women into existing political and economic structures may be insufficient in the attainment of role transformation if they are not accompanied by other changes as well. It has been the contention of this chapter that, coupled with the widespread acceptance of the ideology of gender equality, if not its practice, the absence of independent women's organizations that generate debate regarding sex roles and power in society may be crucial. Despite the real success of many of the highly institutionalized Swedish efforts to eradicate gender inequality, the system appears to have reached an impasse.

9

Conclusion

This study has examined the different directions taken by feminism in three nations, emphasizing the importance of external factors, including political institutions, cultural traits, and values on the resulting movement structures and goals.

Swedish politics, we have found, presents a model of consensus and corporatism, as well as an all-encompassing state that directs most citizen-related activity and tends to incorporate those activities existing outside the boundaries of state policy. The British system is distinguished by a centralized bureaucratic state and a "dichotomous" ideological context in which conflictual politics tend to predominate. In the United States a less organized, somewhat adversarial pluralism reigns in a system distrustful of centralized power and welfare policies. In turn, the character of feminism has been shaped by the character of the state as well as economic factors and the strength of traditional values and attitudes. Thus, we have argued that in Sweden a form of state equality concerning women exists in the absence of an organized movement.In Britain, ideological/left-wing feminism is in part a product of the closed and conflictual political system. In the United States, a less ideological and more pragmatic political setting has led to mass-based liberal/equal rights feminism. The prevalent mode of activism has been interest group lobbying for power rather than integration in parties and unions in the manner of the European movements.

Definitions of what constitutes social movement "success" may vary. Success may refer to legitimization of a group's goals, change in individual or group consciousness, and/or change in public policy outcomes involving redistribution of social goals and changes in power relations.For some, political access for hitherto excluded groups constitutes success. Success may also refer to the mere fact of survival, and/or the creation of alternative sources of power through the development of new organizational forms.It is evident that the movement in each nation has succeeded in different terms, partially because of different goals and the systemic factors that constrain political activism.

We have shown that the most active part of the British feminist movement emphasizes expressiveness, personal transformation, consciousness, and changed belief systems. It eschews formal structure and hierarchy and is centered in small groups that stress life experience and self-help politics. In Gerlach and Hine's terms, it is segmentedlocalized, autonomous, and ever changingand decentralized. Nonetheless, it lacks the reticulate or networking structure that they see as inherent to movement groupings. Largely as a result of ideological conflicts and the consequent failure to coordinate action and permit the sharing of resources, networking efforts, particularly important at the national level, are absent. Social movement organizations in the United States have been far more likely to form coalitions in order to realize their goals.

As several researchers point out, movements adopt different forms depending on their goals, with personal change movements adapting decentralized structures and exclusive membership, while institutional change movements are typically centralized and inclusive. Although the goals of grass-roots participation, service, and transformation of aims are more likely to be realized in decentralized structures, the costs may lie in the failure to influence the larger political system, as in the British case. Bureaucratic structures provide skill and coordination but may sacrifice participatory goals, as is sometimes true of the American movement.One trend in the United Kingdom that may effectively interact with the structure and values that predominate among women's groups is the growing interest of local council governments in aiding feminist efforts.

Clearly, the British movement has succeeded in creating local activities emphasizing consciousness and life-style transformation in numerous centers throughout the country. British feminism has also defied traditional sociological rules regarding the origins and maintenance of social movements. Rather than becoming bureaucratized and less radical, the British movement has retained its ideological fervor and commitment and has continued to seek new alternative structures.The degree of activism and commitment is impressive, even to the casual observer. Movement groupings and activist outposts created in the 1970s survive. These include Women in the Media, NAC, the NWAF, Rights of Women, and the Women's Rights unit of the NCCL, as well as Women Against Violence Against Women (WAVAW).As Jenson has observed, the movement's main contribution may be simply its survival, in contrast to the largely esoteric state of the formerly active French and Italian movements. The British movement remains the most vital and important one in Europe, although the numbers involved in some grass-roots groups may have declined since the 1970s.

Although the British movement's origins were in many ways similar to those in the United States, the movement was never characterized by either mass demonstrations or a strong national presence. Its internecine struggles, largely between sectors of radical and socialist feminism, remain unresolved. One effort in conjunction with the TUCthe march to fight restrictions in the abortion act, demonstrated both the mass potential of the movement and its internal conflicts. This march was probably the largest demonstration over a social issue that Britain had ever seen. Nonetheless; it revealed the chasm between women and the trade union movement and between socialist and radical feminists. The radical feminists resented what they perceived as male usurpation of the movement and ran to the front with their banners. Three women were arrested in a later scuffle with police for hoisting the women's liberation banner; a feeling of hostility was thus one result of the day's effort, though not the only one. The effort at the Greenham Common missile installation three years later resolved some of these conflicts through a separatist, women-only protest. Thirty thousand strong, it helped to bring women from all groups together and to generate widespread awareness of the dangers of nuclear proliferation. A major question for British feminism remains the centrality of "cultural" versus "political" feminism, a question we will return to because of its significance in the movement's failure to create a meaningful national presence.

In the United Kingdom, parties and unions occupy a majorif decliningpolitical role, and a tradition of left/socialist thought has been strong. Although activity in party and trade union politics may be viewed as equivalent to the American liberal/equal rights movement, little evidence for this perspective exists. This analysis is thus in considerable disagreement with the view expressed by Hewlett,who argues that in both England and Sweden the most effective women's groups have been embedded in parties and unions, not in separate feminist organizations.

Rather, it appears that women's participation in established British institutions has been marked by marginalization, with women organized into separate advisory groups and limited to a handful of mandated seats on executive committees. The major union force, the TUC, has endorsed, lobbied for, and even demonstrated for numerous progressive policies on behalf of women.Nonetheless, where issues of economic and political power are involved, there is greater hesitancy.

In addition, tensions exist between socialism and feminism and between the hierarchical unions/parties and feminist ideology, as the march against the Corrie Bill demonstrated. However, at their most effective, women's groups within parties may serve as forums through which women's demands and concerns can be highlighted.

Nonetheless, Jenson's contention that British feminism has emerged from a decade of political isolation and an exclusive grass-roots focus to help unite the Left and the Labour Party seems premature based on the analysis presented here. The energetic activity of women within Labour and the organized Left notwithstanding, thus far their policy- and decision-making impact has been limited.

Despite the existence of numerous progressive policies pertaining to women in the United Kingdom, the absence of a feminist movement that can set a policy agenda, speak for itself, and engage in dialogue regarding specific policy initiatives has resulted in serious gaps between policy and implementation. The upshot: a strangely limited vision of feminist goals and ideals, which has, in fact, led to less societal change than might be expected.

In the United States a tradition of reform, the absence of a strong socialist Left, and the impact of interest groups in decision-making have combined to produce a different type of movement. In part reflecting the increased weakness of parties and unions politically, feminists have organized as separatist or gender-based groups outside established structures.This approach has given them significant autonomy in strategy, as a recent trend in the direction of electoral efforts demonstrates. American feminism is characterized by far greater inclusivity of different views than its British counterpart; coalition building and networking are movement watchwords. The American movement has also forged an accommodation between the more "radical" women's liberation movement and the middle-class reformist one.

The most visible manifestation of American feminism is the traditional interest group, organized as a hierarchical structure with staff dominance. Groups such as NOW have moved in the direction of mass membership, while such feminist groups as WEAL, the Center for Women Policy Studies, and the NWPC fit the McCarthy/Zald model of funded social movement organizations relying on "conscience constituencies" or contributors for resources and staff for day-to-day decision-making and long-term strategizing.As the history of the movement against domestic violence demonstrates, even nontraditional groups with grass-roots origins are pulled toward political engagement and greater professionalization. American feminists have been eclectic and pragmatic in their use of strategiesfrom protest to litigation and campaigning. Nonetheless, although American feminist groups have moved much further than British ones in the direction of traditional organizational structure, they have not abandoned feminist policy goals in the interests of organizational maintenance. Thus, although different from their British counterparts in structure and ideology, the movements have each remained firmly committed to their own feminist vision of the "good society."

In Sweden, feminist movement politics per se has played a minor role, although "equality" and "family" issues have been given primacy by the SDP and other parties. Women's federations in four of Sweden's five parties have provided a context for some policies pertaining to women and for recruitment of women to party and political office. Although various data in this chapter suggest that women are dissatisfied with Swedish efforts to achieve "equality," at present apparently no mechanism exists to capitalize on this discontent and move beyond the egalitarian rhetoric to a new stage of political endeavor on behalf of women.

So far in this chapter, we have examined the role of women's politics in changing individual consciousness, creating alternative political structures, and simply surviving as organizational structures. Hence, we have been concerned with movements primarily at the individual and structural/organizational level. Now, recalling our initial definitions of movement success, we will examine other facets of the success, or impact, of women's politics: 1) the impact on changed policy outcomes and 2) the impact on group and societal consciousness as well as the legitimization of group goals.To assess the latter, in particular, we rely on attitudinal and economic data on the three nations under consideration. We will try to distinguish between those gains that have been made in the welfare state and those that have involved a changed role for women in society because of increased economic opportunities. We will divide our discussion into 1) attitudes that demonstrate consciousness of the women's movement and support for feminist issues, 2) attitudes toward child care and domestic workor the persistence of traditional attitudes toward sex roles, and 3) evidence of changed economic roles for women as a result of more employment opportunities.

Table: 9.1

Impact of Changes in Individual and Group Consciousness			
	Sweden	U.K.	U.S.
Legitimation of group goals	-	-	+
Access to power structure	+	-	+
Changes in power relations	+	-	+
Public policy outcomes	++	+	++
Group survival	-	+	++
Creation of alternative sources of power	-	+	++
NOTE: - = little or none; + = somewhat; ++ = significant.			

Extent of Support for Feminist Movements

We have already noted that the British movement has succeeded in changing the consciousness of its individual members and in creating new, localized alternative power and service structures. With regard to other measures of successfor instance, those involving the larger society and policy outcomesthe movement's achievements have been less impressive. Efforts to increase collective awareness of movement goals and to gain broadened support within the political system may involve potential members, allies, and the general public. Measured by this standard, the total membership of British feminist activists has been estimated as one-tenth of 1 percent of the female population, indicating a huge distance to go to reach even a fraction of the women in the United Kingdom.In contrast, membership in traditional British women's groups is close to a million.Only a small segment of British women have been reached by the women's liberation movement in its various manifestations, and the movement remains isolated, both by deliberate design and because of the obstacles created by British economic and political institutions. Despite the mobilization potential evident in the case of abortion rights and Greenham Common, the movement remains on the fringes of British life, its marginal position reinforced by media emphasis on the movement's domination by antimale radical feminists. The failure to reach more traditional women may be seen in a 1981 Spare Rib poll that compared the responses of Spare Rib readers with women in the more traditional Townswomen's Guilds.

Similarly, despite the media attention given the women's protest at Greenham Common in December 1982, there is little evidence that most women have changed their opinion about the cruise missile as a result of that effort. The balance of women had the same opinion after the demonstrations as they had had three years earlier.A Guardian poll in January 1983 showed about 23 percent of women to be in favor of the Greenham Common activists' goalthat Britain abandon nuclear weaponswhich was actually 10 percent fewer than four months earlier. Spare Rib rightfully concludes that Greenham has not especially raised women's awareness of the nuclear threat, at least as measured by national polls. In conducting their own, more limited poll, most women interviewed by Spare Rib objected to the all-female nature of the protest, and the magazine's survey found that working-class women were less supportive of the Greenham Common protest and of feminism than their middle-class sisters.

The American movement has grown in size and heterogeneity, particularly in the Reagan era, where apparent disaster has been turned to advantage in terms of group mobilization. NOW, for example, grew from 125,000 to 250,000 in several years. This number has fluctuated considerably as the attention of the public has wandered from one issue to another. As of 1985, the dues-paying membership of the feminist movement numbered about 300,000.Despite the relatively small membership,support for feminists among the American populace appears to be far broader and more significant than is the case in Britain.

American women's support for feminism also appears to be substantial: 56 percent of them said in 1986 they considered themselves feminist, 28 percent said they were not, and a mere 4 percent indicated they were antifeminists.A majority of women also indicated that the women's movement had affected their lives positively.A 1981 poll indicated that 4 percent of women and 2 percent of men contributed to the women's rights movement,and that one of every 300 women is active in some type of feminist activity.A survey by Janet Boles as far back as 1974 found that the total membership of women's rights groups (including the NWPC, NOW, the League of Women Voters, and the National Federation of Business and Professional Women's Clubs) was 56.77 per 10,000, indicating a fairly significant pattern of participation, which is likely to be much higher a decade later, given the trends we have outlined.

As Ruth Mandel has noted, "The women's rights movement is in a process of diffusion. It is spread, assimilated and incorporated throughout society at various levels and [has] become part of the social fabric." Underscoring acceptance of many feminist views were the results of a recent New York Times poll. Twenty-eight percent of those surveyed indicated that the women's movement had made their lives better, and these respondents were most likely to be young and educated. Among those who responded favorably, improved job opportunities were cited most often as being a result of the women's movement.Similarly, while strong differences separate college-educated women from their more traditional sisters, over the past decade the more egalitarian views of the former have begun to make inroads among the latter, and we contend that American sex role attitudes have become increasingly egalitarian. Growing numbers of less-educated women were found in a recent study to be more receptive to egalitarian views, although not necessarily to what is perceived as the more "radical" women's liberation movement.

In the United States a 1980 survey found that, on a five-point scale, attitudes changed from 3.2 to 2.9 toward liberation, while in Britain rightward shifts on women's rights, abortion, and welfare were more evident. In Sweden, as we noted earlier, women's liberation is viewed as anathema by many men, hostility to the movement apparently existing out of all proportion to the limited strength of feminist organizations and views, at least among elite males. In any event, Swedish surveys do not reveal women's attitudes regarding feminism, because the movement in Sweden has been oriented differently. In the United Kingdom there appears to be considerable ambivalence regarding the movement, its accomplishments, and the potential role of women,although British women are only a bit less opposed to traditional role constraints than are their American counterparts.While four-fifths of Americans say they would vote for a qualified woman for president,in Britain, after Thatcher's election as prime minister, 64 percent agreed that it made no difference whether a woman held the office, while 25 percent said a woman was "not as good." Support for the notion of "greater confidence" in a woman as a Member of Parliament has dropped, perhaps reflecting some defection of women from Thatcher's social policies.

Table: 9.2

Favorable Feeling Toward Women's Liberation Movement		
Country	Parents	Offspring
United Kingdom	43%	38.1%
United States	45.7%	51.8%
Source: Allerbuck, Jennings, and Rosenmayr 1979:497.		

Studies comparing attitudes toward feminism and women's social role in the United States and Britain also offer some striking differences. One study found British youth much less supportive of women's liberation than their European or American counterparts, suggesting that generational change has been far more limited in the United Kingdom (Table 9.2).

Of particular note is the limited nature of value change that has taken place in the United Kingdom. Inglehart found that Britain exhibited the smallest amount of generational change of any nation in his cross-country survey. Another report of intra-European opinion on feminism reveals British women to hold a higher proportion of negative views than citizens of any other European nation except Italy. The degree of polarization cutting male/female lines is notable.Although strictly comparable data are difficult to obtain, a 1979 poll showed 63 per cent of Americans and only 40 per cent of the British agreeing that the part played by women in their nation had changed a lot.Britons are reported to have the poorest opinion of women's liberation of any Europeans.

Attitudes toward Sex Roles

A 1983 survey found more Britons "disagreeing with women who claim there should be fewer differences between men's and women's role in society" than in any other European nation surveyed, as well as profounder disagreements regarding female family roles than elsewhere in Europe.More British men preferred that their wives not be in paid employment.These findings are confirmed by a recent survey that found that British husbands were not supportive of working wives: only 41 per cent of women said their husbands were enthusiastic about their working. While in many instances working wives were tolerated by their husbands, this was true only if their employment did not interfere with their domestic life or the husband's work.

Female attitudes toward work have undergone considerable transformation, with only 25 per cent of women indicating that women's place should remain in the home; a majority believe that work is beneficial for women.Among younger women; a vast majority say they wish to return to work after having children. However, 53 per cent of British women say that women should quit their jobs when they have children and return to work only after their children are grown up.At the same time, British women accept the view that work is beneficial, but only if it can balance with and accommodate their primary domestic role.Opposition to feminism may combine with the poor economic conditions in

Britain to reinforce the concept of the "family wage" discussed earlier and keep women in a secondary role in the labor force.

British women consider their career less important than their home. Eighty-nine percent of surveyed women of working age felt that a woman's first duty was to home responsibilities, 61 per cent said that a woman's first duty was to her marriage, and only 31 per cent thought they could be loyal both to marriage and to a job. For 69 per cent, their husband's career had priorityand 55 percent of the respondents were under 25! While a poll of Townswomen's Guild respondents did reveal that a majority supported the view that it was good for women to work, 75 per cent indicated that such work was "bad for children" and 71 per cent thought that it was undermining the family.Forty-eight per cent of men and 38 percent of women interviewed in 1979 agreed that women should remain at home with children under 10.

In contrast, in the United States, 63 per cent of women interviewed in one poll indicated that they would want to work outside the home in the future, even if they had enough money to live comfortably without working. Another poll found a majority of American women indicating they wished to combine home and career, while slightly under half of men and women interviewed said they favored a new concept of marriage in which husband and wife share work and domestic responsibilities.

By 1982, 75 per cent of Americans said they approved of women working outside the home, and over 80 per cent favored joint responsibility for raising children.In 1985, only 22 per cent of American college freshmen interviewed said they believe the activities of married women are best confined to the home.Even women's Political Action Committees are increasingly approved by the American publicwith favorable responses rising from 11 percent in November 1982 to 64 percent in May 1984.

In Britain, compulsory military service for women is favored by 35 per cent of the public; in the United States, by 53 percent.In all three of the societies under study, women continue to perform more household tasks than men, but in the United States, particularly; there is some evidence of more equal sharing of tasks, especially child care and economic roles.

Table: 9.3

Attitudes Toward Sex Roles		
	U.S.	Sweden
Traditional roles benefit family	66%	41%
Housework should be shared equally	95%	97%
Not enough women are employed in business	77%	85%

Data collected by the University of Wisconsin's Comparative Project on Class Structure and Class Consciousness indicate similar attitudes by U.S. and Swedish respondents toward sex roles, with one exception. The exception is that whereas 66 per cent of American women believe that traditional learned sex roles benefit the family, almost 60% of Swedish women disagree. Egalitarian attitudes toward housework are similar in both countries. Perhaps reflecting the economic stratification in Sweden that we will discuss later, even more Swedish than American women would like to see a larger role for their sex in business.

Other Swedish data reveal some division between parties on ideological linesand, increasingly, divisions between men and womenon women's issues. The data over time suggest a trend toward conservatism regarding some issues, a trend that may affect women adversely in the welfare state. Growing imbalances in the economy appear to make cuts in public expenditures inevitable.Conflicts in discussions of distributive policy have become sharper as well, so that the very real gains women have enjoyed as beneficiaries of the policies of the progressive Swedish welfare state may be in question. The absence of an organized feminist movement to press for continued commitment of social policies may be critical, although the trend toward advocacy by joint groupings of women's organizations from the different parties may lead to collective action on this front. To date, collective action has been limited to "sexual" or "woman-specific" matters,which do not directly affect the parties' socioeconomic policy commitments.

Since 1976, of the two leftist parties, the VPK has been especially supportive of such issues as day care and the six-hour work day. In 1985 over 80 percent of the VPK and about 70 percent of the SDP favored the building of more day-care centers and the six-hour workday.

Swedish surveys reveal that the concept of equal representation in Parliament for men and women has received little backing from any quarter. Principles loosely related to "affirmative action" are viewed with considerable apprehension by the Swedish public. Interestingly, given the state commitment to economic equality and independence for women, 46 percent of men and 48 percent of women in 1979 indicated that men should get jobs first. Another response that may signal difficulty ahead for the welfare state was the considerable support for reducing the public sector and social welfare commitment in 1982 and 1985. Prohibition of pornography, an issue initially supported by the more conservative parties, has come to reflect a dichotomy between male and female views. From 1979 to 1985 women consistently supported a ban in far greater numbers than men.There appears to be a growing awareness of this issue, which was highlighted by an all-women party demonstration in Stockholm. Eduards has noted that a majority of women also favor the use of quotas to gain election to the Riksdag for women and oppose jobs for men first. Whether these trends augur a new feminist consciousness that may be translated into group activism is questionable, given the continued prevalence of norms related to Swedish political consensus within the corporate state. What is worth noting, however, is the apparent emergence of a separate female consciousness about some key women's concerns.

Opinion polls in the early 1980s found some contradictory responses to survey questions among the three nations.Whereas 63 percent of Swedish respondents and 59 percent of American ones felt that men and women were treated equally, only 47 percent of British respondents thought so.Nonetheless, it is difficult to measure whether these data reflect a more truly egalitarian role for women in Swedish society or simply acceptance of the well-known institutio-nalized rhetoric. Table

9.4 presents a comparison of responses regarding 1) sexual equality in politics and 2) general customs and practices.

The data in the table indicate, perhaps somewhat surprisingly, that a far higher proportion of Swedish than American women perceive that equality has not been attained in politics or social life.

Table: 9.4

Attitudes Toward: General Customs and Practices				
Country	Men Treated More Favorably		Both Sexes Treated Equaly	
United States	(1) 58%	(2) 20%	(1) 38%	(2) 70%
Sweden	(1) 78%	(2) 60%	(1) 15%	(2) 28%
United Kingdom	(1) 94%	(2) 71%	(1) 5%	(2) 22%
Source: Adapted from Hastings and Hastings 1985:707 -128; -147;17.				

Table: 9.5

Distribution of Household Responsiblities		
	U.K.	U.S.
Household repairs:		
Done by men	76	39
Shared partially or equally	11	47
Cleaning house:		
Done by wife	66	46
Shared partially or equally	31	45
Cooking:		
Done by wife	73	55
Shared partially or equally	22	35
Sources: Hastings and Hastings 1982:239; 1983:285.		

A crucial measure of egalitarian views is the distribution of household responsibilities (Table 9.5).

In Sweden, despite the legal encouragement given to sexual equality, few husbands participate in child care, and other traditional sex roles appear to have remained entrenched. Thus, it appears that labor force participation per se has little impact on sharing of customary sex roles, particularly given the high incidence of part-time work among women, which is likely to reinforce existing patterns of domestic responsibility.

According to a 1976 study on Swedes at work by the Swedish Central Bureau of Statistics, in families where husband and wife were both employed full time:

67 Percent of women did all or practically all the cooking:

50 Percent did all or practically all the washing up;

80 Percent did all the laundry;

53 Percent did all or practically all the shopping; and

55Percent did all the cleaning.

As for the time spent by Swedish men who did "some" of the cleaning, shopping, cooking, and so on, a sample survey of 7,000 women made by the Committee on Equality in 1978 revealed that, overall,men spent less than half as much time as women in daily routine household tasks. Sex segregation and "ubiquitous part-time work" have reinforced women's almost full responsibility for the household.

Although the role of women in the domestic sphere still completely overshadows that of men, recent data demonstrate some movement toward leveling. From 1974 to 1981, men doubled their share of the family domestic responsibilities from a minute 7 percent to 14 percent. Differences between age groups are remarkably small and gender roles still very strong, although a larger percentage of men share household tasks with fulltime working wives.Recent Swedish survey data demonstrate that sex role differentiation in the home remains marked. Women are almost exclusively responsible for care of clothing.They are disproportionately involved in cooking, cleaning, and washing up and in child care as well,while men engage in repair work, gardening, and car and boat maintenance.

Nonetheless, the distribution of household responsibilities reveals a more egalitarian division of labor between husbands and wives in Sweden and in the United

States than in Britain, where, for instance, a larger majority of wives clean house. Similar patterns appear with regard to washing dishes, although in the United States, children are the most likely to help out.American women are also the most likely to undertake such male-oriented tasks as gardening and lawn owing. (Nonetheless, in a recent survey of women only a fraction of U.S. respondents thought that real householding decision-making power was shared equally by both partners; and the Swedes were the fewest of all respondents to agree that males should be the major breadwinners and women should stay at home, which at least demonstrates the prevalence of the full-employment philosophy in Swedish culture)

The data suggest that strong patterns of gender polarization and traditional sex role socialization persist even among the sons and daughters of the welfare state. Earlier we noted similar patterns discernible with regard to the taking of parental and sick leave. Data on political participation by women also demonstrate a continued separation between the public and private spheres among all socioeconomic classes in Sweden, although the differences have narrowed somewhat in the last decade.

However, union-meeting activity among women in Class I and the proportion of women holding office in the LO declined from 1974 to 1981perhaps a reflection of the increased growth of the part-time sector and lessened attachments to the workplace. Women's participation in corporate channels lagged behind men's by at least 10 percent. But data from the 1970s reveal decreasing gender differences in union and party activity and other efforts to influence the political process, especially in the 16 -128; -147;24 age group. Whether these patterns may continue to survive the demands of domestic responsibilities and counter prevalent trends in which males "out-participate" women is open to speculation. Clearly, support for some of feminism's basic goals, including sex role modification, has met with great resistance not only in the more traditional United Kingdom but even in the "egalitarian" society that Sweden has forged. In turn, as we have seen, the persistence of traditional values has constrained political opportunities for feminists and, together with the rigid nature of the political system, has limited their options. The British movement in particular has a long way to go in gaining support of women who do not enter into competition with men, and therefore do not feel unequal, and in convincing the vast majority, who are married, have been married, or expect to be married that the feminist movement they perceive as antimale is relevant to their lives.

Impact on Public Policy

Public policy reflecting feminist concerns has resulted in Sweden, the United States, and Britain; in each of the three nations, legislation on equal pay, sex discrimination, abortion, and domestic violence is in effect. However, the policy process both leading to and involving implementation of legislation has been significantly different in each nation, thus influencing policy impact. In the United States, policy has largely been the result of lobbying by gender-based groups. As noted earlier, gender-based policy networks are made possible by the emphasis on coalition formation and the relative openness of the political system to group participation.

Even though public policy in the United Kingdom on such movement goals as equal pay, sex discrimination, abortion, and domestic violence has reflected feminist concerns via trade union and Labour Party politics, the impact of policy change has been minimal. Some of the efforts made toward these goals were prompted at least in part by EEC directives requiring equal pay and job equality. A major exception is in the area of abortion policy, where a coalition of trade unionists, feminists, and Labour Party activists has effectively intervened to prevent weakening of the existing law. (In addition to demonstrating against the Corrie Bill in 1979, mobilized after 1981 to lessen the impact of a restrictive interpretation of the Abortion Act by the DHSS, that would limit circumstances in which doctors could perform abortions.)

The EOC, TUC, and women's groups have also succeeded

in expanding public consciousness about such issues as positive action and "equal value". In Britain the continued efforts by such activists as the women's rights officer of the NCCL,increased strength in white-collar unions like the NUPE (where training courses and baby-sitting services have been established for working women, with a resultant increase in the number of shop stewards and TUC delegates),as well as efforts at the local council level provide evidence of ongoing attempts to achieve policy change. However, whereas in both the United Kingdom and the United States it has been more difficult to secure policy implementation than the legislation itself, in the United States opportunities for intervention in bureaucratic politics are far greater.

In Britain, owing to ideological purism and localized structures, women have not developed political networks comparable to those in the United States. Institutional factors such as the growth of administrative power and executive dominance and secrecy, combined with the strength of parties and Parliament, have limited opportunities for direct intervention in policy-making and made monitoring of implementation well-nigh impossible. The women's liberation movement's emphasis on "women-specific" issues, such as abortion, rape, and domestic violence, while of utmost importance, has sometimes obscured the significance of issues involving work and the family so crucial to change for women.

When the Conservative government came to power in 1979, the tone was one of de-legitimization of women's right to work, as exemplified by the opinions of Lord Spens who, opening a debate on unemployment, said that married women should leave paid employment to make way for men.Shortly thereafter, this view was reinforced by Thatcher's secretary of state for social services, who contended that women should look after their children full time and that state aid be restricted to very needy cases. As noted, state provision of nursery and child care has never been adequate in Britain, and when other benefits were also cut, stipends to dependent mothers and children became even more meager. These events were not greeted with any mass response by the feminist movement in Britain.

In contrast, the positive changes in laws relating to violence against women were in part a response to women's campaigns, although these were often marked by the feminist ambivalence and the inaccesibility to the political system, as discussed earlier. As van der Gaag has correctly pointed out, Women's Aid never perceived legislation as particularly important in altering women's position in society and in the family. Nonetheless, feminists did intervene when they pushed for the Housing Persons Act of 1977, which gave priority in local housing to women who fled their homes because of violence. They also campaigned for changing the law on injunctions, discussed earlier. But there have been massive difficulties with enforcement in the face of a hostile judiciary and police force and the feminists' inability to monitor implementation.Sums made available to the shelter movement by local and central government grants have been minimal, for the same reasons.

Similar difficulties have ensued with regard to the Sexual Offences Act dealing with rape. Funding problems and failures of enforcement and interpretation remain. British feminists have concluded that the act has appreciably affected neither the way in which trials are conducted nor their reporting. Williscroft concludes that legislation at the local and national level has been of marginal importance. The failure of legislation to produce significant gains may result in either political quiescence or heightened cynicism regarding the political process, reinforcing the isolation of British feminists in any case.

We have argued that though the Sex Discrimination Act and the Equal Pay Act were potentially important pieces of legislation, they have not been implemented effectively enough to challenge inequality. The absence of coalitions and the failure to create a feminist infrastructure that might transcend ideological differences have been crucial. These deficiencies have to some degree been averted in the United

States, where affirmative action practices are much more widely practiced than in Britain, reflecting a major difference between the American EEOC and the British EOC created by the Sex Discrimination Act.Affirmative action is viewed with suspicion and hostility in a Britain dominated by high unemployment and economic strain, while in the United States, women have benefitted from more vigorous implementation of equal opportunity and affirmative action directives.

Three factors account for more effective enforcement of sex discrimination laws in the United States than in Britain or Sweden: 1) legislative and judicial commitment to the principle of affirmative action or positive discrimination, including the use of sanctions against offenders; 2) greater public acceptance of and mobilization for affirmative action principles; and 3) monitoring and intervention by a feminist network. In addition, the range of legislation that the EEOC can call on is impressive, as are the resources at its disposal, particularly in comparison with the United Kingdom and Sweden. The EEOC employs 3,100 people in a Washington office and 48 district or local offices.It is thus far more accessible to the public than the minute British office and the even tinier Swedish version.Federal guidelines appear to have produced significant gains in hiring and promotion in companies that do business with government, particularly if supported by vigorous organization and litigation.

The American tradition of litigation for equal rights has provided a securer foundation for equality than has the British approach, even in a period of conservative rule. There has been less erosion in the U.S. public policy arena because it has been buttressed by strong public support for affirmative action, the concept of "indirect discrimination," the ability to bring class action suits, a professional feminist litigation sector, and continual feminist lobbying and networking. As Grant has found, there is extraordinary support among American business for the practice of affirmative action, in part because this provides far more utilization of human resources and opens the workplace to new talent and ideas.Unlike the unions in Britain and Sweden that opposed national legislation against sex discrimination and remain lukewarm toward it today, in the United States the initially hostile business community strongly supports the continuation of aggressive federal affirmative action and equal opportunity guidelines.

In particular, the employment of black women, especially in firms with federal contracts, increased significantly as a result of EEOC policies. The major impact of equal opportunity policy has been at the professional and managerial level. It is at this level, as we shall see, that American women have achieved gains that exceed those made by women in Sweden and Britain.

It is undeniable that because of the largesse of the Swedish welfare state, benefits to single-female heads of families, to female members of the labor force, and to their children are far superior to those offered in the United States and Britain. Over 50 percent of Swedish children were in child-care facilities funded and regulated by the government in 1980, but only 15 percent of American children were similarly advantaged in 1984 (although a large number of American women relied on private-sector group and individual day care, bringing overall coverage to about the same level).While 40 percent of American women have maternity coverage through their employment, 76 percent of Swedish women have that benefit. Generous family rent and maintenance allowances, paid parental and sick leaves, in addition to special subsidies for single parents, have created a system that provides a far higher standard of living, without stigmatization and without long-term dependency and work disincentives, than in the United States.

Swedish parties have proven receptive to women's sections' views on such issues as day care and leaves but in fact the inception of many of these issues predates an active role for women's groups. Because the unions and parties sought to discourage further economic inclusion of immigrant groups, the participation of women in the labor force was encouraged in the 1960s. Policies related to women were therefore not informed by a feminist perspective, although they clearly sought to create equal opportunity for all, primarily through full employment. Both the SDP and the powerful unions, especially the LO, have opposed state intervention in order to strengthen institutional guarantees against sexual discrimination and have continued to view voluntary agreements between labor and employers as more significant than legislation.

As we have noted, "equality" policies on sex discrimination and on lack of employment opportunities for women met with a tepid response from the unions and Social Democrats, so that these policies have been narrowly defined and limited to employment-related issues. Given their lukewarm attitude, there has been scant impetus to gain compliance with anti-sex discrimination efforts through the effective application of government policy since the resumption of political power by the Social Democrats and their labor allies in 1982. At present, in an atmosphere in which the dominant political view is that "equality" already exists, women's sections within the four parties that have them appear to be playing a quiescent role. Though in the past they provided women with an opportunity to voice their special concerns, today women's sections may "ghettoize" participation and prevent fuller inclusion in decision-making.

In the main, women lack independent resources with which to seek further implementation and discussion of their concerns, including intransigent issues such as part-time work, occupational segregation, and limited mobility. We have seen that Sweden represents a society in which women have been politically incorporated without being fully mobilized; so their demands as claimants in the political system have been dealt with by the male-dominated corporatist power structure on its terms. Women, unlike men, have been unable to create a basis for organization in the labor market owing to their lesser numbers and representation and to the active discouragement of women's groups in the labor force. Nor have they effectively created independent groups related to other aspects of their lives.

Despite Sweden's official policies mandating change in men's roles as well as women's, absence from work because of child-care needs is almost exclusively restricted to women. Nearly eight out of ten men transfer their parental leave to women, and family life is organized so that women work part-time in order to care for children and home. Work, society, and politics are still organized on patriarchal lines despite the existence, of "equal opportunity".

Policies concerning we may call the "organization of daily life" has proven costly and difficult to implement in the absence of a significant movement continuously advocating for them. The result: Sweden remains highly sex-segregated in politics, work, and the home. In the absence of a feminist frame of reference, women's issues have been subsumed under "equality" and "family policy" and no longer regarded as a problem. Women-only issues involving "sexual" or "body" concerns have been belatedly recognized and incorporated into state policy mechanisms; they are treated as minor problems despite their relatively high incidence in a society viewed as violence-free. The fact that a grass-roots voluntary movement has arisen with regard to wife abuse indicates that the pervasiveness of male violence against women is a key social issue even in consensus-oriented Sweden. Similarly, the emerging differences on such issues as affirmative action for women may demonstrate increased consciousness of feminist concerns among Swedish women.

Swedish women have in fact not really left their homes; their major domestic responsibilities and very partial attachment to the labor force has resulted in the continuing primacy of traditional sex roles and society. The socialization of traditional women's roles in public-sector paid employment and the existence of benefits that help support women's part-time status may reinforce rather than change sex roles over the long run.

In examining the Swedish policy process, it seems clear

that Swedish unions and parties have "literally preempted feminist demands and have put their political clout behind numerous proposals to advance equality between women and men".Enactment of public policy has in large measure left the unions and parties free to pursue issues of equality in the workplace and in their own decision-making bodies at their own pace and on their own terms, and issues of power sharing and male dominance have largely been left untouched. As Verba and Orren point out, the SDP has worked "deliberately and successfully to make gender equality a subset of the general issue of equality and not a separate, isolated set of demands -128;¦. In Sweden, the Social Democrats -128; ¦ shaped feminist demands; in the United States feminist demands transformed the Democrats."

We have indicated that the issue of wife beating and abuse, identified in the American context as the more neutral policy arena known as "domestic violence," illustrates a good deal about the nature of the American political process and the receptivity of the system to feminist issues. Although the shelter movement began in England and exists belatedly in Sweden as well, it has been most successful in a number of ways in the American setting. The creation of shelters under the aegis of feminist groups legitimized the issue as a policy agenda matter, and by 1982 there were at least 300 shelters in operation.

Coalitions were created to combat treatment of battered women in 48 states. State funds became available, largely owing to pressure from shelter staff and residents, as well as other coalition members. Federal aid was forthcoming from a variety of sources, although it was not until 1984 that federal funding was finally appropriated for shelter support specifically, after several years of strident attacks from the New Right, which feared what was perceived as the weakening of the nuclear family. Since 1985, Congress has appropriated additional funding for shelters, and several additional federal programs have come to the aid of victims of domestic violence. In almost every state as well, laws have been enacted to improve reporting procedures, mandate police intervention, and establish more effective criminal court procedures. As Pleck points out, the process of gaining legitimization for intervention in domestic violence meant some dilution of the original radical feminist ideas that gave rise to the shelter movement. The inclusive coalitions involved in pushing for reform were often pressed to compromise because of the broad-based nature of the movement as it developed strength. Thus, a price was paid for success in gaining funding, legislation, and new legal enforcement: feminist rhetoric and control of shelters and even the movement's direction were affected. Nonetheless, the conclusion reached in this analysis is that the new coalition spurred by autonomous feminist movements allied with legislators, the judicial enforcement process, and other activists, including the social work profession, produced gains that made domestic violence a priority issue and helped achieve significant change. Women as claimants in this policy arena have had considerable success, and the diffusion of feminist ideas into the political culture seems evident.

The reluctance of British feminists to engage the national political system on the issue of battered women provides a clear contrast. The ready co-optation by the Swedish political system of the issue, at the same time as it was placed on the policy agenda, may have muted the important process of conflict and controversy, leaving in question both the fate of the grass-roots voluntary efforts that helped raise the issue initially and the vigor of the implementation process in the absence of an autonomous feminist movement.

In the United States the existence of numerous channels to influence policythe executive, the courts, the states, and the legislaturemay facilitate the diffusion of issues at different levels and permit pressure to initiate and enforce policy. We therefore contend that the relatively permeable American political system permits more choices than that of Britain or Sweden for change-oriented groups such as feminists and helps provide numerous reinforcements for the activity of independently organized and funded groups. Even though the policy process is characterized by incrementalism, with regard to a once "radical" issue such as wife abuse or domestic violence, it seems quite responsive to demands for change.

Changing Economic Roles for Women

A final area for examination is the significance of women's increased presence in the labor force as a vehicle for personal and societal change. Two different types of public policies must be considered to understand the increased mobility of American, as opposed to Swedish, women. Policies of the first type facilitate labor force participationthese are the policies provided much more generously by the Swedish state than by the American one. Policies of the second type foster greater economic opportunity by expanding the possibilities and choices available to women. In this second arena, characterized by commitment to affirmative action and widespread feminist consciousness, the United States appears to have surpassed Sweden.

Table: 9.6

Part-Time Employment of Women and Men		
Country	Women	Men
Sweden	46.2%	7.3%
United Kingdom	42.4%	3.3%
United States	23.3%	7.6%
Source: Equality Ministry 1985:12.		

It was shown that women's labor force participation in each of the three nations discussed has increased phenomenally during the post-World War II period and continues to grow annually in each nation. In 1983, 58 percent of British women, 61 percent of American women, and 77 percent of Swedish women were employed.Nonetheless, although the employment of Swedish women was the highest of all three, so was the percentage of women employed part-time (Table 9.6). As Erikson and Aberg have pointed out, "It is to part-time work in the public sector that newly employed [Swedish] women have moved. Women are overrepresented in unqualified work, have little independence at the job, and are underrepresented in supervisory positions. Both sex segregation and the ubiquitous part-time works are the reasons for their low income." In the United Kingdom and

Sweden, women are disproportionately employed by the public service sector, and there they are increasingly employed in part-time positions.In Sweden, 90 percent of the women who work do so in the service sector, a vast majority being employed by the government, in contrast to about 75 percent in the United States and Britain.Forty-five percent of all women were employed in the social welfare sector in Sweden, 28 percent in the United States, and 26 percent in England. As Rein and others have shown, the social welfare sector is also the most highly segregated, with Sweden and Britain having the highest patterns of sex segregation and the United States the lowest.

Occupational segregation is a problem in all three countries, but probably the greatest amount of change can be discerned in the United States, where there has been a decrease in occupational segregation and downward mobility after childbirth.In Sweden, especially, occupational choice has been very much an extension of the traditional role of women, and sex segregation remains a persistent problem. Another obstinate problem affecting women's role and power is that of wage differentials between men and women, in large measure a function of part-time work and occupational segregation. In Britain, women's hourly earnings were 74 percent of men's, while gross earnings were 61 percent whereas in the United States they were 83 percent and 65 percent, respectively. Among American women ages 26 to 34 this gap has narrowed to 75 percent of men's income, and for ages 20 to 24 it has narrowed even further to about 86 percent.In Sweden, full-time female workers earned about 80 percent of male income, but because of the large part-time component of work force, total female earnings are in fact about half of men's.

A significant measure of the economic role of Swedish, British, and American women is the disparity between women in each country who hold managerial and supervisory positions. Even accounting for differences in data-gathering methodology, the differences are striking. In contrast to the United States, in which over 35 percent of managers and administrators are female, the comparable numbers in the

United Kingdom and Scandinavia are 18.8 and 11 -128; -147; 15 percent.In Sweden, women occupy only 0.2 percent of the managerial positions, 3 percent of executive positions, and less than 1 percent of the top positions in companies and public authorities.Four percent of the senior government executives and officials are women. In the United States the female share of executive, administrative, and managerial jobs rose from 20 percent in 1972 to 35 percent in 1985, almost doubling.The United Kingdom occupies a middle position: women slightly decreased their role as managers in 1983 and now hold 17 percent of the administrative and professional positions.However, in the private sector in 1986, women held only 0.3 percent of the top positions in companies and only six percent of senior managerial posts.British women hold 18.5 percent of appointments to public bodies, but are only 2 percent of the directorates of private sector firms. Only 25 women are found among the top three grades of the senior civil service and only nine women among the boards of the hundred largest companies, while in the United States, 36 percent of corporate boardrooms had female members in 1982. Hernes shows that British women held from 8 to 12 percent of the country's top administrative positions, whereas in Scandinavia in general and Sweden in particular no more than 2 percent of the top managers were women.

Table: 9.7

Occupational Stratification

Occupational category	U.K.		Sweden		U.S.	
	M	F	M	F	M	F
High-prestige professional and technical	4.8	2.3	8.5	6.2	11.1	6.7
Administrative and managerial	6.1	0.9	5.2	0.4	10.4	3.0

Source: Roos 1985: Table 3.3.

A comparative analysis of occupational stratification of women in Britain, Sweden, and the United States suggests trends similar to those described here (Table 9.7).

Although strict comparability is not possible because of the absence of incisive cross-national data, the available data reveal that "professional employment has widened more rapidly and significantly in the United States, as females have during the last generation made serious inroads into a wide range of professional occupations".Although this quotation refers specifically only to Britain and the United States, our analysis indicates that the Swedish case may demonstrate greater resistance to women, particularly in senior administrative and managerial roles. The virtual absence of women in such positions in Sweden may be attributable to women's marginal attachment to the labor forceowing both to occupational segregation and to part-time work, which continually reinforces the role of women as responsible for the domestic sphereand Swedish cultural norms that appear to decry assertive, individualistic women as beyond the pale of consensus politics.

The pattern of higher education in each country buttresses the economic role of women. In Sweden, although 66 per cent of university graduates in 1982 -128; -147; 83 were women, postgraduate work was dominated by men. The proportion of female university students is largest in the United States, and they now reap more than half of the bachelor's and master's degrees and one-third of the doctoral degrees awarded.In the more elitist British educational system, 5 per cent of women held bachelor's or advanced degrees, whereas in the United States the number was 20 per cent.

Women in all three countries have greatly improved their representation in medicine. The high number of Swedish female dentists is particularly notable.However, in the United States, 11 per cent of engineers are women, in the United Kingdom only 3 per cent, while in Sweden women hold about 5 percent of construction-related positions. Only 10 percent of American women planned to major in education in 1985; business was now the most popular undergraduate major for both men and women. The proportion of M.B.A.'s awarded to women rose from 3 per cent in 1965 to 30 percent in 1986.American women have made particular strides in the field of law, where they earned 38 percent of degrees awarded, up from 15 per cent in 1975.In Britain, 11 per cent of the barristers in 1983 were women and 14 per cent of the solicitors.In Sweden, about 11 per cent of lawyers and jurists are women; in the United States, almost 20 per cent.

American women compose 27 per cent of university faculties and about 12 per cent of all professors; in Britain, female professors' number less than 4 per cent. In 1982, 5 percent of Swedish women were professors. The contrast between the growing economic and professional gains of American women and to a lesser degree, their British sisters, seems to highlight continued inequities in Sweden. While as many Swedish women as men interviewed by a survey said they would like to be promoted; only 5 percent thought they would be.Through the division of labor, then, Swedish "men are able to preserve a dominant, superior position. Men still occupy practically all positions conferring power and influence in society -128; ¦. Women do not compete with men because they live on different terms".

Assessment

In this analysis we have argued that structural factors, including political, cultural, and economic constraints, narrow the possibilities for women to become policy claimants. We have marshaled evidence to demonstrate the importance of women articulating on behalf of their own interests and own concerns, contending that the "strident" tones of women's liberation decried by some are a necessary, if not sufficient, condition for societal change.

A causal relationship between movement politics, policy enactments, and the growth of a professionally active group of women with economic and political potential is not fully demonstrable, but it is evident that the American feminist movement has had a profound impact on changing expectations and possibilities. In 1984, 49 per cent of the women surveyed by Ms magazine indicated that they would continue to work even if they did not have to do so for economic reasons, while 57 percent indicated that they felt the "women's movement has just begun." The evidence of the continued vigor of the American feminist movement seems fairly conclusive, suggesting that reports of its demise are premature and unfounded.

This analysis has stressed the significance of several major factors that appear to limit the role of British feminists: the closed and inflexible nature of British government, particularly the administrative process; the reluctance of key institutions such as parties and unions to go beyond rhetoric in meaningfully sharing power; and the localized, purist nature of the women's liberation movement, which has failed to create coalitions and an enduring national presence. In Sweden, the anomaly of progressive policies pertaining to women, despite the lack of an independent, feminist movement, has resulted in a set of political contradictions.

Not withstanding the greater hospitableness of the Swedish party system in particular to pressure, in practice the system permits little ideological or political space for nonproducer groups. Issues drawn from the feminist agenda have found their way into the public policy arena and have profoundly influenced expectations, particularly regarding women's role as labor force participants. But in the absence of an autonomous independent movement that could structure dialogue on its own terms, much of the policy enacted appears to have had little impact on gender-based roles. The continued existence of a huge part-time female work force, the extraordinarily high degree of labor force segregation based on sex, and the apparent persistence of traditional sex roles imply that the general labor force policy that benefits women is not enough.

This analysis has sought to demonstrate the interaction between the "political opportunity structures" and mobilization by feminist social movements. In turn, the product of this interaction has affected the success of feminist claims and the degree of social change possible in each nation. Although the concept of success utilized here has emphasized policy outcomes, it has not neglected other manifestations, such as movement survival, changes in individual consciousness, and diffusion of group values. The results of these developments include acceptance of the group as a legitimate political organization, with ensuing gains for its members.

We have argued that policy impact may often rely on implementation efforts by a coalition of feminists and their political allies, and that the efforts may best succeed if these feminists are members of autonomous groupings that enjoy access to the political process, as is the case in the United States. American feminists also seem to have achieved the most public support for movement goals and ideals, now broadly diffused throughout the culture. With regard to individual consciousness, we contend that feminist ideology has had a profound impact on women in all three nations, although it has sprung from different sources. In the context of its self-defined goals British nondirected "liberationist" movement politics is remarkable for its continued vigor and survival. In his analysis of social movements and policy change, Tarrow has observed that "the range and flexibility of its tactical repertory is often a good predictor of movement success." We have contended that the American movement has enjoyed the greatest autonomy in choice of tactics because it has been unconstrained by the necessity to work through the intermediation of existing groups, such as parties and unions. This freedom has permitted the use of a variety of tactics from protest to participation in existing power groupings. British feminist participation has been constrained by the rigidity of the political system and the ambivalence of movement activists about engaging in national politics in a coordinated fashion. Swedish women have, in the main, been limited to behaving as participants in existing institutions.

In all three nations, the relatively unstable nature of traditional electoral coalitions and the declining relationship between unions and the working class have produced new opportunities for women as potential recruits and bases of strength. In Sweden and the United States, these new opportunities appear to have produced the most responsiveness to new policies for women, although they have created different results. The crucial factor appears to be the greater availability of allies or coalition partners in these two countries. In the United States in the last two decades, relationships have been cemented between feminists, other like-minded groups, and the Democratic Party, while in Sweden electoral instability created new opportunities for political access for women, particularly in the 1970s.

As Tarrow puts it, political "reforms may be more reversible when they are substantive only, creating no new vested rights of participation or veto in the population groups newly enjoying them." This hypothesis argues, then, for the idea that reforms producing institutionalized participation may be the most significant of all, largely because they help create resources for future mobilization and ensure continued attention to substantive policy concerns. Seen from this perspective, the American movement, now recognized as a legitimate group in the pluralist system, may be in the strongest position to endure as a significant political force.

From the examination of substantive policy gains, this analysis has found that Americans have achieved the most in expanding economic opportunities, while the Swedes have been most successful in creating a support structure that facilitates female labor force participation. Substantive rights, such as access to equal employment, are, as we have seen, limited by support from government and willingness to use sanctions, the sympathetic response of the public and political allies, and continued intervention by an activist feminist policy network. Legislation, it appears, is not enough, as it is necessary to have continued access to the implementation process in order to consolidate policy gains and achieve further political success. In the final analysis, all three nations demonstrate the limitations of their "political opportunity structure" as it affects the role of women. In the case of Sweden, gender-neutral policies have not yet been able to encompass the special needs and experiences of women and liberate them from their traditional roles. And, in the United States and in Britain despite the strength of the independent feminist tradition that has acted from a collective position in the name of collective goals, individual women have been forced to struggle with family responsibilities still squarely rooted in the private sphere.

Bibliography

Andrews, Peggy. *Sisters Listening to Sisters: Women of the World Share Stories of Personal Empowerment.* Bergin and Garvey, 1996.

Awkward, Michael. *Negotiating Difference: Race, Gender, and the Politics of Positionality.* University of Chicago Press, 1995.

Bannerji, Himani. *Thinking Through: Essays on Feminism, Marxism, and Anti-Racism.* Women's Press, 1995.

Basu, Amrita, ed. *The Challenge of Local Feminisms: Women's Movements in Global Perspective.* Westview Press, 1995.

Butler, Judith and Joan W. Scott, ed. *Feminists Theorize the Political.* Routledge, 1992.

Carver, Terrell and Veronique Mottier, ed. *Politics of Sexuality.* NY: Routledge, 1998.

Chapman, Jennifer. *Politics, Feminism and the Reformation of Gender.* Routledge, 1992.

Chapman, Jenny. *Politics, Feminism and the Reformation of Gender.* Routledge, 1993.

Cocks, Joan. *The Oppositional Imagination: Feminism, Critique, and PoliticalTheory.* (out of print)

Elshtain, Jean Bethke. *Meditations on Modern Political Thought: Masculine/Feminine Themes from Luther to Arendt.* Penn State Univ. Press, 1992.

Fowlkes, Diane L. *White Political Women: Paths from Privilege to Empowerment.* Univ. of Tennessee Press, 1992.

Fraser, Nancy. *Justice Interruptus: Critical Reflections on the "Postsocialist" Condition.* Routledge, 1997.

Gottfried, Heidi, ed. *Feminism and Social Change: Bridging Theory and Practice.* Univ. of Illinois Press, 1996.

Hughes-Freeland, Felicia and Nickie Charles, ed. *Practising Feminism: Identity, Difference and Power.* Routledge, 1996.

Jones, Kathleen B., ed. *Citizenship in Feminism: Identity, Action, and Locale.* Indiana University Press, 1998.

Kenney, Sally J. and Helen Kinsella, ed. *Politics and Feminist Standpoint Theories.* Haworth Press, 1997.

King, Katie. *Theory in Its Feminist Travels: Conversations in U.S. Women's Movements.* Indiana Univ. Press, 1994.

Meehan, Elizabeth and Selma Sevenhuijsen, ed. *Equality Politics and Gender.* Sage, 1991.

Meyers, Diana Tietjens, ed. *Feminist Social Thought: A Reader.* Routledge, 1997.

Naples, Nancy A., ed. *Community Activism and Feminist Politics: Organizing Across Race, Class, and Gender.* Routledge, 1997

Okin, Susan Moller. *Women in Western Political Thought.* Princeton Univ. Press, 1992.

Pascall, Gillian. *Social Policy: A New Feminist Analysis.* 1997.

Pateman, Carole and Elizabeth Gross, ed. *Feminist Challenges: Social and Political Theory.* Northeastern Univ. Press, 1987.

Phillips, Anne. *Engendering Democracy.* Penn State Univ. Press, 1991.

Phillips, Anne. *Feminism and Politics.* Oxford, 1998.

Randall, Vicky and Georgina Waylen, ed. *Gender, Politics and the State.* NY: Routledge, 1998.

Rocheleau, Dianne, Barbara Thomas-Slayter, and Esther Wangari, ed. *Femininst Political Ecology: Global Issues and Local Experiences.* 1996.

Sapiro, Virginia. *A Vindication of Political Virtue: The Political Theory of Mary Wollstonecraft.* Univ. of Chicago Press, 1992.

Simon, Sherry. *Gender in Translation: Cultural Identity and the Politics of Transmission.* Routledge, 1996.

Sunstein, Cass R., ed. *Feminism and Political Theory.* Univ. of Chicago Press, 1990.

Thomas, Sue and Clyde Wilcox, ed. *Women and Elective Office.* Oxford, 1997.

Waring, Wendy, ed. *By, For and About: Feminist Cultural Politics.* Women's Press, 1994.

Warren, Karen J. and Duane L. Cady, ed. *Bringing Peace Home: Feminism, Violence, and Nature.* Indiana Univ. Press, 1996.

Wolf, Naomi. *Fire with Fire: The New Female Power and How It Will Change the 21st Century.* Fawcett Books, 1993.

Young, Iris Marion. *Justice and the Politics of Difference.* Princeton, 1998.

Young, Stacey. *Changing the wor(l)d: Discourse, Politics, and the Feminist Movement.* Routledge, 1997.

Zack, Naomi, ed. *American Mixed Race: The Culture of Microdiversity.* Rowman and Littlefield, 1995.

Index